"This welcome book is a reminder that history always impacts theology and in turn shapes spirituality. Jimmy Tan's insightful comparative study of Ignatius of Loyola and John Calvin provides rich wisdom for both Christian spirituality and spiritual direction. I hope this excellent resource will guide ecumenical conversations in spiritual direction. The church will be the healthier for it. Strongly recommended!"

—Tom Schwanda
Associate professor emeritus of Christian formation and ministry, Wheaton College

"In this comparative study of Ignatius Loyola and John Calvin as spiritual guides, Jimmy Tan has shown that there are deep spiritual affinities as well as significant differences. The study is especially important in our day when spiritual guides tend to be rather careless in their use of sources. They would do well, following the lead of the author, to engage in some spiritual exercises in Ignatian and Calvinist discernment."

—Simon Chan
Editor, *Asia Journal of Theology*

"This is a very important, substantial, and well-written book in the area of spiritual direction and formation. It clearly and helpfully describes and compares the spiritual guidance approaches of Ignatius of Loyola and John Calvin from the triperspective of history, theology, and method. Highly recommended as essential reading!"

—Siang-Yang Tan
Senior professor of clinical psychology, Fuller Theological Seminary, and senior pastor emeritus, First Evangelical Church Glendale

"In response to the common tendency to take a smorgasbord approach to a buffet spread of spiritual direction practices, Jimmy Tan's timely and essential book offers an approach that takes seriously the historical and theological roots of various models so that these can be faithfully and effectively employed. He demonstrates this by examining the Ignatian and Reformed traditions, showing their similarities and differences, and how bridges can be built for mutual enrichment."

—Robert Solomon
Bishop emeritus, The Methodist Church in Singapore

"We urgently need a recovery of biblical spirituality and a rediscovery of spiritual disciplines, unencumbered by misconception and prejudice. In this book, Jimmy Tan helps us navigate our way through the Catholic and Protestant milieu, bringing history, theology, and methodology into what he calls 'a trinocular vision' arising from both Ignatian and Reformed traditions."

—David Wong
General secretary, Bible-Presbyterian Church in Singapore

"Burgeoning interest in Christian spirituality is no evidence of its informed practice. Jimmy Tan's timely book addresses the neglect of historical context and theological foundations in the practice of spiritual guidance. Offering critical and comparative accounts of Ignatius and Calvin on spiritual direction, Tan demonstrates how the threefold perspective of method, history, and theology enriches its practice across the Ignatian and Reformed traditions. I commend this sure-footed study that recovers themes of considerable importance for anyone interested in spiritual theology and formation."

—Edwin Tay
Principal, Trinity Theological College

How Then Shall We Guide?

How Then Shall We Guide?

A Comparative Study of Ignatius of Loyola
and John Calvin as Spiritual Guides

JIMMY BOON-CHAI TAN

PICKWICK *Publications* · Eugene, Oregon

HOW THEN SHALL WE GUIDE?
A Comparative Study of Ignatius of Loyola and John Calvin as Spiritual Guides

Pickwick Publications
An Imprint of Wipf and Stock Publishers
199 W. 8th Ave., Suite 3
Eugene, OR 97401

www.wipfandstock.com

PAPERBACK ISBN: 978-1-6667-3525-3
HARDCOVER ISBN: 978-1-6667-9214-0
EBOOK ISBN: 978-1-6667-9215-7

Cataloguing-in-Publication data:

Names: Tan, Jimmy Boon-Chai, author.

Title: How then shall we guide? : a comparative study of Ignatius of Loyola and John Calvin as spiritual guides / Jimmy Boon-Chai Tan.

Description: Eugene, OR: Pickwick Publications, 2023. | Includes bibliographical references and indexes.

Identifiers: ISBN 978-1-6667-3525-3 (paperback). | ISBN 978-1-6667-9214-0 (hardcover). | ISBN 978-1-6667-9215-7 (ebook).

Subjects: LSCH: Spiritual direction—Study and teaching. | Spiritual directors—Supervision of. | Ignatius, of Loyola, Saint, 1491–1556. | Calvin, Jean, 1509–1564. | Spiritual formation.

Classification: BX2350.7 T12 2023 (print). | BX2350.7 (ebook).

VERSION NUMBER 062323

To my wife,
Soh Kwan,
who lives our marriage covenant in God to the full,

and

to our children and their spouses,
Hannah and Justin, Rachel and Andre, and Deborah,
our pride and our joy,
who journeyed together till the completion of this project.

Contents

Acknowledgments

THE COMPLETION OF THIS work represents a slice of a much larger endeavor for my family and me—one that is made possible by communities of faith in America and in Singapore. It is, as such, a humbling experience to try to express my appreciation for all who have contributed in one way or another to see us through the years of academic and spiritual formation in the United States and in Singapore. We are surrounded by a host of faithful witnesses to whom we are deeply indebted. To all who contributed in one way or another, my family and I are deeply grateful to you. May God be praised for his glorious grace in Christ through his Holy Spirit.

Much of this book is based on my doctoral dissertation and so I wish to thank my mentors who guided me through the process. I am deeply grateful to my primary mentor, James E. Bradley, whose penetrating insights on the historical and theological developments of the Christian Church opened for me many vistas that shaped the contours of this work. His expert guidance and eye for detail, communicated with grace and precision, profoundly influenced me as a steward of knowledge. His humble disposition and untiring efforts at mentoring me leaves an indelible mark that I can only hope to emulate. I am deeply grateful to Siang-Yang Tan, who served both as a doctoral committee member and as my pastor. His academic excellence and passion for this work's focus spurred me on, and his loving pastoral care sustained me through some of the most challenging moments in this journey. I am very grateful to Scott Sunquist for his guidance and contribution at a critical juncture in this study. Only God could orchestrate the renewal of a teacher-student relationship that began some thirty years ago on the other side of the Pacific. His commitment to integrate Christian spiritual formation and mission blazes a trail for me to pursue. I am deeply grateful to Tom Schwanda who, as the external reader, shared many helpful suggestions to further improve this work. It was his spiritual friendship and guidance that both spurred and sustained me to the completion of this work. Special mention goes to Simon Chan who guided me untiringly on spiritual theology and prayed unceasingly for my family and me.

There were many more who contributed to my development at Fuller and in Singapore through the years. I give thanks to God for them, and they are specially mentioned in the acknowledgments in my dissertation.

I wish to make special mention of those who helped to spur this book project from its inception to completion: my colleagues, Roland Chia and Mark Chan, who, from the early days after I joined Trinity, encouraged me to get the dissertation published; and Mark connected me with John Wipf; my mentors Jim Bradley, Siang-Yang Tan, Scott Sunquist, and Simon Chan, who all encouraged me to "get the book out"; David Wong, who helped me visualize the possibility of this book project; Robert Solomon, who served as guide and conversation partner during my sabbatical; Edwin Tay, who encouraged and pointed to available funding; Tom Schwanda, who kept pace from beginning to end—sponsoring, praying, sustaining, and connecting me to endorsers; and my two faithful brothers in the Lord, Kenny Chee and Koh Seng Chor, who journeyed alongside all through this work. To every one of them, I am deeply grateful.

I wish, finally, to thank my editor, K. C. Hanson, who guided me along, and bore with each delay, on the long process of preparing the manuscript for publication.

The best is yet to be.

To God be the glory.

Abbreviations

CALVIN

Institutes 1559: To minimize the number of notes, I have included all citations from the McNeill-Battles (1960 edition) in the body of the text itself, following the standard citation format (Book, Chapter, Section; e.g. 1.5.2) unless otherwise specified.

Comm. Commentary

Letters: The Letters of John Calvin, trans. Jules Bonnet, 4 vols. New York: Franklin, 1973

Selected Works: Selected Works of John Calvin: Tracts and Letters. Translated by Jules Bonnet. Edited by Henry Beveridge. Grand Rapids: Baker, 1983

IGNATIUS OF LOYOLA

The Spiritual Exercises of Saint Ignatius: To minimize the number of notes, I have included all citations from the Puhl, Louis J (2000 edition) in the body of the text itself, following the standard citation format in reference to the annotations (e.g., annotation 23, [23]).

Letters: The Letters of St. Ignatius of Loyola. Translated by William J. Young. Chicago: Loyola University Press, 1959.

Autobiography: All citations on the autobiography are from *A Pilgrim's Journey: The Autobiography of Ignatius of Loyola.* Translated by Joseph N. Tylenda. Collegeville, MN: Liturgical, 1985. Citations follow the standard citation format (*Autobiography* 12 = paragraph 12).

1

Recent Developments in Spiritual Direction

SPIRITUAL DIRECTION IS IN vogue today.[1] So great is the current wave of interest in this ministry that it is tempting to see it as a new discovery at the dawn of a new century. "Such an ahistorical view," warns veteran spiritual director Lavinia Byrne, "risks cutting off present-day practice from its honorable roots."[2] Furthermore, Christian spiritual direction is regarded as the integrative art that brings the study of Christian spiritual theology to its proper conclusion.[3] Yet, in some contemporary expressions of spiritual direction, especially interfaith spiritual direction, it is unclear what forms of spiritual theology undergirds its practice.[4] This tendency in contemporary

---

1. From what was estimated at just over a few hundred members some thirty years ago, Spiritual Directors International, arguably the largest international organization on spiritual direction, now boasts of "a vibrant membership of more than six thousand individuals on six continents who represent more than fifty spiritual traditions, from Anabaptists to Zen Buddhists and many spiritual traditions in between." See "About" in http://sdiworld.org.

See also Evangelical Spiritual Directors Association (ESDA), https://www.graftedlife.org/spiritual-direction/esda, for spiritual directors committed to an evangelical theological perspective.

The term "spiritual direction" is variously defined by different traditions and persons. I will discuss its usage along with terms like "interfaith spiritual direction," "contemporary spiritual direction" and "Christian spiritual direction" as this work progresses.

2. Byrne, *Traditions of Spiritual Guidance*, vii.

3. Chan, *Spiritual Theology*, 225–26.

4. See, for example, Neafsey, "The Human Experience of God," 19–26, where

spiritual direction to divorce its practice from a tradition's history and theology is the presenting impetus for this work. My specific concern is on how this tendency affects Christian spiritual direction, especially in an ecumenical setting.[5] A brief survey of recent literature by Christians engaged in Christian spiritual direction will help to orient us to the discussion.

The Roman Catholic Church has witnessed an increased in demand for its resources and expertise in spiritual retreats and direction both from its members and those beyond. Publications such as those by Thomas Merton–Trappist,[6] John Sullivan–Carmelite,[7] William Barry and William Connolly,[8] and Thomas Green–Ignatian,[9] Henri Nouwen–Dutch Catholic Priest,[10] Joan Chittister–Benedictine,[11] and Thomas Dubay–Society of Mary,[12] to name but a few, reveal that the historic ministry of spiritual direction continues to receive significant attention in the Roman Catholic Church. The

---

Neafsey's reference to God as Mystery is denoted by many names, not all of which are Christian, making the theological grounds for reflection on human experience unclear.

See also Mabry's introduction to and advocacy for the practice of interfaith spiritual guidance. While he rightly observed that his students in interfaith spiritual guidance would need to have a good grounding in the world's religions so that "they would feel comfortable and prepared no matter *who* stepped through their doors," he nevertheless acknowledges the challenge of arriving at a suitable term for one "transcendent reality" across the religions. He asks, "what do we call the transcendent reality to which we are trying to help people orient their lives? Should I use a rotating set of terms, such as God, Brahma, Buddha Nature, Allah, the Tao, the Goddess, the *Èlan vital*, and the Universe? I toyed with the idea, but I feared such a kaleidoscopic approach would prove disorienting and fragmented." Mabry, *Noticing the Divine*, iv–x. See also Mabry, *Spiritual Guidance across Religions*.

See Addison, *Show Me Your Way*, 85–107, for Addison's discussion of the pitfalls in interfaith spiritual direction where the reality of historical and theological differences in religious faiths and traditions are not easily circumvented.

5. Authors who share this concern include James Houston and Philip Sheldrake. See Houston, "Christian Spirituality: A Contextual Perspective," 27–38; and Sheldrake, *Spirituality and History*, 1.

6. Merton, *Spiritual Direction and Meditation*.

7. Sullivan, *Spiritual Direction*.

8. Barry and Connolly, *The Practice of Spiritual Direction*.

9. Green, *Weeds among the Wheat*.

10. Nouwen, *Reaching Out*; and Nouwen et al, *Spiritual Direction*.

11. Chittister, *Wisdom Distilled from the Daily*.

12. Dubay, *Seeking Spiritual Direction*.

major approaches in spiritual direction, such as the Ignatian,[13] Benedictine, Franciscan,[14] and Carmelite, all continue to enjoy healthy development.[15]

The Orthodox tradition also witnessed fresh expressions as exemplified in works by Joseph Allen,[16] Irénée Hausherr,[17] and John Chryssavgis.[18] The practice of spiritual direction within the Orthodox tradition enjoys a lengthy continuity since the Early Church as the Orthodox were not significantly affected by the schisms of the Protestant and Catholic Reformations. Its form of spiritual direction is primarily hierarchical, and its essence is anchored in its theological understanding of the church, its sacraments, and liturgy.

The Protestant interest is signaled by major publications from Anglicans Kenneth Leech[19] and Martin Thornton,[20] Episcopalians Tilden Edwards,[21] Morton Kelsey,[22] Margaret Guenther,[23] and Alan Jones,[24] Christian Psychiatrist Gerald May,[25] Presbyterian Eugene Peterson,[26] James Houston (Plymouth Brethren),[27] Gordon T. Smith (Christian Missionary

---

13. In recent decades, there is a surge in demand for retreats and literature in the Ignatian way. See, for example, Malloy, *Spiritual Direction: A Beginner's Guide*; Gallagher, *A Handbook for Spiritual Directors*; and Thibodeaux, *Ignatian Discernment of Spirits for Spiritual Direction and Pastoral Care*. For examples of Jesuits Prayer Ministry resources in Singapore see https://www.jesuit.org.sg/ .

14. An example is The Center for Action and Contemplation founded by Franciscan Fr. Richard Rohr. See https://cac.org/

15. There are numerous online spiritual direction resources in the Catholic tradition. See, for example, https://www.discerninghearts.com/. For resources in Singapore, see, https://www.montfortcentre.org/, http://kingsmeadcentre.sg/, http://www.lifespringscanossian.com/, and https://www.franciscans.sg/

16. Allen, *Inner way.*

17. Hausherr, *Spiritual Direction in the Ancient Christian East.*

18. Chryssavgis, *Soul Mending.*

19. Leech, *Soul Friend.*

20. Thornton, *Spiritual Direction.*

21. Edwards, *Spiritual Director.*

22. Kelsey, *Companions on the Inner Way.*

23. Guenther, *Holy Listening.*

24. Jones, *Exploring Spiritual Direction.*

25. May, *Care of Mind, Care of Spirit.*

26. Peterson, *The Contemplative Pastor.*

27. Houston and Pearson, *Alive to the Love of God.* Houston was a founding member of Regent College and who exercised an extensive ministry in spiritual direction there for more than three decades.

Alliance),[28] Jeannette Bakke,[29] Susan Philips,[30] and Alice Fryling.[31] Recently, Angela Reed, Richard Osmer, and Marcus Smucker joined in the discussion too.[32] It appears that the Protestants are retrieving historical and theological insights from the Christian Tradition and learning to adapt from both the Catholic and Orthodox traditions. In addition, there are increasing efforts to reclaim insights from its own heritage such as the Reformed and Puritan traditions.[33] These developments contribute to a renaissance of sorts in this unique ministry described by Gregory Nazianzen as "the art of arts and the science of sciences."[34]

Before we consider the challenges that confront the practice of spiritual direction across the traditions, it would help to first note how this ministry is perceived within the major Christian traditions.[35] Beginning with the Catholic tradition, Thomas Merton, writing as a Trappist Monk from the Abbey of Gethsemani, proposes that spiritual direction was a monastic concept. He reasons that "the original, primitive meaning of spiritual direction suggests a particular need connected with a special ascetic task, a peculiar vocation for which a professional formation is required."[36] Consequently, he defines spiritual direction as "a continuous process of formation and guidance, in which a Christian is led and encouraged *in his special vocation*, so that by faithful correspondence to the graces of the Holy Spirit he may attain to the particular end of his vocation and to union with God."[37]

Writing from the Ignatian tradition, William Barry and William Connolly place spiritual direction within the realm of pastoral care. They describe it as generally a one-to-one helping relationship between the director and the directed, entered upon on a quasi-contractual basis, and with the

---

28. Smith, *Spiritual Direction*; Smith, *The Voice of Jesus*; Smith, *Listening to God in Times of Choice.*

29. Bakke, *Holy Invitations.*

30. Phillips, *Candlelight.*

31. Fryling, *Seeking God Together.*

32. Reed, et.al., *Spiritual Companioning.*

33. See, for example, Boulton, *Life in God*; Schwanda, *Soul recreation*; and Canlis, *Calvin's Ladder.*

34. Nazianzen, Oration 2:16. Gregory the Great borrowed the phrase in the *Pastoral Rule*. See Demacopoulos, *The book of pastoral rule*, 29.

35. While the term "spiritual direction" has gained increased familiarity today, its origins remain unclear. See May, *Care of Mind, Care of Spirit*, and Barry and Connolly, *The Practice of Spiritual Direction*, on this concern. My work includes a brief history of spiritual direction in chapter two.

36. Merton, *Spiritual Direction and Meditation*, 11.

37. Merton, *Spiritual Direction and Meditation*, 13.

aim of centering their lives in God.[38] By definition, they understand spiritual direction "as help given by one believer to another that enables the latter to pay attention to God's personal communication to him or her, to respond to this personally communicating God, to grow in intimacy with this God, and to live out the consequences of the relationship."[39]

From an Orthodox perspective, Joseph Allen proposes that spiritual direction should be studied as one of the varieties of ministries given to the Church by God. He calls it a ministry of healing and reconciliation, concepts that are drawn from Scripture. Although he argues that the roots of spiritual direction can be traced to Eastern Christianity, especially with the monastic elder as spiritual physicians, he cautions against a total identification of the spiritual director with that of the elder. As a ministry, he adds, it is known as a gift of God—one of the *charismata*, and hence to be used to serve the people of God. Allen thus proposes that "spiritual direction must include the components common to all ministries: given by God and used for others."[40] The problem, as he notes, is the considerable debate as to whom the gift is given to and the way it should be used.

Martin Thornton, an influential Anglican pastoral and spiritual theologian, defines spiritual direction as "the application of theology to the life of prayer."[41] He argues that since prayer, "as progressive relationship with God in Christ, is carried on in the world, [and] ultimately controls all aspects of life," spiritual direction is that ministry which bridges the learning of theology to the applying of theology in all aspects of life as an act of prayer.

Tilden Edwards, founder, and senior fellow at the Shalem Institute for Spiritual Formation, shares a similar perspective with Martin Thornton. His description of spiritual direction is noteworthy for its comprehensiveness:

> The ministry of spiritual direction can be understood as the meeting of two or more people whose desire is to prayerfully listen for the movements of the Holy Spirit in all areas of a person's life (not just in their formal prayer life). It is a three-way relationship: among the *true* director who is the Holy Spirit (which in Christian tradition is the Spirit of Christ present in and among us), and the human director (who listens for the *directions* of the Spirit with the directee), and the directee. The interpretive framework of this relationship is seeded by understandings of the spiritual life found in scripture and in the

38. Barry and Connolly, *The Practice of Spiritual Direction*, 11–12.

39. Barry and Connolly, *The Practice of Spiritual Direction*, 8.

40. Allen, *Inner Way*, 6–7.

41. Thornton, *Spiritual Direction*, 1.

lives and writings of great saints and theologians. The director
is a companion along the pilgrim's way, wanting to be directly
open along with the directee to the Spirit-undercurrents flowing
through the happenings of the directee's life.[42]

Edwards explains that the ministry of spiritual direction takes place
within an "interpretive framework" of the Holy Spirit's movements in the
director's and directee's lives, a framework that is seeded by "understandings
of the spiritual life found in scripture and in the lives and writings of great
saints and theologians." These understandings serve as the spiritual theology for the ministry. The director is "companion" and spiritual direction is
spiritual companionship.

We also note that Edwards describes spiritual direction as possibly
involving two or more people; not necessarily a one-to-one as described by
Leech and Max Thurian.[43] In this regard, Rose Mary Dougherty, a member
of the School Sisters of Notre Dame and director at the Shalem Institute
for Spiritual Formation, and Alice Fryling, an evangelical spiritual director,
have written books that discuss the practice of group spiritual direction.[44]

Finally, a work by the late Bruce Demarest (1935–2021), senior professor of Christian theology and spiritual formation at Denver Seminary,
offers an evangelical perspective of spiritual direction. Demarest describes
it as "the ministry of soul care in which a gifted and experienced Christian
helps another person to grow in relationship with and obedience to God by
following the example of Jesus Christ."[45] Here, Demarest describes growing
in relationship and obedience to God as the goal of spiritual direction and
following the example of Jesus Christ as the process. He also describes the
spiritual director to be a "gifted and experienced Christian," an important
quality that is shared by most authors on this subject.

There is clearly a range of definitions, with many overlapping aspects,
across the traditions. As my work is a comparative study, I will not offer
another definition of spiritual direction. Instead, I will refer to the preceding definitions and, at this point, propose that the terms spiritual direction
and spiritual guidance may be used interchangeably although the latter has,
arguably, a somewhat broader reference.

42. Edwards, *Spiritual Director*, 2–3.
43. Leech, *Soul Friend*, 30.
44. Dougherty, *Group Spiritual Direction*; Fryling, *Seeking God Together*.
45. Demarest, *Soul Guide*.

ECUMENICAL SPIRITUAL DIRECTION

As interest grew on how spiritual direction is practiced within each tradition, there is an accompanying curiosity about how it can be enriched across the traditions. This signaled the dawn of ecumenical spiritual direction: the interaction and sharing of resources across different Christian spiritual traditions in a friendly ecumenical spirit. Works by Lavinia Byrne,[46] Norvene Vest,[47] Gary Moon and David Benner,[48] and Suzanne Buckley[49] are examples that signal the interest here.

Byrne's work consists of a collection of articles previously published in *The Way*, an international review of contemporary Christian spirituality.[50] It is entirely focused on spiritual guidance and has two parts: the first treats the practice in various Christian traditions, including the desert fathers and mothers, Benedictine, Celtic, Carthusian, Carmelite, Ignatian, and several contemporary directors such as Evelyn Underhill and C.S. Lewis; and the second examines several world faiths, such as Hinduism, Zen Buddhism, and Islam. My interest at this point is on part one. I will refer to part two in the next section.

Byrne's purpose is two-fold: the first is to illumine how spiritual direction is practiced within each of these traditions. As she notes, spiritual direction is both an art and a science, and so each tradition's practice stems from its own spiritual theology. Further, she urges that each tradition's wisdom of the past should not be forgotten in our enthusiasm for the present. Hence, she makes the connection between each tradition's history, theology, and practice of spiritual direction. Her first priority for spiritual directors is that one's practice must be rooted in a deep understanding of the history and theology of one's tradition.

Byrne's second purpose is to promote mutual understanding across the traditions. "Where this reflection and training are underpinned by an understanding of the tradition, they stand a chance both of contributing to the ministry of those involved and of promoting respect and understanding when genuine differences emerge."[51] Here, Byrne notes the contemporary need to engage beyond one's tradition and sounds the call to do so. But she

---

46. Byrne, *Traditions of Spiritual Guidance.*
47. Vest, *Tending the Holy.*
48. Moon and Benner, *Spiritual Direction and the Care of Souls.*
49. Buckley, *Sacred Is the Call.*
50. See http://www.theway.org.uk/.
51. Byrne, *Traditions of Spiritual Guidance*, viii.

recognizes that mutual respect and understanding is only possible when we have first gained an in-depth understanding of our own tradition.

Vest's work is similar. Organized in three parts, she touches first on four worldwide faith traditions including Buddhism, Sufi Islam, Hinduism, and Judaism; then on four Christian traditions: Ignatian, Evangelical, Carmelite, and Benedictine; before extending beyond to several special perspectives such as how Franciscan spirituality ministers to the poor, reaching out to the Gen-X soul, and feminist spiritual direction. As with Byrne's work, my attention at this point is given to Vest's focus on the Christian traditions. Like Byrne, she sounds the call to reach across the traditions, in large part inspired by Spiritual Directors International's call to "[tend] the holy around the world and across traditions."[52] Nevertheless, she sought first to illumine the practice within each tradition before extending beyond them. These studies are helpful as they demonstrate how each tradition's practice flows out of its particular history and theology.

Another work with a similar regard is that by Gary Moon and David Benner.[53] Their contribution was a study of spiritual direction in seven major traditions in Christian spirituality that also extended to how Christian spiritual direction can, together with psychotherapy and pastoral counseling, become a formidable triad in Christian soul care. Concerned about the "one-dimensional" nature of recent literature in spiritual direction, they hope that their work, inspired by Richard Foster's classification of six major Christian traditions,[54] will lend support to "the challenge of reintegrating streams of soul care that have been separated for nearly a century."[55] Hence, like Byrne and Vest, they encourage "respectful interdisciplinary dialogue and ecumenical openness."[56]

Thus far, these three works have all sought to illumine how spiritual direction is practiced within a Christian tradition before sounding the call for ecumenical interaction. As a priority, they first make the connection between each tradition's history, spiritual theology, and its practice of spiritual direction before attempting to engage another Christian tradition.

Buckley's contribution is a collection of articles by experienced spiritual directors that treats all the major aspects of spiritual direction from a broadly ecumenical perspective. These are all very helpful as training

---

52. Vest, *Tending*, vii.

53. Moon and Benner, *Spiritual Direction and the Care of Souls*.

54. Foster, *Streams of Living Water*.

55. Moon and Benner, *Spiritual Direction and the Care of Souls*, 9.

56. Moon and Benner, *Spiritual Direction and the Care of Souls*, 9.

material for spiritual directors. However, the challenge comes with the call to extend the practice across the traditions.[57]

In her chapter on "Widening the Tent: spiritual practice across traditions," Sandra Lommasson, past president of Spiritual Directors International, notes the shifting spiritual landscape that changed the orientation of spiritual directors training programs from what were typically Roman Catholic, with clear institutional connections and heritage, to new ones that included candidates from the different traditions within the Christian church as well as some from entirely different faith traditions. She notes that "spiritual directors found themselves approached by growing numbers of people outside their own traditions or any tradition, [with] the one commonality being an evident hunger for something "more.""[58] She described this as "the creative evolutionary spirit" that is moving powerfully in human consciousness and that crosses traditional boundaries. It is this recognition that moves her to make the call to widen the tent.

While the call to Christian spiritual directors to widen their tent can enrich our understanding of God's diverse ways of relating across the traditions, it also raises important considerations for the practice of spiritual direction in an ecumenical setting. As Byrne, Vest, and Moon and Benner have demonstrated, it is important for spiritual directors to first be firmly grounded in their own traditions before engaging another, for the lack of knowledge of one's own tradition inhibits true engagement with another. It also exposes one to inappropriate mixing and matching of practices that are inconsistent with a tradition's history and theology. Aware of this danger, Lommasson cautions: "We need to find ways of honoring other and emerging traditions without losing the integrity that comes from depth of location in a particular tradition."[59]

However, it is a constant challenge in an ecumenical setting to retain the depth of location in one's spiritual tradition while respectfully engaging another. Hence Lommasson was quick to add that "shaping the director's gifts toward holding these tensions within themselves in creative partnership with the Spirit is an awesome charge." As she sees it, directors "need to be firmly rooted but not rigid and be capable of discerning authentic movements of Spirit in a realm where ego can masquerade as enlightenment."[60]

As it appears, the call to ecumenical openness requires that one "be firmly rooted but not rigid." Despite the overarching Christian theological

57. Buckley, Sacred Is the Call.
58. Lommasson, "Widening the Tent," 162.
59. Lommasson, "Widening the Tent," 162.
60. Lommasson, "Widening the Tent," 162.

center in ecumenical spiritual direction, the challenge remains on how to honor each other's tradition's history and spiritual theology while remaining firmly grounded in one's own tradition. It requires that all spiritual directors be diligent and faithful in retrieving another tradition's history and theology. Clearly, the challenge in ecumenical spiritual direction requires that spiritual directors possess a robust knowledge of their own spiritual traditions and at least an adequate appreciation of another's.

INTERFAITH SPIRITUAL DIRECTION

The complexity increases when we extend the tent beyond the ecumenical to the interfaith. Interfaith spiritual direction, as the term suggests, is the practice of spiritual direction across different world faiths, including Christianity. Its impetus is a shared universal spirituality that transcends the boundaries of a singular religious tradition. Edwards describes it as that place "where we can embrace that diversity within the Unity that is God."[61] For Edwards, when we do not seem to find help from our faith tradition for our present spiritual experience, it may be reason enough to "find a spiritual companion from a more sympathetic tradition."[62]

In this regard, Byrne's and Vest's contributions already included a discussion of how spiritual direction is done in other world faith traditions. While they were careful to respect the historical and theological boundaries between each world religion, they nevertheless echo the evocative call by Spiritual Directors International to "[tend] the holy around the world and across traditions"[63]—a call that is also echoed in Buckley's work.[64]

Show Me Your Way is Rabbi Addison's call to exploring interfaith spiritual direction. In it, he posits some of the historical roots of interfaith spiritual direction and contemporary reasons why people seek it. He recounts how interfaith spiritual direction from a Catholic spiritual director helped him to "recognize God's transforming presence" during a period of crisis in his life. Likening his experience to Hagar at the well, he felt that his eyes were "finally being opened to the unfolding wonder of intimacy with God."[65] Addison also described how a Christian transpersonal psychologist and spiritual director benefitted from interfaith spiritual direction as she

61. Addison, *Show Me Your Way*, 107.

62. Addison, *Show Me Your Way*, 107.

63. Vest, *Tending the Holy*, vii.

64. See also Mabry, *Noticing the Divine*, and Mabry, *Spiritual Guidance across Religions*, for works on interfaith spiritual guidance.

65. Addison, *Show Me Your Way*, 57.

described how guidance from a Buddhist "literally rescued her Christian faith."[66]

Apparently, interfaith spiritual direction has been of benefit to some of its advocates. But Rabbi Addison was quick to add that it has its drawbacks.[67] One Jewish girl who sought spiritual guidance from Christianity reflects on its difficulties: "Language was certainly a big one. Even the same words–like grace, spirit, discernment–can have different meaning for people with different religious experiences."[68] Interfaith spiritual direction certainly has to contend with the different theologies or philosophies, and the religious histories and distinct practices that each faith tradition brings.

Interfaith spiritual direction may be an avenue for a seeker from one spiritual tradition to learn from a guide of another, but when the relationship leads to the "mixing and matching" of different faith traditions, the outcome may be more harmful than helpful. As interfaith spiritual director Dr. Mary Ann Woodman of the Center for Spiritual Practice warns; "those who selectively appropriate practices from here and there wind up with a faith 'like a cut bouquet, beautiful–but without roots and ungrounded, ultimately fated to wither.'"[69]

Woodman's comment drives the point home. Interfaith spiritual direction can wind up without a clear theological center and certainly not a shared history. As spiritual direction is the effort to reflect on spiritual experience in search of the Holy, the absence of clear theological criteria makes the practice untenable. Gordon Smith makes a pertinent point: "As with all ministries of the church, it is vital that we establish the theological vision or perspective by which we enter into the good work of spiritual direction."[70] In the same vein, veteran Jesuit spiritual director, William Barry believes that "the practice of spiritual direction needs to become theologically more grounded." He elaborates that "[an] adequate theology of prayer and of spiritual direction must take into account the trinitarian dimension of the encounter with God in this world . . . Moreover, we shall also come to see that, in spite of the relative isolation of the direction relationship as one-on-one, it must be seen as part of the community not only of the Trinity, but also of the church."[71] Clearly, the separation of theology and practice in interfaith

---

66. Addison, *Show Me Your Way*, 87.

67. See especially Addison's discussion in his preface and chapter on "Blessings and Drawbacks."

68. Addison, *Show Me Your Way*, 101.

69. Addison, *Show Me Your Way*, 103–4.

70. Smith, *Spiritual Direction*, 19.

71. Barry, *Spiritual direction and the encounter with God*, 2–3.

spiritual direction is a matter of grave concern. It brings into sharp focus the need to ground each Christian tradition's practice of spiritual direction in its particular history and Christian spiritual theology.

CONTEMPORARY SPIRITUALITY

Extending further afield, we discover the nebulous climate of contemporary spirituality. As Episcopalian Bishop Steven Charleston observes, the contemporary hunger for spirituality over traditional forms of religion is fertile ground for the proliferation of new spiritualities, many of which offer the spiritual consumer the flexibility of a customized spirituality without the perceived encumbrances of a prescriptive spiritual theology. One finds a tendency to focus purely on religious experience as it seeks to connect with Mystery rather than coherence in theological reflection on how Mystery informs religious experience. Practices are foremost in the search for a lifestyle, and these seem at times to be in conflict with a comprehensive theology of the spiritual life. While these spiritualities may possess their own values, they tend to be root-less and theologically shallow.[72]

Consistent with Charleston's observations, Philip Sheldrake, author of *Spirituality and History*, notes that the "contemporary interest in spirituality is frequently accompanied by what might be called a theological vacuum."[73] He argues that there is a "radical pluralism" that stands in the place of what is viewed as the "old consensus" of the classical spiritual traditions.[74] Unfortunately, though, there is clearly a breach between theology and practice in contemporary spirituality.

So, the problem gets worse with each widening of the tent. The tendency in contemporary spirituality to focus on experience apart from theological reflection or historical antecedents is not conducive to dialogue. Suffice it to say, the distinct tendency in contemporary spirituality is eclectic, ahistorical, and atheological, and it does not take well to Christian spiritual direction.

72. See Charleston, "A graph of spirituality: understanding where we are going by knowing where we have been," 183–98, for a discussion of these spiritualities and their challenge to spiritual directors.

73. Sheldrake, *Spirituality and History*, 1

74. See Sheldrake, *Spirituality and History*, 1–10, for a discussion of the issues in spirituality brought on by postmodernity.

A PRESENTING PROBLEM
ON ECUMENICAL SPIRITUAL DIRECTION

As we extend the tent across the traditions and faiths, the need to be firmly grounded in one's tradition is paramount before meaningful engagement with another is possible. Whether we trace the problem from the micro perspective of ecumenical spiritual direction to the macro perspective of contemporary spirituality or vice versa, the challenge is the same, we need an in-depth understanding of our own spiritual tradition before we can meaningfully engage another.

We also need to be precise in retrieving another tradition's history and spiritual theology if true ecumenical dialogue is to be achieved.[75] Disconnected from its tradition's history and theology, the practice of spiritual direction runs the risk of reflecting on experience without clear historical points of reference or theological criteria. When Christian spiritual direction fails to be historically faithful and theologically truthful to a tradition's heritage, it becomes ungrounded and will not stand the test of time.

It is my contention that the practice of Christian spiritual direction, as reflection on religious experience, must honor the connection to one's historical roots and theological foundations before help can be discerningly offered to others across the traditions. My work, therefore, seeks to demonstrate the integral connections between a tradition's history, spiritual theology, and its ensuing practice of spiritual direction. Making and retaining this perspective is not only important to ecumenical spiritual direction, it also furnishes both the directee and director with a tri-perspective that reflects on experience in the light of one's personal history and theology.[76]

---

75. See Williams, *Retrieving the Tradition and Renewing Evangelicalism*, for a discussion on the issues surrounding the retrieval of the Christian tradition, especially by Evangelicals, in a pastorally sensitive and academically rigorous work.

76. See Browning, *A Fundamental Practical Theology*. The eminent theologian of practical theology Don Browning has proposed that the rhythms of descriptive, historical, systematic, and strategic practical theology are important "movements of theological reflection in all practical religious activity," including the activity of care. While Browning utilizes the four rhythms or movements in his approach to practical theology, I utilize the triple perspectives of history, theology, and reflection on experience for the practice of spiritual direction.

ECUMENICAL OPENNESS ACROSS THE IGNATIAN AND REFORMED TRADITIONS

Specific to my concern with ecumenical spiritual direction is the challenge when Protestants embrace the practice of spiritual direction from a Roman Catholic tradition. In recent decades, we have seen a sharp increase in the number of Protestants receiving training in spiritual direction from a variety of Roman Catholic traditions.[77] This healthy development has enriched both the Catholic and the Protestant churches in their understanding of the spiritual life and its growth. However, this development is not without its difficulties. As Christian spiritual direction is seen as the logical end of Christian spiritual theology, Protestant practitioners of spiritual direction are often confronted with having to resolve differences between Roman Catholic and Protestant theologies of the spiritual life despite finding many areas of common emphasis.[78]

The points of continuity and discontinuity between Catholic and Protestant theologies of the spiritual life therefore become an important consideration in view of this recent development. Points of continuity will help to reinforce shared convictions for practice, while points of discontinuity will require respectful dialogue rather than being simply brushed aside. However, not all directees or aspiring directors are careful to honor the traditional denominational boundaries. As Sheldrake observed, "exclusive systems are increasingly giving way to an eclectic approach to spirituality that is prepared to 'borrow' not only from across denominational boundaries, but also from other world faiths."[79] This development raises the questions on how we might appropriate these practices in a manner that is historically faithful and theologically coherent.

Two streams from the Catholic and Protestant traditions have received particular attention in recent decades. From within the Catholic Church, the *Spiritual Exercises of Saint Ignatius* has enjoyed a very warm reception

77. See Grafted Life Ministries and its resource Evangelical Spiritual Directors Association, and SDI and its publications.

78. The conference papers on John Calvin and Ignatius of Loyola presented at St. Patrick's College, Maynooth, Ireland is an example of how pastors and theologians from the Reformed and Ignatian traditions share respective understandings and common emphases of the Christian life. See McConvery, *Living in Union with Christ in Today's World*.

79. Sheldrake, *Spirituality and History*, 1–10. A number of works on the Christian spiritual traditions have all emphasized that a proper hermeneutic requires that these traditions be read within their historical context and theological framework. See, for example, O'Donnell and Maas, *Spiritual Traditions for the Contemporary Church*, and Goggin and Strobel, *Reading the Christian Spiritual Classics*.

not only from among Catholics but also among Protestants as a guide to spiritual formation and direction. Examples of retrievals of this tradition include those by Jesuits John English,[80] Gilles Cusson,[81] George Ganss,[82] Francis Houdek,[83] George Aschenbrenner,[84] and recently, Richard Malloy,[85] Mark Thibodeaux,[86] and Timothy Gallagher, O.M.V.[87] to name but a few. Protestants who retrieved the *Spiritual Exercises* include James Wakefield,[88] Alex Aronis,[89] and Larry Warner.[90]

Within the Protestant church, the spirituality of John Calvin has enjoyed renewed interest among those in the Reformed tradition for practical faith formation and guidance. These studies include a work by a lay Catholic Lucien Richard,[91] and by Protestants Ford Lewis Battles,[92] Dennis Tamburello,[93] Elsie McKee,[94] Randall Zachman,[95] Julie Canlis,[96] Todd Billings,[97] and Matthew Bolton.[98]

---

80. English, *Spiritual Freedom*.

81. Cusson, *Biblical Theology and the Spiritual Exercises*.

82. Ganss, *Ignatius of Loyola: The Spiritual Exercises and Selected Works*.

83. Houdek, *Guided by the Spirit*.

84. Aschenbrenner, *Stretched for Greater Glory*.

85. Malloy, *Spiritual Direction*.

86. Thibodeaux, *Ignatian Discernment of Spirits*.

87. Gallagher, *A Handbook for Spiritual Directors*.

88. Wakefield, *Sacred Listening*.

89. Aronis, *Developing Intimacy with God*.

90. Warner, *Journey with Jesus*.

91. Richard, *The Spirituality of John Calvin*.

92. Battles and Tagg, *The Piety of John Calvin*.

93. Tamburello, *Union with Christ*.

94. Calvin, *John Calvin: Writings on Pastoral Piety*.

95. Zachman, *John Calvin*.

96. Canlis, *Calvin's Ladder*. In her outstanding comparative study of Calvin and Irenaeus, Canlis offers a spiritual theology of ascent and ascension that is firmly grounded in Calvin's understanding of God's work in Christ. Christ came to us as man (*descent*) and having accomplished his mission, he went back to the Father (*ascent*). Consequently, "the entire Christian life is an outworking of this ascent—the appropriate response to God's descent to us—that has already taken place in Christ. Thus, for Calvin, the only appropriate human ascent is a matter of participating in Christ." Communion with God is, therefore, "a participation in Christ's own response to the Father, whether that be desire for God, prayer, obedience, vocation, or worship." See Canlis, *Calvin's Ladder*, 3.

97. Billings, *Union with Christ*.

98. Boulton, *Life in God*.

WORKS RETRIEVING THE IGNATIAN
AND REFORMED TRADITIONS

In Wakefield's helpful guide, he adapts the *Spiritual Exercises* into a day-to-day format for personal use in collaboration with a listening group. His introduction includes an overview on Ignatius and the history of the *Exercises*, as well as how the *Exercises* were adapted for daily use and embraced by Protestants early in its history. Wakefield was careful to craft four movements in his format that correspond to the Four Weeks of the *Exercises*. Emphasis was given to Scripture and the role of the Holy Spirit as the primary Guide, imaginative prayer and journaling as means for receiving guidance, while utilizing the four movements of *Lectio Divina* as a framework. The listening group served as human helpers in the sacred task of listening for the Holy Spirit's voice in one's life.[99]

Wakefield's contribution is significant as it avails itself of an Ignatian spiritual classic for contemporary Protestant use. However, Wakefield acknowledges that he "incorporates small revisions to avoid unnecessarily alienating Protestants."[100] One of the revisions was the rephrasing of the first sentence in the Principle and Foundation, a construct that is central to Ignatian spirituality.[101] Wakefield's justification for this revision was that he adapted it from John English, a noted Jesuit spiritual director and author. While I will address English's own justification in this matter, my concern here is that this manner of revision raises questions about being faithful to the historical and theological context of the *Exercises* and Ignatian spirituality. Sometimes it is easy, in the eagerness to appropriate the *Exercises* for a Protestant audience, to overlook important aspects in its underlying theology.

Warner's significant contribution is the fruit of years of experience guiding students at Biola University through the *Exercises*. He includes a more substantial introduction to Ignatius and the history of the *Exercises*, especially elaborating on certain key elements in its dynamics, and the format he uses for the *Exercises* proper corresponds to that of the *Spiritual Exercises*. In bridging it to his Protestant audience, he included some preparatory exercises and extended times in the Principle and Foundation to properly ground an exercitant before embarking on the Weeks of the *Exercises*.

---

99. Wakefield, *Sacred Listening*.

100. Wakefield, *Sacred Listening*, 16.

101. Wakefield, *Sacred Listening*, 179, 203n2.

Despite these strengths, there were two aspects that were less well accomplished in his work. He left out the phrase "and by this means to attain salvation" in the Principle and Foundation,[102] and diminished the importance of several "structural meditations"[103] which are regarded as core to Ignatian discernment. These unfortunate blemishes to what is otherwise an excellent guide to the *Spiritual Exercises* once more emphasize the need for great precision and care in the matter of retrieving a spiritual classic for contemporary use. Once again, it is tempting, and easy, to overlook Ignatius' own theological paradigm and historical constructs in the effort to made it more palatable to a Protestant audience. These matters require careful attention when spiritual direction is exercised in an ecumenical setting.

Apart from these two Protestant retrievals of Ignatian spirituality, many noted scholars of Ignatian spirituality have also retrieved the *Exercises* for a contemporary audience. As I have noted above, a few examples are those by John English, George Ganss, and Gilles Cusson, along with one by a former lay catholic Margaret Silf.[104] Even with these noted Ignatian scholars, there appears to be occasions in which liberty is taken when representing the *Exercises* for the contemporary audience. In our earlier reference to English's work, he rephrases the first sentence of the Principle and Foundation from the original translation by Louis Puhl, "Man is created to praise, reverence, and serve God our Lord, and by this means to save his soul"[105] to "Human persons are created to praise, reverence, and serve God, and so embrace salvation."[106] While it may be argued that English was using inclusive language, Ganss does the same but retains the latter phrase in the Foundation as "and by means of doing this to save their souls." This incident of liberty notwithstanding, it is apparent that Ignatian scholars by and large were careful to attend to the historical context and theological paradigm in their work. Cusson and Ivens are two examples where great care is taken to be faithful to Ignatius' sixteenth-century historical and theological context.

Similarly, noted Calvin scholars have retrieved Calvin's spirituality for the contemporary audience. I have listed the examples in Lucien Richard,

102. Warner, *Journey with Jesus*, 80.

103. The meditations are "Call of the King," "Two Standards," "Three Classes of Persons," and "Three Kinds of Humility." In his book review, theologian Wilkie Au notes that "practitioners of Ignatian spirituality generally consider these "structural meditations" to be crucial for maintaining the Exercises' thrust towards the "Election," (i.e., the making of a choice in which God is *the* telling influence)." See Au, "Review of *Journey with Jesus*," 3.

104. Silf, *Inner Compass*.

105. Ignatius and Puhl, *The Spiritual Exercises of St. Ignatius*, 12.

106. English, *Spiritual Freedom*, 28.

Ford Lewis Battles, Elsie McKee, Randall Zachman, Julie Canlis, Todd Billings and Matthew Boulton. All these scholars have taken care to attend
to the historical and theological context of sixteenth-century France and
Switzerland. For example, Lucien Richard, a Roman Catholic, discusses the
spiritualities of the sixteenth century as he considers the context of John
Calvin's spirituality. He also includes a linguistic analysis of Calvin's differentiation between *devotio* and *pietas*. Further, he examined Calvin's episte-
mology through the correlation of Word and Holy Spirit, before concluding
with the implications of Calvin's spirituality for today. This manner of careful analysis reflects Richard's effort at being historically and theologically
precise.

The other authors listed have, likewise, sought to be faithful to Calvin's
historical context and theological climate. McKee adopts an autobiographical introduction to Calvin to paint his historical setting, then provides a section on his theological orientation before going on to discuss his liturgical
and sacramental practices. Battles drew significant portions from Calvin's
Institutes to sketch Calvin's pilgrimage before introducing Calvin's faith and
teachings on the Christian life. Likewise, Zachman paid close attention to
Calvin's historical and theological location, especially his relationships with
contemporary reformers, and his exegetical method in his efforts to present Calvin as teacher, pastor and theologian. Finally, Boulton was careful
to attend to Calvin's historical and theological context even as he attempts a
"rereading" of the *Institutes* with a particular focus on practical formation.
In this regard, all these scholars have attempted to be faithful to Calvin's
life and times in the context of the sixteenth century. Still, Calvin scholar
Richard Muller warns that quite a number of contemporary scholars have
ignored Calvin's historical and theological context in their eagerness to use
Calvin as an advocate for their cause.[107]

A case in point is a recent conference on the spirituality of John Calvin
and Ignatius Loyola held at St. Patrick's College in Maynooth, Ireland. It
brought together scholars, pastors, and laity from the Reformed, Roman
Catholic and other traditions for a weekend of interactions in a friendly
ecumenical climate–an effort that is to be praised. Among the papers presented were those that sought to be faithful to Calvin and Ignatius as they
were known in their historical and theological context in the sixteenth century. The papers presented at the conference have since been edited and
published by Brendan McConvery.[108]

107. Muller, *Calvin and the Reformed Tradition.*
108. McConvery, *Living in Union with Christ in Today's World.*

Specific to my concern, however, is the workshop on the spirituality of John Calvin and Ignatius Loyola. In a helpful way, it drew attention to the emphasis that both Calvin and Ignatius gave to an experiential knowledge of God and highlighted ten areas of similarities in their spiritualities. But in their effort to engender a spirit of unity across the broadly ecumenical setting, some of the discontinuities between Calvin and Ignatius were clearly glossed over.[109] As a result, one may leave the workshop thinking that Calvin and Ignatius shared the same theological bases on their theology of union with God when in fact they did not. While the ecumenical spirit of unity was helpful, glossing over the finer nuances in history and theology may in fact hurt rather than help in ecumenical dialogue when these differences eventually come to light.

On a more positive note, a 1994 doctor of ministry study possesses greater rigor in its comparison of Ignatius and Calvin as spiritual guides.[110] Bennett's helpful study posits that both Ignatius and Calvin were heavily influenced by sixteenth-century humanism, especially in its cry to return to the sources. He identified areas of similarities and differences between Calvin and Ignatius that included their shared focus on the Scriptures, their commitment to prayer and reflection, their missional focus on the world, and their different perspectives on confession. My work seeks to carry the discussion further by analyzing the finer details on how their personal histories shaped their theological persuasions which in turn shaped their particular method of spiritual guidance. In making these connections, my study seeks not only to emphasize the importance of careful retrieval but also, through its comparative analysis, to make a contribution by highlighting the continuities and discontinuities between their histories, theologies and methodologies.

THIS WORK'S FOCUS

It is in view of these developments that this comparative study of Ignatius' and Calvin's history, theology, and practice of spiritual direction addresses the danger of being ahistorical and atheological in spiritual direction, especially in an ecumenical setting. I intentionally focus my research on a

---

109. See "The Spirituality of John Calvin and Ignatius of Loyola: A Workshop," in McConvery, ed., *Living in Union with Christ in Today's World*, on important discontinuities like those of union with Christ and appeals to Mary in prayer were not treated. It is important to acknowledge these discontinuities even in the effort to participate respectfully in an ecumenical conference.

110. Bennett, *John Calvin and Ignatius of Loyola as Spiritual Guides for Today*.

retrieval of Ignatius of Loyola and John Calvin that interprets them in their sixteenth-century historical and theological contexts, investigating their understanding of the theological criteria and practice of spiritual guidance for insights for the ministry of spiritual direction today. I propose that spiritual direction in an ecumenical setting will gain from, rather than be hindered by, clarity on the continuities and discontinuities in their history, theology, and practice of spiritual direction.

I will demonstrate that each tradition's practice of spiritual direction stems from its particular history, from which evolves its particular theology, and from which emerges its particular methodology.[111] Hence it is important to make, and retain, the connections in a tradition's history, theology, and practice of spiritual direction before comparisons, and enrichment, across traditions can be honestly and fruitfully made. When spiritual directors take care to be properly grounded in their tradition's historical and theological distinctives, then their efforts at reaching across traditions will be less inclined to run the risk of confusion but rather, hopefully, will truly enrich the ecumenical spirit.

THIS WORK'S METHODOLOGY

This study adopts the hermeneutical approach for the study of spirituality by Sandra Schneiders.[112] It is a three-step approach that first seeks to *describe* the phenomena of the Christian spiritual life under investigation. Second, it seeks to *critically analyze* the phenomena. Thirdly, it works towards a *constructive interpretation*. Schneiders explains that "the objective of the study of spirituality is not simply to describe or explain the spiritual experience but to understand it in the fullest sense of that word." "The point here is that studies in spirituality are, ideally, neither purely descriptive nor merely critical but also constructive, even though any given study might focus more directly, or even exclusively, on one or another dimension of the project."

In the endeavor to *describe* the phenomena in the practice of spiritual direction, the historical context surrounding the lives of Ignatius of Loyola and John Calvin will be carefully studied. This necessarily pertains to the "matrix of ideas"[113] in their cultural, political, and religious milieu, as well

---

111. In this regard, I share Allen's position but do not include the psychological perspective in my historical and theological study. See Allen, *Inner Way*.

112. Schneiders, "A Hermeneutical Approach to the Study of Christian Spirituality," 49–64.

113. Bradley and Muller, *Church History*, 24.

as the personal and corporate factors, that shaped their theology and identity and that influenced their contributions to their respective traditions, especially their practice of spiritual guidance. As a historical study, I pay careful attention to the integral or synchronic model as elaborated by James E. Bradley and Richard A. Muller. In this regard, I attend not only to the "force of personality" of these two giants of the Catholic and Protestant Reformations, but also to the "broader dialogue [that] took place with other theological topics and other issues, such as social concerns, politics, and the interaction of parties in the church in confrontation with one another. This approach provides a more complex view of history, but the complexity belongs to the materials themselves and ultimately yields a clearer sense of why ideas developed as they did."[114]

In attending to the contexts and theological forms contemporary to Ignatius of Loyola and John Calvin, I will describe the historical forces that shaped them. This will involve the "intersection of different grids" as I explore how Ignatius of Loyola as a sixteenth-century Catholic Reformer influenced the course of spiritual direction through his theological paradigm and way of proceeding, particularly through the *Spiritual Exercises*. Similarly, I explore how John Calvin as a sixteenth-century Protestant Reformer influenced the course of spiritual guidance through his theological paradigm and method as seen, in particular, in the *Institutes of the Christian Religion*.

The phenomena of spiritual direction and its theological criteria, as they were employed by Ignatius of Loyola and John Calvin, will then receive *critical analysis*. I compare and contrast the theological criteria and method of practice in spiritual guidance and analyze their continuities and discontinuities. I then offer a *constructive interpretation* on how the points of continuity and discontinuity can be navigated so that they can be of mutual benefit to both the traditions.

The primary texts that I seek to interpret are Ignatius' *Spiritual Exercises* and Calvin's *Institutes of the Christian Religion*, which I will demonstrate are their primary texts for an understanding of the spiritual life and its progress. My interpretation of these primary texts will be supplemented by insights from their other primary sources. For Ignatius, these will include his spiritual autobiography, spiritual diary, Constitutions of the Society of Jesus, and letters. For Calvin, these sources will include his commentaries, sermons, letters, and shorter theological writings. In addition, I will also refer to secondary sources for their interpretation on specific aspects in my

---

114. Bradley and Muller, *Church History*, 24.

investigation, considering the various interpretations before offering my own.

THIS WORK'S CONTRIBUTION

It is anticipated that this study's findings will illumine the art of spiritual guidance by demonstrating the pertinent relationship of historical experience on core theological criteria and their resultant methodology–and that these vectors together make for a foundational tri-perspective of a Christian practice of spiritual guidance. As I also seek to highlight the points of continuity and discontinuity in theological criteria and practice of spiritual guidance between the Ignatian and Reformed traditions, these insights will illumine how similarly, or differently spiritual guidance is practiced between the traditions and how spiritual guidance can be further enriched in each tradition and across the traditions.

The significance of this work lies in its emphasis on retaining the connections between the history, theology, and the practice of spiritual direction. In particular, the insights derived from an understanding of the points of continuity and discontinuity between the history, theology, and methodology in Ignatius of Loyola's and John Calvin's understanding of the spiritual life and its growth can offer a more comprehensive theology and methodology for use by practitioners of spiritual guidance, both from the Ignatian and Reformed traditions. While the points of continuity serve as mutual bonds to strengthen each other, the points of discontinuity offer alternative insights that help to refine an understanding of theology or methodology and thus serve to further strengthen the art of spiritual guidance for both the Ignatian and Reformed traditions.

HOW THIS WORK UNFOLDS

In chapter two, I retrieve the practice of Christian spiritual direction in historical perspective and show the connection between each period's history, theology, and practice of spiritual guidance. Beginning with the Early Church, I discuss how each period's historical context shaped its theological assumptions which in turn shaped its practice of spiritual direction.

In chapter three, I discuss the question of spiritual experience, which is central to the practice of spiritual direction, and then the theological criteria for its reflection. I discuss perspectives on what makes for a robust spiritual theology, their relationship to history, and how they are foundational to spiritual direction.

I then examine Ignatius' history, theology and practice of spiritual direction over two chapters. I begin, in chapter four, with Ignatius' own spiritual experiences in historical context, before I examine Ignatius' theological criteria in his interpretation of his experiences. Then, in chapter five, I point out the connections between Ignatius' method of spiritual direction and his theological framework.

Likewise, I examine Calvin's history, theology and practice of spiritual guidance over two chapters. I begin, in chapter six, with Calvin's religious experience in historical context followed by his theological criteria for guidance in the light of his perspective on experience. I then explicate the connections in Calvin's approach to spiritual guidance in the light of his theology in chapter seven.

In chapter eight, I examine the continuities and discontinuities between Ignatius and Calvin in historical context, especially for their theology and practice of spiritual guidance. I illuminate how continuities and discontinuities in their theological criteria account for their method of guidance.

In the concluding chapter, I offer a constructive interpretation on the continuities and discontinuities between Ignatius and Calvin and discuss how the preceding insights apply to the practice of spiritual guidance today, particularly in an ecumenical context.

2

Spiritual Guidance
in Historical Perspective

Retrieving the History
behind the Theology and Practice

THE CALL TO REACH across the traditions in ecumenical spiritual direction entails a prior understanding of its practice within each tradition. It is easy to project a popular contemporary understanding of spiritual direction, as a quasi-contractual one-with-one director-directee relationship, onto its history and assume that spiritual direction has always been as we know it today.[1] Donald Corcoran brings to our attention that, strictly speaking, spiritual direction "was not a formalized and self-conscious practice in early Christianity."[2] Moreover, as Corcoran adds, "the guidance and care of souls in its widest sense was certainly a major theme in much early Christian literature–sermons, letters, treatises of moral exhortation, etc."[3] If Corcoran is right, then it is important that we do not project a particular perspective of spiritual direction onto its past but seek to gain an understanding of its varied practice in historical and theological context. Such an approach will

1. This study recognizes that in contemporary practice, the term "spiritual direction" is often interpreted as a one-with-one quasi-contractual practice of spiritual accompaniment, while "spiritual guidance" refers to a broader concept that includes spiritual direction and other means of guidance, including sermons, letters, treatises, and liturgy, done individually or in groups.

2. McGinn et al., *Christian Spirituality: Origins to the Twelfth Century*, 444.

3. McGinn et al., *Christian Spirituality: Origins to the Twelfth Century*, 444.

enable a more historically faithful appropriation of the practice of spiritual direction for today.

This chapter seeks to retrieve the various expressions of spiritual guidance in its historical and theological context in the Christian tradition. There exists no connected narrative of the entire history of spiritual guidance. Hence I synthesize a range of works that have appeared on specific topics and eras as I make the connections between each period's history, theology and practice of spiritual guidance. As we make the connections, we will discover that each period's practice of spiritual guidance emerged out of its particular historical and theological context. It is beyond the scope of this study to elaborate in detail on the precipitating factors surrounding each period's history and theology, but I hope to uncover the variety of expressions of spiritual guidance that accompany the uniqueness of each period's history and theology. With this in mind, we embark on our retrieval from the early Church.

SPIRITUAL GUIDANCE IN EARLY CHRISTIANITY

George Demacopoulos observes that "like many things in early Christianity, there was significant variation in the approaches to spiritual direction" in the early Church.[4] His study of five monks who became clerics–Athanasius of Alexandria, Gregory of Nazainzen, Augustine of Hippo, John Cassian, and Pope Gregory I–revealed how each one struggled to reconcile their ascetic idealism with the reality of pastoral responsibility. The contrasting realities between the exponential growth of monks and monasteries in the fourth century and the growing lay movement in the institutionalized church meant that these clerics had to accommodate the differentiated pastoral needs of these communities. Each one responded differently. The outcome was five different models of spiritual direction.

Demacopoulos suggests that when we carefully examine the criteria for authority and the techniques of religious formation, we will discover different patterns on how spiritual direction operated in the lay and ascetic communities. He argues that these patterns evolved along two distinct trajectories. The first focuses on the lay community and emphasized doctrinal instruction, the distribution of charity, and the celebration of sacraments. The second, which was developed in a monastic setting, took on a more personal and interactive approach through the spiritual father and spiritual disciple relationship, and typically stresses the specific activities of one's

---

4. Demacopoulos, *Five Models of Spiritual Direction*, 1.

renunciation.[5] These helpful observations set the tone for an exploration on how each historical era and theological climate shaped its form of spiritual direction.

As we consider the desert fathers and mothers, we are greeted by Thomas Merton's comment that spiritual direction was "a monastic concept" and that it "was unnecessary until men withdrew from the Christian community in order to live as solitaries in the desert."[6] There, especially confronted with the need to discern the variety of spirits in the desert, these novices sought the help of a spiritual *abba* or *amma* who, because of their gift of discernment (*diakrisis* in Greek; *discretio* in Latin), became both an exemplar and a guide. Hence Leech proposes that the earliest signs of spiritual direction within the Christian tradition on any sizeable scale can be found in the Desert Fathers in Egypt, Syria and Palestine in the fourth and fifth centuries.[7] This seems to be the dominant perspective on the emergence of spiritual direction.

Yet Benedicta Ward warns that "it would be an anachronism to talk about "spiritual direction" among the desert fathers if we envisage a regular appointment as we would today. For Ward clarifies that the desert fathers "were very clear that the process of turning towards God . . . was given in direction only by Christ."[8] Hence, any words spoken between them were sparing and few and, when necessary, they were for "the attainment of that stillness in which the Spirit of God alone guides the monk."[9] Consequently, it would be "wrong to look for a coherent program of spiritual direction" from the literature we have of the fathers and mothers although "it is possible to see something of their expectations and experiences through some of the *Sayings*."[10]

The historical circumstances surrounding the emergence of the desert fathers and mothers were traced to a massive exodus to the desert in search of an authentic faith. In part, it was a reaction to a perceived decline in spiritual authenticity following the rapid numerical growth of state-sponsored Christianity after 313 CE. This massive exodus to the desert meant that special guidance was needed. Now confronted with the harsh physical and spiritual conditions of the desert, the novices must not attempt nor expect to make progress in the spiritual life independently but sought the help of

---

5. Demacopoulos, *Five Models of Spiritual Direction*, 3.

6. Merton, *Spiritual Direction and Meditation*, 11–12.

7. Leech, *Soul Friend*, 37.

8. Ward, "Spiritual Direction," 4–5.

9. Ward, "Spiritual Direction," 4–5.

10. Ward, "Spiritual Direction," 4–5.

one who is more experienced–an *abba* or an *amma* who would guide them in the way.

There was not a formal structure in desert spirituality, although three main types of desert monastic experiments were noted: Lower Egypt—the hermit life; Upper Egypt—coenobitic monasticism; and Nitria and Scetis— groups of ascetics. Developments were also noted in Syria, Asia Minor and Palestine. Antony the Great (251–356), a Copt and a layman, was tradition- ally seen as the prototype of the hermit life. In coenobitic monasticism, it was common for communities of brothers to unite around each other in work and prayer, while groups of ascetics were often several monks living together as "disciples" of an *abba*. The Egyptian monks tended to live in groups and revolved their lives around regular patterns of prayer and man- ual labor. Syrian monks, on the other hand, tended to be individualist and imposed on themselves the most severe forms of asceticism. Those in Asia Minor were more inclined to be theologians and writers, while those who lived in the Judean deserts tended to follow the asceticism of the Egyptian tradition.[11]

We owe our understanding of this period chiefly to several individu- als: Athanasius (296–373), bishop of Alexandria, who was credited to have written *The life of Antony*;[12] Evagrius Ponticus (345–399), who was both an abba and a writer. His trilogy, *Monachikos*, mirrors his basic structure of the mystical life. It consists of *Praktikos*—about the ascetic life, *Gnostiko*— on spiritual knowledge, and *Kephalaia Gnostica*—on Evagrius' speculative mysticism;[13] and John Cassian (360–435), who was credited for systematiz- ing the teachings of Evagrius and the major ideas of desert spirituality and bringing them to the West.[14]

Cassian's main works, the *Institutes* and the *Conferences*, were largely the product of his conversations with the desert fathers.[15] They were prob- ably written sometime between 420 and 430 for the new monks of Gaul, where he was then.[16] Casiday notes that these works became "normative accounts of the Desert Fathers" and classics in the West.[17] They serve as source material for an understanding of monastic spiritual direction. There

11. Ward, *The Sayings of the Desert Fathers*, xvii–xix.

12. See Athanasius., *The Life of Antony*.

13. See McGinn and McGinn, *Early Christian Mystics*.

14. See Allen, *Inner Way*; Chryssavgis, *Soul Mending*.

15. See Cassian and Ramsey, *John Cassian, the Conferences*; and Cassian and Ramsey, *John Cassian, the Institutes*.

16. See Chadwick, *John Cassian*; and Stewart, *Cassian the Monk*.

17. Casiday, *Tradition and Theology in St John Cassian*, 1.

is sufficient consensus that the eight deadly vices discussed in both the *Institutes* and the *Conferences* were passed on from Evagrius to Cassian. These conversations between Cassian, his traveling companion Germanus, and the desert fathers reflects the kind of teaching that is typical of the oral-aural culture of ancient Egypt. Ramsey notes that the *Conferences* "may be reduced to the passing on of Christian ascetic wisdom from masters to disciples, and both masters and disciples are intended by Cassian to appear as models of their types."[18]

Desert Spirituality

Theologically, the conviction that the kingdom of God is to be discovered within the human heart lies at the center of desert spirituality. It is in the "conversions of the heart" that a monk develops virtue and experiences salvation. Sin, like "a serpent deeply coiled" around one's heart, demanded the daily practice of repentance before an inner stillness can be experienced.[19] Hence, one must be quick to act when God moves the heart, as Arsenius attests in the *Sayings of the Fathers*–the *Apophthegmata Patrum*.[20] This pattern of being moved by the action of God first, of leaving the familiar place, going away and giving oneself over to the action of God in silence and solitude is the gateway in the desert to prayer and conversion of the heart.[21]

While some of the actions of the hermits might appear esoteric, we are reminded that the Scriptures and the wise counsel of a spiritual father support to discern these movements of the Spirit. Athanasius testifies to the shared Scriptural foundation in the spiritual father and son relationship.[22] The fathers rested their wisdom and authority on the Scriptures. They knew the Scriptures well, discussed them, memorized them and meditated on them.[23] Christ is their hermeneutical key to the Scriptures, and they sought to obey what Christ instructed.

Thus informed, they lived a radically simple lifestyle of strict asceticism. "A stone hut with a roof of branches, a reed mat for a bed, a sheep-skin, a lamp, a vessel for water or oil" was enough.[24] Though strict, their asceticism was not an end in itself but a means to greater attentiveness to God.

18. Cassian and Ramsey, *John Cassian, the Conferences*, 16.
19. Byrne, *Traditions*, 3, 11.
20. Ward, *The Sayings*, 9.
21. Ward, "Spiritual Direction," 7
22. Athanasius, *The Life of Antony*, 97.
23. Sittser, "The Desert Fathers," 199.
24. Ward, *The Sayings*, xxiii.

The monks went without sleep because they were watching for the Lord; they did not speak because they were listening to God; they fasted because they were fed by the Word of God. Still, these forms of asceticism seem to have placed the burden of their salvation on their own shoulders. While some in their midst, particular those of the Syrian tradition, displayed quite outlandish behavior, others exercised their common sense and attended to the rule of love. They balanced work and prayer as a saying attributed to Antony attests.[25]

The form of spiritual guidance that emerges out of the theological worldview of desert spirituality thus places a special emphasis on the locale of the cell, the central role of the Scriptures, and the guidance of an *abba* or *amma*. The cell is the place where one returns again and again to learn the conversion of the heart. "Go, sit in your cell, and give your body in pledge to the walls of your cell, and do not come out of it."[26] "A brother came to Scetis to visit Abba Moses and asked him for a word. The old man said to him, "Go, sit in your cell and your cell will teach you everything."[27] Strange as it may sound, the rationale behind these sayings is the insight that God can be encountered in the cell. In the silence and stillness of that solitary place, the human heart becomes more supple and ready to meet God—hence, rendering in time not the physical space of the cell per se that is so formative but, more so, the emotional and spiritual space that it engenders in the one who prays.

The desert way of wisdom, therefore, does not just leave one in the cell. It also advises one to seek the counsel of a father as the following account by Antony underscores:

> Nine monks fell after many labors and were obsessed with spiritual pride, for they put their trust in their own works and being deceived they did not give due heed to the commandment that says, "Ask your father and he will tell you." (Deut. 32:7)[28]

For this reason, desert spirituality is often described as the wisdom of the fathers and mothers. Young ascetics would seek out these elders for their guidance and exemplary lives. Perhaps they were revered more for their holiness and purity of heart than for their teaching.[29] Yet these el-

25. Ward, *The Sayings*, 1–2.
26. Systematic Series 73
27. Ward, *The Sayings*, 139.
28. Ward, *The Sayings*, 8–9.
29. Leech, *Soul Friend*.

ders possessed the gift of discernment, which is so foundational to spiritual direction.

Still, desert spirituality was a whole way of life. Leech notes that "the spiritual director was not simply someone who taught a spiritual technique, but was a father who helped to shape the inner life of his children through his prayer, concern and pastoral care."[30] Antony was described as one who was disciplined yet was tender in service. He lived simply as a hermit and advised, reconciled, healed, and encouraged those who came to him for help.[31] Though the *Sayings* come down to us in chronicled form, they were not systematically given but were occasional words given in response to a special need. They must always be read within the context in which they were given.[32] Thus the desert form of spiritual direction came to be known as spiritual fatherhood and motherhood. Although these accounts may be treated as hagiography they do, nevertheless, provide a glimpse into how spiritual guidance is dispensed during this period in the Christian tradition.[33]

The Cappadocian Fathers

While the desert fathers and mothers were exercising a form of charismatic eldership in Egypt, the Cappadocian Fathers in Asia Minor provided spiritual guidance in the form of ecclesiastical leadership. Its form, Demacopoulos proposes, was a synthesis of the ascetic and the cleric.[34] Basil of Caesarea (330–379), Gregory of Nazianzus (329–390), and Basil's brother, Gregory of Nyssa (331–395) belonged to the aristocracy and were well educated. Basil and Nazianzus studied at Athens and became close friends, but they chose to give up their earthly riches for an ascetic life of poverty and of the pursuit of God.[35]

Apparently, Basil visited the desert fathers in Egypt and Syria and lived as an ascetic among them for some time.[36] When he returned to Caesarea in 370 to become bishop, he organized the monastic life in and around that region, bringing structure and organization into the way of life learnt in

30. Leech, *Soul Friend*, 37.

31. Holt, *Thirsty for God*, 62

32. Ward, *The Sayings*.

33. Athanasius., *The Life of Antony*.

34. Demacopoulos, *Five Models of Spiritual Direction*.

35. McGinn et al., *Christian Spirituality: Origins to the Twelfth Century*, 61–88. See also Meredith, *The Cappadocians*.

36. Louth, "The Cappadocians," 162.

Egypt.[37] From that center, Basil became a major influence in ecclesiastical administration and controversy. While Gregory of Nazianzus shared Basil's education and calling to the ascetic life, he apparently had a temperament that was more suited to a life of withdrawal and only with reluctance became involved in matters of ecclesiastical politics.[38] Gregory of Nyssa did not seem to have a formal education like his brother Basil nor was there evidence that he lived as a monastic. Yet, he was the most intellectually brilliant of the Cappadocian Fathers and seemed to have wielded quite an influence at the Second Ecumenical Council (ca 381) and in the years after that.[39]

The theological polemics that dominated the religious climate meant that spiritual guidance took on a particular theological rigor. The council that met at Nicaea (ca 325), before their birth, condemned the Arian heresy and formulated the Nicene Creed. Still, offshoots from the Arian heresy lingered in their lifetime and demanded theologically clear and firm responses from the Cappadocian Fathers, so spiritual authority demanded both theological mastery and ascetical proficiency.

According to Andrew Louth, the Cappadocian Fathers manifest the influence of Origen and Neoplatonism as well as Athanasius and the contemporary ascetic movement.[40] Gregory Nazianzen blended the clerical and ascetic traditions and expected bishops and priests to be well-educated and also purified through renunciation and contemplation.[41] Consequently, the form of spiritual guidance from the Cappadocian Fathers required both theological precision and ascetical rigor. The theological polemics required the former, while progress in the spiritual life entailed the latter. Given these demands, the Cappadocian Fathers provided spiritual guidance through a broad range of means that included theological treatises, homilies, letters, and personal counsel.

Basil served as spiritual guide through his wide-ranging literary works. Besides several books, he wrote monastic *Rules* in response to questions put to him by monks and nuns. Comprising two sections: the *Longer Rules* and the *Shorter Rules*, they provided guidance on prayer and matters related to asceticism; practices which the monks and nuns apparently tended to overdo. These Rules became the basic manuals of spiritual direction in Eastern monasticism.

37. Ward, *The Sayings*, 39.

38. Louth, "The Cappadocians," 162.

39. Louth, "The Cappadocians," 163.

40. Louth, "The Cappadocians," 163.

41. Demacopoulos, *Five Models of Spiritual Direction*, 54.

His collection of forty homilies served as a guide for lay people on similar matters pertaining to progress in the spiritual life. Of special note are his numerous letters that reflected his pastoral initiatives and care for his family, friends, and members. He tells his readers to find a man "'who may serve you as a very guide in the work of leading a holy life," one who knows "the straight road to God." He warns that "to believe that one does not need counsel is great pride."[42]

For Gregory of Nazianzus, the spiritual guide must be one who had "the dignity and education of the privileged class" and at the same time, "rejected the advantages of nobility." He is one who is both theologically astute and ascetically rigorous. Gregory of Nazianzus wrote "no fewer than four hundred poems, which reflected historical, dogmatic, and autobiographical needs . . . [His] epistolary legacy remains unchallenged in the Greek-speaking church."[43] Yet, he was also known for his ascetic pursuits.

Gregory of Nyssa had many mystical writings, most of which were composed during the last ten years of his life. To him belong both the distinction of being the most systematic thinker among the Cappadocian fathers and who elaborated the richest doctrine of Christian mysticism in the ancient Greek-speaking churches.[44]

From these observations, we discover that the form that spiritual guidance took among the Cappadocian Fathers encompassed a variety of modes that were sensitive to the historical and theological dictates of their time. They exercised a form of ecclesiastical leadership that synthesized the clerical and ascetical traditions. Spiritual authority was vested in the abbot, formalized in the *Rules* and treatises, and applied through homilies, letters, and personal counsel.

The Latin Church Fathers

As we turn to consider the history, theology and method of spiritual guidance of the Latin Church Fathers, we discover that, like the Cappadocian Fathers, the Latin Fathers were providing spiritual guidance through their ecclesiastical leadership in the monasteries. The historical context was similar to that of the East as it was a time when theological battles were fought to establish the orthodox teaching of the Church. In the synods and the ecumenical councils, these Christian leaders exposed the threat of severe doctrinal distortions and heresies. They laid the groundwork for true

---

42. Leech, *Soul Friend*, 37.

43. McGinn et al., *Christian Spirituality: Origins to the Twelfth Century*, 70.

44. McGinn et al., *Christian Spirituality: Origins to the Twelfth Century*, 71.

orthodoxy and led the way in formulating the creeds. Hence, they were honored as fathers of the church for their guidance in shaping Christian orthodoxy.[45] Prominent among them were Ambrose of Milan (340–397), Jerome (347–420), and Augustine of Hippo (354–430).

The theological climate during Ambrose's, Jerome's and Augustine's time was largely shaped by the polemics over foundational doctrines of the Church, such as the Arian heresy in the Alexandrian Church and the Pelagian heresy in Rome. Hence, their priority, like the Cappadocians, was to guide toward orthodoxy and orthopraxy. They based their theology on the Nicene faith and emphasized the priority of grace in salvation. Like the Cappadocian Fathers, spiritual authority rests in the abbot, which was derived from Scripture and the Creeds. The teaching of dogma was a priority, and it was accomplished through treatises, sermons, and letters of counsel along with the occasional personal guidance.

Consequently, the form of spiritual guidance just as with the Cappadocian Fathers was significantly concerned with correcting heresy and teaching right doctrine. Ambrose certainly served as a spiritual guide not only for his influence over Augustine but also through his ecclesial leadership and preaching. He was an accomplished writer, editing sermons and exhortations collected in three books entitled *Concerning Virgins*, and complemented by *Concerning Widows*, for a woman attracted by a second marriage, among others.[46] Ambrose's influence over Augustine was unmistakable as he not only baptized him in 387 but also influenced Augustine's understanding of the doctrine of original sin, the sacraments, biblical hermeneutics and principles of ecclesiology.[47]

Augustine spent at least two decades of his life refuting the heresy of Pelagius and his defective doctrine of grace. He provided ecclesiastical leadership in this respect by laying a new foundation for the doctrine of grace in the light of the doctrine of original sin and clarified the relationship between grace and merit. His spiritual guidance in this doctrine impacted the Church through the Middle Ages until now. Augustine also guided through his teaching on the Trinity. His treatise, *On the Trinity*, comprises two parts. The first part is an exposition of the doctrine of the Trinity based on Scripture and tradition and is like a statement of faith. The second part is an exercise at understanding primarily by drawing the soul to contemplate God the Trinity. In this sense, it is a guide on integrating theological reflection and prayer.

---

45. Kannengiesser, "The Spiritual Message of the Great Fathers."

46. Kannengiesser, "The Spiritual Message of the Great Fathers," 81.

47. Kannengiesser, "The Spiritual Message of the Great Fathers," 82.

Jerome also guided in response to theological concerns and wrote a number of important literary works. His *Letters* and three *Lives* of Saints have been described as "the most significant corpus of ascetic literature in the West" of his time. "The letters reveal him as a sensitive spiritual director, and contain interesting ideas about the education of young Christians," notes Yarnold.[48]

The Orthodox Tradition

A survey of the history, theology and practice of spiritual direction in the Orthodox tradition reveals a certain consistency through the centuries.[49] It traces its origin to Athanasius and the Cappadocian Fathers down through John of Damascus and the Middle Ages. Maintained as a ministry with apostolic heritage, the spiritual elder or father serves as a living bond that dispenses wisdom and discretion that is empowered by the Holy Spirit. The framework for the spiritual guidance relationship tends to be more hierarchical though not necessarily authoritarian. The practice of spiritual direction is intricately woven into the theological and ecclesial framework of the Church, undergirded by Scripture and aided by literature such as the *Philokalia*, a collection of writings by the spiritual masters. The Orthodox Church has preserved an expression of spiritual direction unique to its tradition.

The Orthodox tradition appeals to apostolic continuity for its history in spiritual direction. Ivan Kontzevich, a spiritual son of the Elder Nektary of the famous Optino Monastery in Russia, argues that in its nascent form–"eldership"–spiritual direction can be traced back to the apostolic age itself.[50] John Chryssavgis elaborates:

> The figure of the spiritual elder illustrates the two levels on which the Church exists and functions in the world: the hierarchical and the spiritual, the outward and the inner, the institutional and the inspirational, ultimately the organizational and the charismatic. In this sense, the *geron* (Greek) or *staretz* (Russian) exists alongside the Apostles.[51]

48. Jones et al., *The Study of Spirituality*, 133.

49. I have not included the Syriac (Persian) tradition, which was also very ascetic, in this work as it was virtually unknown in the West until very recently.

50. Allen, *Inner Way*, 15.

51. Chryssavgis, *Soul Mending*, 49–50.

The spiritual elder thus serves as a living bond between the Apostles and the Christian–and in him rests spiritual authority. While he may not be ordained, the elder serves as spiritual guide on the basis of his gift from the Holy Spirit. "Such an elder merits the title *pneumatophoros* or "Spirit-bearer" because he strives to be led as perfectly as possible through the immediate guidance of the Holy Spirit, rather than through his own individual powers or ambitions."[52] Eldership thus occupies a central role in the practice of spiritual direction within this tradition.

Theologically, the Orthodox tradition's goal for the Christian life is to attain *theosis* or deification, which is brought on through the process of *karthasis* (purification) and *theoria* (contemplation). The Early Fathers understand this to be realized only at the resurrection after death, but in time Christian thinkers associate it with growth in "saving knowledge" (gnosis) brought by Christ.[53] The doctrine of divinization attained a central place in the teachings of Athanasius, who was often quoted as saying "God became man, so that man might become God." His teaching has been passed on through the centuries in the Orthodox tradition.[54]

In a recent work on spiritual direction in the Orthodox tradition, however, Allen does not so much emphasize the idea of *theosis* but rather communion with Christ. He argues that spiritual direction in the Eastern tradition is an inner way of healing and reconciliation–to God, to oneself and to others. It is a relational ministry within the broader context of total care for the person, but with the specific goal of reconciliation to God, distinctively marked by communion with Christ through the Holy Spirit.[55]

The Orthodox tradition places special emphasis on the virtues of humility, discernment and gentleness over all other virtues. The spiritual elder, as one endowed with experience and the gift of discernment, guides the directee through the dynamics of repentance and confession, self-disclosure and trust, and obedience and freedom. "Repentance is a continual enactment of freedom, a bold movement forward leading toward greater spiritual liberty." As Chryssavgis notes in St. Isaac the Syrian's words, to repent is "to accept with joy." It is "the humility and humiliation of nature" that involves a fundamental change of heart (*metanoia*) that leads to reconciliation and renewal.[56]

---

52. Chryssavgis, *Soul Mending*, 51.

53. McGinn, *The Essential Writings*, 397.

54. McGinn, *The Essential Writings*, 400.

55. Allen, *Inner Way*, 86.

56. Chryssavgis, *Soul Mending*, 20.

Repentance, however, is differentiated from confession. Chryssavgis notes that historically repentance leads to a sinner being readmitted into the worshipping community—the Church. Confession, however, takes place within the Church.[57] Allen describes spiritual direction as the hard work of guidance in repentance before the fruit of confession is reaped.[58]

Obedience is highly esteemed in the Orthodox tradition. John Climacus (579–649) adheres to the notion of obedience as expressed by Abba Hyperechios:

> Obedience is the best ornament of the monk. He who has acquired it will be heard by God, and he will stand beside the crucified with confidence, for the crucified Lord became obedient unto death. (Phil 2:8)[59]

However, Allen clarifies that even with the emphasis on obedience the directee is not deprived of all power of rational judgment and choice or a total lack of free will. Rather, the point is made that the invitation to obedience is based on a relationship of deep trust and love between the director and directee. The elder's intention is to heal and give hope, even when this demands obedience. "It is this humble love in the relationship which protects the freedom of the directee."[60]

The Orthodox insistence on spiritual guidance reflects an awareness of the potential dangers involved with ascetic practices. The practice of the Jesus Prayer from the seventh century in Mount Sinai through the fifteenth century in Russia, where it has come to be associated with spiritual direction and its spiritual guides, or *staretz* (plural *startzy*), is an example. Theophan the Recluse (1815–94) warns: "How important it is to have experienced instructors here, and how very harmful it can be to guide and direct oneself."[61] St. Mark the Ascetic (fifth century) counsels the monk Nicholas to "question other servants of God . . . in order to know how and where to direct [one's] steps, and not walk in the dark without a bright lamp."[62] St. Dorotheos, in his *Directions on Spiritual Training*, warned of the grave danger of not having a guide or teacher on the way of God. One who has no guide is like a leaf, at first green, flourishing and beautiful, but gradually withers, falls, and is eventually trampled underfoot. Likewise, St Isaac the Syrian in the seventh

57. Chryssavgis, *Soul Mending*.
58. Allen, *Inner Way*.
59. Chryssavgis, *Soul Mending*, 62.
60. Allen, *Inner Way*, 49.
61. Leech, *Soul Friend*, 41–42.
62. Leech, *Soul Friend*, 40.

century urged one to confide his thoughts to an experienced man who is able to judge patiently and discern what is truly useful.[63]

Apart from the authority of Scripture, the Orthodox tradition utilizes a major guide for its practice of the contemplative life–the *Philokalia*. The *Philokalia* is a collection of writings of the spiritual masters of the Orthodox Christian tradition from the fourth century to the fifteenth century.[64] St. Nikodemos describes it as "a mystical school of inward prayer."[65]

The Orthodox tradition laid great stress on hesychasm–the practice of silence in prayer and meditation. The practice of hesychasm, however, entails an ecclesiology: a particular understanding of the Church and a view of salvation inextricably bound up with its sacramental and liturgical life. Hesychasm is therefore part and parcel of the sacramental and liturgical life of the Orthodox Church.[66]

Hesychasm shows the way to awaken attention and consciousness, and to develop them; it provides the means of acquiring the quickest and most effective conditions for training in spiritual direction. Nicodemus emphasized that "[like] all attempts to reach a certain spiritual level the practices described require a man's care, attention and constant watchfulness, to evade the very real and unsuspected dangers of trying anything *in his own way*; the lack of spiritual leaders in our days necessitates the constant study of these sacred writings in order to follow without harm this wonderful way of the art of arts and science of sciences."[67]

Celtic Spirituality

As we turn to consider Celtic spiritual guidance, perhaps the prominence of the Celtic proverb, "Anyone without a soul-friend is a body without a head," comes first to mind. It harks back to the deep religiosity of this land prior to the arrival of the gospel, for the Celts believed in the immortality of the soul and possessed many stories that tell of their journeys and the efforts to guide them.[68] As it appears, the figure of the "soul-friend" already existed in Celtic tradition even before the arrival of Christianity. Every Celtic chief had his counselor or druid–the soothsayers who held a rapport with the gods and spoke in their name, discerning days or explaining dreams and

---

63. Leech, *Soul Friend*, 40.

64. Nicodemus et al., *The Philokalia*, 11.

65. Nicodemus et al., *The Philokalia*, 14.

66. Nicodemus et al., *The Philokalia*.

67. Macario and Nicodemo, *Early Fathers*, 13.

68. Riche, "Spirituality in Celtic," 163–64.

visions. However, after St. Patrick returned to evangelize the land that had previously held him as a slave, the Christian cleric replaced the druid as the king's chief advisor, and the title *"anmchara"* or "soul-friend" took on a Christian meaning.[69]

St. Patrick (385–461), regarded as the apostle to Ireland, was a Roman Briton who was kidnapped and shipped to Ireland as slave when he was barely sixteen years old. He managed to escape and return to his homeland six years later. However, two years after his ordination at age forty-five, he decided to return to evangelize the Celts, and he remained there till he died at age seventy-six. His evangelistic zeal and spiritual fervor left a deep imprint on Celtic spirituality and made being on exile and pilgrimage for Christ a major theme in Celtic asceticism.[70]

Unfortunately, the Celt's religious zeal and the ascetic heroism rendered the new converts rather susceptible to the ideas of Pelagius, who propagated his ideas in Britain before going to the Continent.[71] It is not unusual for the Irish penitents to adopt austere forms of asceticism to express their love for God. Nevertheless, they also carried over their love for nature and the land, for learning and manual labor into their Christian monastic expressions.

The theological value placed on the concept of soul-friendship reflected their general attitude toward the spiritual and monastic life. Their heavy emphasis on asceticism meant that no one could traverse the Christian way without the guidance of an *anamchara*.[72] Even St. Columba (521–597), who evangelized Scotland and founded the monastery at Iona, had his soul-friend in St. Laisren.[73]

That is not to say that all authority was in the hand of the spiritual guide. For as Liebert notes, "the office [of *anmchara*] consisted of counseling and guiding [and] was generally non-sacramental in nature and stressed the mutuality of the relationship."[74] Instead, the Scriptures provide the foundational criteria for guidance, and the Celts derived their emphasis on prayer, study and manual labor from it.

Still, their zeal for Christ often found expression in corporeal austerities. Thus, the *Penitentials* or manuals to guide the process of penance and monastic Rules became distinctive of Irish spirituality. The theological assumption is that, whether it is the human guide or the written manual, these

69. Leech, *Soul Friend*, 45.

70. Ó Laoghaire, "Celtic Spirituality," 219.

71. Riche, "Spirituality in Celtic," 165.

72. Ó Laoghaire, "Celtic Spirituality," 222.

73. Leech, *Soul Friend*, 45.

74. Liebert, *The Process of Change in Spiritual Direction*, 30.

serve as guides for progress in the spiritual life. Following the example of St. Patrick, many went on pilgrimage or exile for the sake of Christ–perhaps not always motivated by missionary zeal, but certainly by ascetic aspirations.[75]

So, the dominant form of guidance in Celtic spirituality came from a combination of the Irish *Penitentials* and the guidance of a soul-friend, at times in the person of the monastery's abbot. Their penchant for private penance often meant that the abbot imposes an appropriate penalty from the *Penitentials*. Somewhat bizarre, these penances are described as red, white, and blue (or green) "martyrdom." Red involved the shedding of blood and death for Christ's sake, white implied renouncing the world in the daily living of the ascetic life, and blue denotes devoting themselves to severe austerities as the expression of their penitence.[76]

Nevertheless, the Celtic monks sought to balance prayer and work as a form of guidance for their spiritual growth. They tilled the land, reared cattle and made jewelry, even as they learned to read the Bible and celebrate the Liturgy in Latin. They meditated on Scripture and especially prayed the Psalter on a daily basis. Their zeal for learning also meant they paid close attention to the education of children entrusted to their care.[77] These activities broaden their scope of guidance.

The Celtics possess a large body of prayer, especially beautifully expressed in the *lorica* or breastplate prayer. Together with their dedication to study and manual labor, these prayers contain some of the most beautiful expressions of their spiritual lives. Though the *lorica* may have been pagan in origin, they now contain Christian values and perspectives. As O'laoghaire notes, "these prayers convey a sense of completeness, for example, in enumerating the members of the body, external circumstances, all the various groups of the heavenly and earthly Church, represented by the outstanding saints. Everything, external and internal, was to be under the sway of God."[78]

The development of spiritual direction through the Celtic Church in Britain was a major development in the history of spiritual direction. This could be a period where the term "spiritual direction" came into a more formal use. Leech notes that as the Celtic church became increasingly monastic in structure, centers such as Iona and Lindisfarne seem to have become bases for spiritual direction. It has also been suggested that there was a close connection between Celtic spirituality and the eastern desert

75. Ó Laoghaire, "Celtic Spirituality," 218–25.

76. Ó Laoghaire, "Celtic Spirituality," 221; Riche, "Spirituality in Celtic" 167–68.

77. Riche, "Spirituality in Celtic," 166.

78. Ó Laoghaire, "Celtic Spirituality," 223.

movement. He notes that *"The Rule for Monks* written by St Columbanus contained a chapter which is not found in the Benedictine or other rules, entitled "On Discretion." Discretion, that quality which was valued so highly by the Desert Fathers, was described as "a moderating science," a gift by which God gives the light of discernment."[79] Chester Michael notes that "the Irish monks who evangelized northern Europe in the eighth and ninth centuries introduced spiritual direction to the laity of France and the Germanic countries."[80]

Our exploration of spiritual guidance in Celtic spirituality brings our examination of spiritual guidance in the early Church to a tentative conclusion. As we observed, there are a variety of forms of spiritual guidance during the first five centuries of the Christian Church, each influenced by its particular history and theology. Celtic spirituality is sometimes rendered as an insular tradition, but its form of guidance through a soul friend would find a similar expression in the spiritual friendships of the twelfth century. The desert fathers and mothers's way of guidance through one who possessed the gift of discernment laid the foundation for the Orthodox tradition and defined their "inner way" of guidance through the *geron* and *staretz*, whose authority is derived from Scripture and the Holy Spirit. The Orthodox emphasized the practice of hesychasm and the *Philokalia* serves as a major text for spiritual training. Cassian's systemization of desert spirituality, together with the theology and praxis of the Latin Fathers, carried the Christian West on a somewhat different trajectory. In the early Church, their form of spiritual guidance took on a decidedly theological emphasis even as they sought to balance it with ascetical progress.

SPIRITUAL GUIDANCE IN THE MEDIEVAL PERIOD

We are challenged by its sure length of time as we transition to consider the history, theology and method of spiritual guidance in the medieval period. Frequently, scholars of the Western European Middle Ages date the beginning of this era from 604, with the death of Pope Gregory the Great, to 1517, the year when Martin Luther posted his "Ninety-five Theses" at Wittenberg—a period of about a thousand years.[81] Given this long duration, I will be highly selective and discuss only the major turning points and people in my retrieval of spiritual guidance in this era. I will divide the period into three major sections, the early Middle Ages (500–1000), high Middle Ages

79. Leech, *Soul Friend*, 46.
80. Michael, *An Introduction to Spiritual Direction*, 6.
81. Peters, "The Medieval Traditions."

(1000–1300), and late Middle Ages (1300–1500), and choose to begin with Benedict of Nursia (480–547) and Gregory the Great (540–604) because of their profound influence on the Middle Ages.[82]

Perhaps more than any others, St. Benedict and Pope Gregory impacted Western monasticism through the way of their spiritual guidance. Benedict was often regarded as the "father" of Western monasticism for the influence of his *Rule*, while Gregory the Great, from whom we mostly know about Benedict through his *Dialogues*, effectively fused the ascetic and the clerical in the person of the abbot most evidently through his *Pastoral Rule*.[83]

The Benedictine Tradition

The circumstances surrounding Benedict's involvement in spiritual direction can arguably be traced to his flight from Rome to live as a hermit in Subiaco, Italy. At that time, the Roman Empire had virtually collapsed, and Rome was in a decadent state while Benedict was a student there. Sought by his disciples for his exemplary life, he formed them into a colony of twelve monasteries, each with twelve monks and an abbot. He directed these monasteries until an assassination attempt on his life forced him to flee to Monte Cassino. There he established a new monastic community and during his seventeen years as abbot wrote his *Rule* for monks.[84]

It is probable that the chaos of the outside world made Benedict emphasize strongly the desert virtues of stability and obedience to one's Abba.[85] Hence, through Benedict, Western monasticism inherited much of desert spirituality and modified them for its new circumstances.[86]

Theologically, Benedict's dictum of *ora et labora* reflected the need for balance during this chaotic time. He observed that "idleness is the enemy of the soul."[87] His theology called for times of prayer interspersed with times of manual labor—a feature manifest in his *Rule* and wrought from the wisdom of the desert. Benedict "felt that intellectual study was important, but more

---

82. I am aware that there are variations among historians on how they divide the Middle Ages into different time periods. My decision to partition it into the three time periods is influence by Kenneth Latourette and Greg Peters.

83. Demacopoulos, *Five Models of Spiritual Direction*, 163.

84. Spearritt, "Benedict."

85. Reynolds and De Waal, "St Benedict," 148.

86. Liebert, *The Process of Change in Spiritual Direction*, 30.

87. Rule of St Benedict, Chapter 48.

important was the wisdom of the heart."[88] So, we find the emphasis on the contemplative interiorizing of Scripture, most evident in the recitation of the Psalms and sacred reading.[89]

Also reflective of Benedict's times is his emphasis on peace, (Latin, *Pax*).[90] In the Prologue, he exalts: "Seek peace and pursue it." Again, "In the love of Christ to pray for enemies; to make peace with opponents before the setting of the sun."[91] Another virtue that Benedict calls his monks to is obedience. This is laid forth at the fore in the Prologue: "*Listen, O my son to the precepts of the master, and incline the ear* of your heart: *willingly* receive and faithfully fulfill the *admonition* of your *loving father*; (*cf.* Prov. 1:8, 4:20, 6:20) that you may return by the labor of obedience to him from whom you had departed through the laziness of disobedience." Apparently, obedience is greatly emphasized because it is rendered as "a means of grace."[92]

Hence, Stefan Reynolds proposes four principles on which the common life in the monastery is grounded and through which Benedict orientates his disciples to God: obedience, peace, faith and works together, and humility.[93] Benedict calls his monks to the "labor of obedience," the quest of peace, the "work of God"- which includes both prayer and manual labor, and the cultivation of humility under the *Rule*.

Emerging from Benedict's historical circumstances and theological emphases, his way of spiritual guidance is most evidently expressed through his *Rule*. It provided for a balance structure of life so that they could live together in a way that makes prayer, *Opus Dei*, central, whilst engaging in manual labor and the study of Scripture. It is within this "orderly and happy community" that the guidance of souls is carefully provided for.[94]

As Demarest observed, spiritual direction took on an institutional flavor in the monastic communities.[95] The *Rule*, appropriately applied by the abbot, offered guidelines for the spiritual formation of the community. So great was the influence of Benedict's *Rule*, that "from the seventh century onwards, it replaced all earlier monastic rules, which were regarded as severe, and was universally adopted in the West."[96] Nevertheless, Spearritt

88. Reynolds and De Waal, "St Benedict," 149.

89. Rule of St Benedict, Chapter 48.

90. Rule of St Benedict, Prologue, Chapter 4, 34.

91. Rule of St Benedict, Chapter 4.

92. McNeill, *A History of the Cure of Souls*, 108.

93. Reynolds and De Waal, "St Benedict," 156–57.

94. McNeill, *A History of the Cure of Souls*, 108.

95. Demarest, *Soul Guide*, 46.

96. Reynolds and De Waal, "St Benedict," 149.

makes the point that Benedict regarded his *Rule*, as a document, to be subordinate to the wider monastic tradition, which further saw itself as wholly subordinate to a higher rule: the Word of God himself as contained in the Scriptures.[97] "All the ancient monks considered their real rule, in the sense of the ultimate determinant of their lives, to be not some product of human effort but the Word of God himself as contained in the Scriptures[98]"

While the influence of the *Rule of St. Benedict* may be significant, Jean Leclercq notes that "[personal] spiritual guidance has not been a favorite theme of Benedictine spiritual literature."[99] Benedict "speaks of the relations the monk must have with one or two other people concerning his progress to God, but he does not treat these in as much detail as previous authors had done before him," Leclercq explains.[100] On the contrary, much of the *Rule* is presented "as though personal guidance had lost something of the importance it enjoyed in the lives of those who lived alone, now that the way of God is pursued in the common life."[101]

So, it seems that guidance has generally been offered at a communal rather than at an individual level in the Benedictine tradition. "The prioress and abbot provide an environment that confronts the monastic with the presence of God, that shows them the Way. After that it is up to the monastic to let the practices of the community and the rhythm of the prayer life work their way until the piercing good of God rises in them like yeast in bread."[102]

Nevertheless, Chapter 2 of the *Rule* describes the prioress and abbot as ones who have "undertaken the care of souls for whom they must give an account." In this regard, then, the prioress and the abbot seek to guide both the community at large and also the members within. Liebert notes that the *Rule* includes a treatment of discernment, "which, following Cassian, meant a kind of moderation, a control on the other virtues, a sensitivity concerning subjects' strengths and weaknesses."[103] Although the emphasis in the Benedictine tradition is on community, discretion is also exercised for the individual need.

Turning to Gregory the Great (590–604), we discover that the historical climate that confronts him has changed significantly through the lifetime of Benedict. The massive migrations of "barbarians" have transformed

97. Spearritt, "Benedict." 151.
98. Spearritt, "Benedict," 151.
99. Leclercq, "Western Christianity," 16.
100. Leclercq, "Western Christianity," 17.
101. Leclercq, "Western Christianity," 17.
102. Chittister, *The Rule of Benedict*, 37.
103. Liebert, *The Process of Change in Spiritual Direction*, 30.

the political landscape of Western Europe. While the vestiges of Roman rule remained, the imperial government was now located in the East and Rome was left to fend for itself. Christianity also evolved dramatically during through this period, and so great was the change in religious perspective that historian Robert Markus said that it marked the end of ancient Christianity.[104] Gregory's pontificate thus occurred in the middle of the transition from the world of the late antique Christian Roman Empire to the Christendom of the Middle Ages.[105]

This historical climate shaped the way Gregory exercised his leadership and with it, the way spiritual direction was practiced through the Middle Ages. Gregory's decisive action as Pope led him to conclude an agreement with the Lombard invaders of Italy in 592. It further established the independence of Rome from the Emperor in Constantinople. Then, Gregory's able administration of the lands of the Church led to the establishment of the machinery of the medieval papacy and the articulation of its authority in the West.[106] These developments meant that Pope Gregory had to appoint many bishops to shepherd his flock. Given his ascetic ideals, he appointed many monks to the clerical office, thereby initiating an integration of the ascetic and clerical traditions and shaping the way spiritual direction was exercised.[107]

Theologically, Gregory bridges the gap between the patristic world and the Middle Ages. His teaching on prayer "reflects the influence of Augustine of Hippo but with a practical bent, suited to his own temperament and times."[108] He also applies his ascetic perspectives to the laity. As Greg Peters explains, one of the most important theological assumptions during this time is that the contemplative life was by far a better endeavor than those who pursued the active life.[109] He translated his concept of the Christian life as exile and pilgrimage into his doctrine of prayer, making it a process of detachment from the world marked by the desire for God.[110] Hence he emphasizes that the whole life is a life of prayer lived towards God. Though aware of the tension between asceticism and the life of the laity, he sought to close the gap between them. He stressed the contemplative life of the monks

---

104. Demacopoulos, *Five Models of Spiritual Direction*, 129.

105. McGinn and McGinn, *Early Christian Mystics*, 77.

106. Ward, "Gregory the Great," 277–78.

107. Demacopoulos, *Five Models of Spiritual Direction*.

108. Ward, "Gregory the Great," 278.

109. Peters, "The Medieval Traditions," 255.

110. Ward, "Gregory the Great," 278.

while he entrusted to them pastoral duties.[111] In this way, Gregory completed the merger between the ascetic and clerical traditions in his solution to the tension between personal contemplation and the service of ministry.[112] Spiritual authority is now vested in a shepherd who possessed ascetic ideals.

Hence, methodologically, Gregory's *Book of Pastoral Rule* provided a new vision for spiritual direction for the Middle Ages. It is regarded as "the most thorough pastoral treatise of the patristic era" and conveys the ascetic perspective in at least three ways. First, it established ascetic criteria for the selection of clerics. Second, it sought to transform the average priest into a spiritual father who uses the pastoral techniques of an abbot. Third, it communicated a vision of spiritual direction through decidedly ascetic language.[113] Though originally intended primarily for bishops, its counsel was also applied to all who served as pastoral guides or spiritual directors.[114]

Gregory's approach to spiritual direction thus encourages many of the pastoral practices from the ascetic community. He utilizes the spiritual father/spiritual disciple hierarchy as the model for the way his abbots would diagnose the spiritual condition and the appropriate care for their parishioners. Book Three of the *Pastoral Rule*, in particular, develops many of the techniques employed by the desert *abbas*. These initiatives made Pope Gregory "the first bishop in the Christian West to articulate a distinctively ascetic approach for the spiritual direction of the laity."[115]

Spiritual Guidance among the Laity

As we turn our attention to the latter centuries of the first millennium, we meet what Kenneth Latourette described as a period of "great recession." He remarks that "by the middle of the tenth century Christianity in Western Europe was at a lower ebb than it was ever again to be."[116] The peril was a progressive secularization and corruption that accompanied the denaturing of the Christian name. Thankfully, the decline was neither sudden nor continuous. There were many attempts to stem the tide by Irish monks, who evangelized northern Europe in the eighth and ninth centuries and introduced spiritual direction to the laity in France and the Germanic

111. Leclercq, "Western Christianity," 119.

112. Demacopoulos, *Five Models of Spiritual Direction*, 130.

113. Demacopoulos, *Five Models of Spiritual Direction*, 130.

114. Oden and Browning, *Care of Souls*, 49.

115. Demacopoulos, *Five Models of Spiritual Direction*, 163.

116. Latourette, *A History of Christianity*, 330.

countries.[117] This development contributed significantly to the shaping of spiritual direction for there is now a great need among the penitents and oblates that practiced confession regularly. As a result, many manuals for lay training were produced to help with these practices.

Theologically, great value was placed on regular self-examination and confession. Leech records a quote from Alcuin (735–804) that urges the penitent to "lay bare by confession the secret of [one's] iniquity," for the things that are wrought in secret, though the tongue have not spoken, the conscience will not be able to conceal. Confession is a remedy for a troubled conscience. Through it comes the healing for the soul.[118]

Hence, during the Carolingian period, confraternities of clergy grew up in the urban areas with the main purpose of providing material and spiritual support for the new converts. Jonas of Orleans' wrote a lay training manual, *De Institutione Laicali*, which stressed the value of regular self-examination and confession, while others were concerned, less with "sin list," but more with motives and interior responsibility.[119] The lay movement's practice of self-examination and interior awareness seems to have an affinity with the attention given to ones interiority in contemporary spiritual direction. It is differentiated from the sacramental confession and spiritual direction that was practiced in the monastic tradition, which was sometimes administered by the same person.[120] The lay movement's practice seemed to have separated sacramental confession from the giving of spiritual direction.

Spiritual Guidance in the High Middle Ages

The High Middle Ages experienced "four centuries of resurgence and advance" between the middle of the tenth and fourteenth centuries. Certainly, the Crusades stimulated growth, but as Latourette observed, they "weakened rather than strengthened the Greek Church and the Eastern Empire in their resistance to aggressive Islam." It also deepened the widening rift between the Western and Eastern wings of the Catholic Church.[121]

The monastic movement, however, continued to multiply during this period and "reached a crest" in the thirteenth century. Perhaps rather significant was the development at Cluny, France. The unique development of affiliate monasteries with Cluny made it "the centre of a "congregation" of

---

117. Michael, *An Introduction to Spiritual Direction*.

118. Leech, *Soul Friend*, 47.

119. Leech, *Soul Friend*, 47.

120. Allen, *Inner Way*.

121. Latourette, *A History of Christianity*, 408–15.

monasteries, the precursor of such orders as the Franciscans, Dominicans, and Jesuits. Through Cluny a family of monasteries arose.[122]

Apart from its monastic reforms, the High Middle Ages was also known for the birth of scholasticism. It witnessed the formation of the first universities in Europe, for example the cathedral schools in Paris and the University of Oxford in England. With it, the scholastic way of theological method begins to pose a challenge to the monastic method, which until now was dominant.[123]

Theologically, there was an apparent rift between the monastic way and the scholastic way, although there were scholastics that belonged to monastic orders. Two examples were the Dominican, St. Thomas Aquinas and the Franciscan, St. Bonaventure. For many Christians, however, the monastic way was the preferred road to pursue the perfect Christian life and to attain the goal of the salvation of one's soul.[124] For them, the monastery was where one finds the "oxygen" of faith, hope, and love.[125] Among the monastic vows that include chastity and obedience, poverty was especially embraced as a form of union with the poor Christ of the gospel.[126]

Set against this historical and theological climate, we discover three prominent expressions of spiritual direction. They were spiritual direction by letters, through spiritual friendships, and through the Cistercians in the eleventh and twelfth centuries and the mendicant orders, the Franciscan and Dominican Friars, in the twelfth and thirteenth centuries.

The eleventh and twelfth centuries during this period were regarded as the "Golden Age of medieval epistolography."[127] As it appears, letters became a means for the practice of spiritual direction. Anselm (1033–1109) was one who enjoyed an enormous network of literary correspondence during this time. Leech describes Anselm as one who is "a wise director,"[128] and it appears that much of his spiritual guidance was offered in the form of letters. Nearly sixty percent of Anselm's letters were addressed to monks and nuns. They offered spiritual advice to his flock and dealt with a variety of themes, including the reading of Scripture and the Fathers, the fleeting nature of transitory things and the constant need to progress towards perfection in the spiritual life. He also treated subjects such as the need to

---

122. Latourette, *A History of Christianity*, 419.

123. Peters, "The Medieval Traditions."

124. Latourette, *A History of Christianity*.

125. O'Donnell, "Monastic Life," 70.

126. O'Donnell, "Monastic Life," 68.

127. Anselm and Fröhlich, *The Letters of Saint Anselm*, 1.

128. Leech, *Soul Friend*, 48.

accept suffering, to show compassion, to express mutual charity and love, to obey one's superiors as God's representatives, and to live a life of humility and prayer.[129]

During this same period, Bernard of Clairvaux (1090–1153) of the Cistercian tradition contributed to the ministry of spiritual direction through monastic reforms and spiritual friendship through conversations and letters. Bernard administered a vast network of monasteries, and his reforms returned the monastic tradition to the simplicity of the *Rule of St. Benedict*,[130] and with it, strict poverty. Bernard promoted the practice of "confession": which "was not the sacrament of penance as we know it, but the manifestation of conscience to a spiritual guide." Hence, he encouraged spiritual conversations between spiritual brothers likened to the Benedictine idea of *spirituales seniores*. This non-sacramental form of confession is similar to the form of examination of conscience that we know to be associated in a spiritual direction relationship that attends to the inner movements of the Spirit.

The twelfth century witnessed an expression of spiritual direction in the form of spiritual friendships. William of St. Thierry (1085–1148) and Bernard of Clairvaux exemplified this form of friendship within the Cistercian tradition. Leech notes that from him comes the theme of the importance of obedience to a guide.[131] We see this dynamic played out in William's own life as he was establishing his friendship with Bernard. Though already an abbot at St. Thierry, and older in years than Bernard, William wanted to be a "spiritual son" to Bernard in the Benedictine sense. "For him St Bernard was the "Abbas," a loving father appointed to condense the honey of heavenly doctrine for him, let him share his experience of the things of God, and lead his soul to the heights of the mystical life."[132] When Bernard perceived this desire, "he readily became the spiritual father as desired."[133]

Another prominent example on the subject of spiritual friendship is that of Aelred of Rievaulx (1109–1167). We read in the opening lines of his famous work, *On Spiritual Friendship*: "Here we are, you and I, and I hope a third, Christ, is in our midst."[134] This declaration expresses succinctly Aelred's understanding of true Christian friendship: that is two persons sharing a deepening bond with the living Christ. This three-dimensional

---

129. Anselm and Fröhlich, *The Letters of Saint Anselm*, 3–4.

130. Holt, *Thirsty for God*, 86.

131. Leech, *Soul Friend*, 48.

132. Déchanet, *William of St. Thierry*, 28.

133. Déchanet, *William of St. Thierry*, 28.

134. Aelred, *Spiritual Friendship*, 51.

friendship is analogous to our contemporary definition of spiritual direction involving one, the director, the other, the directee, and the Spirit of Christ in their midst and as their Guide.

As we read Aelred's work within the context of twelfth century "Christian humanism" and the flowering of friendship within monasticism, we gain an appreciation of the many opportunities Aelred had to serve as friend, encourager, and guide to many who meet him in person or read his letters and works. The flowering of spiritual friendship was in fact not limited to the twelfth century. In the sixteenth and seventeenth centuries, we witness deep friendships cultivated around a mutual spiritual quest. Teresa of Avila (1515–1582) and John of the Cross (1542–1591),[135] and Francis de Sales (1567–1622) and Jane de Chantal (1572–1641)[136] were sterling examples of these virtuous spiritual friendships.

Spiritual Direction in Mendicant Spirituality

As we have noted, the Middles Ages also witnessed the flowering of spiritual direction among the laity. The hallmark of this century was "the quest for a simple Christian life lived in poverty of spirit and in common with others for the sake of preaching the gospel of Jesus Christ."[137] The spread of the Franciscan and Dominican movements in the thirteenth century accounted for much of this development. Their apostolic ministry and exemplary lives accounted much for their influence. It was reported that on one occasion, a doctor of Sacred Theology sought the opinion of St. Francis (1181–1226) regarding a verse from the book of Ezekiel. In his humility, St Francis initially declined to comment and chose to defer to the expert training that the theologian has received. However, upon the insistence of the theologian, he gave such a profound reply that the theologian returned to his friends with this remark: "My brother, the theology of this man, held aloft by purity and contemplation, is a soaring eagle, while our learning crawls on its belly on the ground."[138] St. Francis' integration of theology and prayer, lived in poverty and simplicity, became a model of spiritual guidance.

St. Bonaventure (1221–1274) was regarded as the most significant spiritual writer of the Franciscan movement and his work *De Triplici Via* was regarded as the first detailed treatment of the three-fold path in the life of prayer. He emphasized regular examination of conscience and frequent

---

135. See Dubay, *Fire Within*.

136. Francis et al, *Francis de Sales, Jane de Chantal*.

137. O'Donnell, "Mendicant Spirituality," 86.

138. Armstrong, *Francis of Assisi*, 315.

confession. However, he did not regard frequent meetings with a spiritual director as necessary except in the early stages of spiritual growth.[139]

It was with the Dominicans that spiritual direction was directed more at the laity. As their ministry spread to the urban centers in Germany and the Lowlands, particularly among the Beguines, Beghards, and Fraticelli; the laymen themselves acted as spiritual directors as in the early monastic movement.[140] Holmes proposes that the Dominicans were "the first to train seriously for spiritual direction."[141] Previously, the practice of spiritual direction had been in the monastic model, and was generally believed to be needed only by beginners. "But now, with the Dominicans, spiritual direction was prescribed for everyone."[142]

Spiritual Guidance in the Late Middle Ages

As we consider the late Middle Ages, we are struck by the somber and pessimistic mood of a period that witnessed the horrors of droughts, famines, plagues and warfare. Both centuries were afflicted by droughts which led to the Great Famine in 1315–1317 that saw the deaths of millions. It was estimated that as many as 25 million died during the bubonic plague in the mid-fourteenth century. Further, the conflict around the papacy (1378–1418) and the Hundred Years' War (1337–1453) between England and France, all contributed to make these two centuries particularly gloomy and dark.[143]

Latourette described the mood of the fourteenth and fifteenth centuries as one of decline and of vitality. The papacy declined as a political, moral, and spiritual force, the climax which was witnessed in the Great Schism (1378–1417). Monastic life, too, was in decay. Deterioration in discipline and morals seemed to be especially marked during this period. Latourette observed that conditions appear not to have been generally as bad as they had been before the reform movements of the eleventh, twelfth, and thirteenth centuries. Still, it is significant that the only fresh monastic or semi-monastic movement that emerged between 1350 and 1500 was the Brethren of the Common Life.[144]

Meanwhile, intellectual pursuit in the universities was overrun by skepticism as late medieval theologians accorded a primary role to reason

139. Leech, *Soul Friend*, 50.
140. Leech, *Soul Friend*, 50–51.
141. Holmes, *A History of Christian Spirituality*, 68.
142. Holmes, *A History of Christian Spirituality*, 68.
143. Peters, "The Medieval Traditions."
144. Latourette, *A History of Christianity*, 640.

and diminished the role of faith. By this time, the role of reason, and with it the pursuit of logic and comprehensiveness, has overtaken the universities and began to displace monastic theology and ascetic practices, and the practice of spiritual direction.

Hence, one can understand why English Mystic Walter Hilton (1340–1396) insists that one must have a guide for the spiritual life:

> I speak of those seculars who do not fear to set out on the way of the spiritual life without a director or capable guide, whether a man or a book, obeying their own impulses . . . If not even the least of the arts can be learned without some teacher and instructor, how much more difficult it is to acquire the Art of Arts, the perfect service of God in the spiritual life, without a guide.[145]

Walter Hilton's book, *The Scale of Perfection*, was written with spiritual directors in mind. He stresses the need for discretion and discernment of spirits in the contemplative life, and urges recourse to a spiritual director especially in the early stages of the spiritual life. Thornton regards Hilton as "primarily an ascetical theologian, a director of souls," adding that *The Scale of Perfection* is primary pastoral in tenor.[146]

We find in English Anchorite Julian of Norwich (1342–1416) a different message set against the pessimism and gloom of this period. Julian guides through her mystical *Revelations of Divine Love*. It is noteworthy that in contrast to the writers of her day who made their audience feel horrendous guilt and shame, Julian "uniquely and brilliantly, turns her vision of the suffering humanity of Jesus into a matter for gratitude and joy."[147] Julian offers these words she received from Jesus: "Sin is inevitable, but all shall be well, and all shall be well, and all manner of thing shall be well."[148]

In Catherine of Siena (1347–1380), a member of the third order of Dominic, we find a "practical mystic" who guided through an exemplary life founded, mystically, in solitary meditation and prayer as a virgin celibate betrothed to Christ, and practically, in giving herself to the service of the poor and the sick, including a year when the Black Death swept across Siena. Catherine wrote hundreds of letters, some of spiritual counsel to humble folk and some to those prominent in Church and state, including the Pope. Amidst this era's gloom, Catherine's exemplary life of mystical

145. Leech, *Soul Friend*, 51.

146. Thornton, *English Spirituality*, 201.

147. John-Julian, *The Complete Julian of Norwich*, 16.

148. John-Julian, *The Complete Julian of Norwich*, 147.

devotion to Christ and practical service to the weak and the powerful, shone as a guiding light.[149]

Perhaps the most significant development set against the scholasticism of the fourteenth century is the birth of the *Devotio Moderna*, which found expression through movements such as the Brethren of the Common Life, chiefly led by Dutchman Gerard Groote (1340–1384). As the name suggest, their contribution to spiritual guidance was expressed through their common life that combined principles of monasticism with the non-monastic life.[150] The primary focus of the *Devotio Moderna* was not a reform of the monastery but a "renewal of piety among individuals, and eventually communities, in their journey toward God."[151]

The crowning influence of the *Devotio Moderna* was through *The Imitation of Christ*, whose authorship was popularly attributed to Thomas a Kempis (1380–1471). It became one of the most widely used aids to devotion, prayer, and meditation. The ideal of the imitation of Christ reflects the resurgence of interest, in this period, in Christ's humanness and suffering, and reflects the devotionalist emphasis upon the affective life.[152] Kempis instructed his readers to "take counsel with a wise and conscientious man; and seek to be instructed by one better than oneself, rather than to follow one's own inclinations."[153]

The Middles Ages witnessed the diverse developments of spiritual direction. From the monastic to the lay, from men to women, confession and direction, in person or through letters, friendly advice or authoritative counsel, treatises on the spiritual life, the ministry of spiritual direction was exercised across a broad spectrum of the Christian Church. Unfortunately, spiritual direction was both practiced in excess or absent at some points during this period.

SUMMARY OBSERVATIONS

Our survey of the connections between the histories, theologies, and practices of spiritual direction over fifteen hundred years of the Christian tradition brings us to the eve of the Reformation. It was at the Reformation that the fault lines between Protestant and Catholic theologies of spiritual guidance were most evident. The variations in the practices of spiritual direction

149. Latourette, *A History of Christianity*, 643–44.
150. Latourette, *A History of Christianity*, 648–50.
151. Burrows, "Devotio Moderna," 110.
152. Burrows, "Devotio Moderna," 122.
153. a Kempis, *The Imitation of Christ*, I.4.

over the past fifteen hundred years have largely been within the monastic and semi-monastic movements. The outcome of the Reformations will lead to significantly different approaches in spiritual guidance: the Roman Catholic way expressing a greater continuity with its history, while the Protestant expression proceeds upon a different theological basis of salvation. It is here that a study of two representative figures from two traditions within the Christian Church, Ignatius of Loyola and John Calvin of Geneva, serves to enlighten us on the continuities and discontinuities between Roman Catholic and Reformed theologies and practices of spiritual guidance. Before we do so, however, we will consider another major aspect in our retrieval of the practice of spiritual direction; it is the theological criteria that guide the reflection on religious experience.

3

Spiritual Guidance
in Theological Perspective

Discerning the Theology that Shapes the Practice

IN CHAPTER TWO, I underscored the importance of making the connections between a period's history, theology, and practice of spiritual direction. I did so by illustrating how a period's historical context influenced its theology, which in turn shapes its practice of spiritual direction. As each tradition's practice of spiritual direction is premised upon its theological assumptions, in this chapter I examine some of these assumptions and what makes for robust theological criteria for the practice of Christian spiritual direction. Jesuit theologian David Lonsdale has observed that many contemporary courses in spiritual direction have been "predominantly practical"—retrieving and developing traditional models for contemporary use. However, he argues that if the ministry is to be to effective and faithful it "needs to be accompanied by regular theological reflection," for "the primary framework of ideas, beliefs and language which shapes Christian spiritual direction is theological" rather than, for example, practical, or psychological.[1]

I will explain why Christian spiritual theology serves as a guiding science for the art of spiritual direction before going on to an in-depth discussion of five major theological doctrines that serve as guiding criteria for spiritual direction. I do so, not so much to discuss the theological criteria themselves but especially to bring out their implications for the practice of Christian spiritual direction. I adopt Simon Chan's theological framework

---

1. Lonsdale, "Traditions of Spiritual Guidance," 312–13.

as a guide and bring it to bear on other theological perspectives.[2] The five theological loci that I will discuss are the doctrine of the triune God; sin and human nature; salvation and progress in the spiritual life; ecclesial foundations on the community of the saints; and missiological and eschatological horizons. Taken together, they provide for a comprehensive theological framework to guide the practice of spiritual direction. It is important for both spiritual director and directee to be attentive to and clear about their theological assumptions, including their points of convergence and divergence, as they reflect on their spiritual experiences, especially in an ecumenical setting.

As it has been largely recognized that Christian experience is essential to the practice of spiritual direction,[3] I will not elaborate more on it but point the reader to the sources that discuss the subject.[4] Here, I am primarily concerned with the theological assumptions that undergird the practice of spiritual direction and so form the criteria that we bring to the evaluation of our spiritual experiences. As our experiences are often fragmentary, reflecting on them in the light of a comprehensive set of criteria from Christian spiritual theology helps us to gain a more holistic understanding of how progress in the Christian life is made. The work of reflection applies to both the director and the directee, first, as they reflect on the directee's experience, and then, as the spiritual director reflects with a supervisor on his experience of providing guidance.[5]

2. Chan has done some of the best integrative work on bringing theology to bear on spiritual direction and is an excellent choice for serving as a guiding framework. Here I am guided by two of Chan's books: Chan, *Spiritual Theology*, and Chan, *Liturgical Theology*.

3. See, for example, Barry and Connolly, *The Practice of Spiritual Direction*, 8— who posit that "the religious dimension of experience is to spiritual direction what foodstuff is to cooking."; Edwards, *Spiritual director*, 45—who regards "spiritual experience as events that have a particular capacity to show us the nature and guidance of God in our souls and in life around us."; and Bakke, *Holy Invitations*, 152—who challenges us to notice our own experiences of God rather than paying attention only to what we have read or heard from others.

4. In addition to the preceding footnote, see also Tidball, "Christian Theology," on the need to bring greater precision to an understanding of religious experience; Runia, "Towards a Biblical Theology of Experience," 175—on the "tremendous importance" of experience in Christian life and theology; Howard, "Experience," 176—on differentiating between different experiences and defining Christian experience as "the interaction of the living Christ with each and all dimensions of human existence."; Lane, *The Experience of God*, 3—on "the revelation of God that takes place in human experience through faith."; and Allen, *Inner Way*, 69—on the priority of God's initiative in our experience of him.

5. As it is beyond the scope of this study to discuss the subject of supervision, I point the reader to the following works. See, for example, Conroy, *Looking into the Well*;

Along with David Lonsdale, many authors have emphasized the need to reflect theologically on spiritual experience. For example, Evan Howard emphasizes the need for "theological reflection that honors the historical and semantic diversity of Christian experience in the context of a basic theology of the Holy Spirit and the Christian life."[6] Tilden Edwards proposes that the "interpretive framework" for spiritual direction is "seeded by understandings of the spiritual life found in scripture and in the lives and writings of great saints and theologians."[7] Dermot Lane sees the task of theological interpretation as "the critical unpacking of the revelation of God that takes place in human experience through faith."[8] Consequently, the question that confronts us is not so much whether theology is needed for reflecting on experience as the kind of theological criteria we bring to our practice of reflecting on experience.

Janet Ruffing describes the attention we give to the theological themes that surface in spiritual direction as "panning for gold." She explains that by attending to these themes both the director and directee will gain a heightened awareness of their espoused and operative theologies. They become more aware of what they say they believe (espoused) as opposed to the actual beliefs which their actions reveal (operative).[9] The awareness of a gap between these theologies is what one theologian refer to as the "sanctification gap."[10] It is the goal of spiritual direction to address and close this gap.

CHRISTIAN SPIRITUAL THEOLOGY AS THE FOUNDATION FOR REFLECTING ON EXPERIENCE

Consequently, Spiritual theology takes seriously the inductive and experiential dimensions of doing theology. John Coe, professor of spiritual theology at Talbot School of Theology, proposes a "theological-experiential methodology" that defines spiritual theology in "its fullest sense as a theological discipline in its own right." It attempts to integrate Scriptural

---

and Bumpus, *Supervision of Spiritual Directors.*

6. Howard, "Experience," 175.

7. Edwards, *Spiritual Director*, 2–3.

8. Lane, *The Experience of God*, 3. Lane's book is dedicated "to explore the religious dimension of human experience, to discover in faith the reality of God co-present in human experience, to situate the gracious revelation of God to man within experience, to ground the activity of faith as a response to the experience of God and to live life more fully by participating passionately in the revelatory orientation of human experience," p.3.

9. Ruffing, *Spiritual Direction*, 57–94.

10. Lovelace, "The Sanctification Gap."

teaching on sanctification with observations and reflections on the Spirit's actual work in the believer's spirit and experience.[11] In a recent primer on Spiritual Theology, Peters posits that the task of spiritual theology is "not only strictly theological, positive, and deductive, but also inductive, resting upon observation and experience."[12] He adds that it is because of this "experiential aspect" that spiritual theology is distinguished from moral and dogmatic theology.[13] Similarly, Chan notes that spiritual theology seeks to understand and guide spiritual growth by attending to biblical and experiential data.[14] The distinguishing feature that sets spiritual theology apart from its predecessors is the attention that its gives to experiential data.[15]

A brief historical review will shed more light on this emphasis. The roots of spiritual theology have been traced to the early Christian essays, medieval mystical theology, and modern ascetical theology of the Catholic Church.[16] Early Christian essays, such as those by Clement of Alexandria (150–215), often presented the spiritual life via a tripartite division of beginner, advanced and perfected, while medieval mystical theology, such as that by Bonaventure (1221–1274), described the spiritual life as progressing from purgation, through illumination, to perfection. Bonaventure's tripartite way, derived from Dionysius, became so influential and pervasive that it absorbed the earlier triad to produce "a remarkable duplication": the way of purification for beginners, the way of illumination for the advanced, and the way of union for the perfect.[17] Subsequently, the presence of the triple way of purgation, illumination, and union became a *sine qua non* of mystical theologies. This schema retained its place in the writings of the greatest Catholic Reformation spiritual authors of the sixteenth century, such as St. Ignatius of Loyola (1491–1556), St. John of the Cross (1542–1591) and St. Teresa of Avila (1515–1582), and even continued past the era of the Catholic Reformation and into the twentieth century.[18]

Contemporary examples of spiritual theology that utilizes this schema include those by Catholic theologians Reginald Garrigou-Lagrange *The*

11. Coe, "Spiritual Theology," 4–43.

12. Peters, "On Spiritual Theology," 16.

13. Peters, "On Spiritual Theology," 16.

14. Chan, *Spiritual Theology*, 18.

15. Susan Philips describes spiritual direction as "a navigational aid" in sanctification. See Philips, *Candlelight*.

16. See Peters, "On Spiritual Theology," for a primer on spiritual theology; and Peters, "Spiritual Theology: A Historical Overview," for a historical overview of spiritual theology.

17. Peters, "On Spiritual Theology," 9.

18. Peters, "On Spiritual Theology," 9.

Three Ages of the Interior Life,[19] Adolpe Tanquerey *The Spiritual Life*,[20] Joseph de Guibert *The Theology of the Spiritual life*,[21] and Jordan Aumann *Spiritual Theology*.[22] Tanquerey utilizes the words mystical and ascetical in his subtitle but demonstrates the shift to spiritual theology when he emphasizes that Christian dogma is the foundation of ascetical theology.[23] He sees the task of spiritual theology "as laying the theological or dogmatic foundation of the spiritual life and only *then* venture into the areas of ascetical and mystical theology."[24] De Guibert defined spiritual theology as "the science which deduces from revealed principles *what* constitutes the perfection of the spiritual life and *how* man can advance towards and obtain it."[25] Like Tanquerey, we notice the progression; first, on the principles that constitute the "what," and then the "how" of advancing. Finally, Aumann defined spiritual theology as "that part of theology that, proceeding from the truths of divine revelation and the religious experience of individual persons, defines the nature of the supernatural life, formulates directives for its growth and development, and explains the process by which souls advance from the beginning of the spiritual life to its full perfection."[26] Aumann provides a more elaborate definition that includes religious experience but retains the same foundational emphasis on divine revelation upon which directives for growth are formulated. From these preceding definitions, we ascertained that spiritual theology attends both to the revealed principles from the diverse riches of Christian theology, as well as the dynamics of religious experience. These twin emphases are what make spiritual theology the guiding science behind the art of spiritual direction.

Recently, a number of evangelical theologians have contributed to the discussion on spiritual theology from a Protestant perspective. We have already noted the contributions of John Coe[27] and Greg Peters.[28] Diogenes Allen retrieves much of the history we discussed earlier and differentiates spiritual theology from doctrinal theology by noting that the theological

19. Garrigou-Lagrange, *The Three Ages*.

20. Tanquerey, *The Spiritual Life*.

21. Guibert, *The Theology of the Spiritual life*.

22. Aumann, *Spiritual Theology*.

23. Tanquerey, *The Spiritual Life*, vii.

24. Peters, "On Spiritual Theology," 12.

25. Guibert, *The Theology of the Spiritual Life*, 11.

26. Aumann, *Spiritual Theology*, 22.

27. Coe, "Spiritual Theology," 4–43.

28. Peters, "On Spiritual Theology;" and Peters, "Spiritual Theology: A Historical Overview."

questions it asks are especially focused on the investigation of the spiritual life. He poses seven questions that investigate the goal of the spiritual life, its path of progress, the helps and hindrances to progress, and its eventual fruit.[29]

Asian theologian Simon Chan carries the discussion further by explicating the formal and material criteria that makes for a robust spiritual theology before going on to discuss its constitutive foundational doctrines.[30] His discussion on the formal and material criteria bears paying attention to in greater detail. He argues that the formal criteria must include the qualities of comprehensiveness, coherence, and evocability. To be comprehensive, it must draw on all the spiritual resources that are available to the Church. These include Scripture and the Christian Tradition—which is "the church's humble reception and faithful embodiment of the primary revelation of God in Jesus Christ."[31] A comprehensive spiritual theology, Chan adds, consequently "stresses a balanced approach to the cultivation of the spiritual life."[32] For example, it does not stress the exercise of the will to the exclusion of grace or vice versa. Instead, it seeks to keep a fine balance between the roles of grace and human effort in the pursuit of the spiritual life. The criterion of coherence implies that there is "internal consistency," where each part relates meaningfully to each other, forming a coherent whole, a total structure.[33] Chan clarifies that it does not mean that every aspect of faith needs to be rationalistically explained but that it possesses a structure that is able to hold the explainable and the mysterious in tension. Finally, evocability refers to the quality of a spiritual work that is able to direct our attention beyond the rational formulations to the spiritual realities they express. In a spiritual theology that possesses the element of evocability, "theological reflection and prayer are no longer discrete activities but exist in a dynamic, ongoing relationship in which one activity enriches the other, stimulating the Christian to new insights and greater fervor."[34]

A robust spiritual theology should also possess three interconnected material criteria. They are the global-contextual, the evangelical and the charismatic. First, the global-contextual criterion recognizes that the world is complex and so reaches out to both the universal and the historical in its

29. Allen, *Spiritual Theology*.
30. Chan, *Spiritual Theology*.
31. Chan, *Spiritual Theology*, 23.
32. Chan, *Spiritual Theology*, 23.
33. Chan, *Spiritual Theology*, 23–24.
34. Chan, *Spiritual Theology*, 24.

consideration of spiritual experience.[35] It considers the synchronic scale of diverse experiences universally together with the diachronic scale of the historical riches of the Christian tradition. In other words, individual spiritual experience is authentically pondered in the light of a much broader-ranging set of historical experience. Second, the evangelical criterion is important in two ways. First, it "reflects a persistent strain within the Christian tradition of telling the Christian story concerning the life, death and resurrection of Jesus Christ."[36] Second, by retrieving this evangelical heritage, we recover resources that can be used to develop a more integrated and comprehensive spirituality. The evangelical criterion thus helps us to discern more clearly the gospel story and so shapes an evangelical spirituality that distinguishes the church as a worshipping and missional community that bears the character of Jesus.[37] Finally, the charismatic criterion is important because it enlarges our doctrine of grace. "It reminds us that the Christian life is not restricted to a predictable pattern of spiritual operations predicated on the Thomistic principle *gratia non tollit sed attolit naturam* (grace does not destroy nature but lifts it up)."[38] On the contrary, it recognizes that God sometimes works in surprising and unpredictable ways, so the doctrine of grace in our spiritual theology must include this element of divine operation.

These explications make the vital point that the practice of spiritual direction must be founded upon a comprehensive and coherent spiritual theology so that its reflection on Christian experience is guided by Christian dogmas that are attested through the Christian tradition. The two major spheres in spiritual theology are the principles from divine revelation and the experience of the saints. In a sense, these two major spheres correspond to the gospel and religious experience. That is why the Christian story revolving around the life, death and resurrection of Jesus gives shape to our lives and defines the nature of our existence as members of a Christian community.[39] In spiritual direction, we reflect on the story of our lives in the light of the larger Christian story that revolves around Jesus, and its testimony through the history of Christianity.

We shall now proceed to consider several foundational doctrines for Christian Spiritual Theology. We do not so much discuss the doctrines in-depth, as it is not the intent of this work, but rather draw out their implications for the Christian life and the practice of Christian spiritual direction.

35. Chan, *Spiritual Theology*, 25.
36. Chan, *Spiritual Theology*, 25.
37. Chan, *Spiritual Theology*, 25.
38. Chan, *Spiritual Theology*, 25.
39. Chan, *Spiritual Theology*, 15–16.

FOUNDATIONAL DOCTRINES
IN CHRISTIAN SPIRITUAL THEOLOGY

The Christian Doctrine of the Triune God

As a ministry of nurturing life in relation to God, spiritual direction must be practiced as a response to God's self-revelation. Consequently, the Christian doctrine of the triune God provides it with its most essential foundation. Chan explains that the doctrine of the triune God is "the Christian way of schematizing the basic self-revelation of God" and so serves as its foundational doctrine.[40] That being the case, spiritual direction ceases to be distinctively Christian when it is not founded upon the doctrine of the triune God.

I find Vanhoozer's comment that "at the heart of Christian faith lie neither principles, piety nor practices but rather the work of three persons: Father, Son and Spirit" rather significant.[41] When we reflect on the shared mission of the Father, Son, and Holy Spirit in the economy of salvation, we gain a deeper grasp on how God profoundly permeates our lives. As Christian spiritual direction is concerned with working out the full ramifications of the gospel in Christian experience, the doctrine of the triune God fundamentally serves as the grounds and guiding framework for its practice.[42]

While Christian spiritual direction ordinarily places special emphasis on the guidance of the Holy Spirit, the doctrine of the Trinity guards against any tendency to over emphasize any one Person within the Trinity. On the contrary, it communicates to us "the mystery of the God who is both one and yet three, both a God-in-himself and a God-for-us in his trinitarian existence."[43] Hence, it calls us to attend to the "full range of God's self-revelation" rather than focusing exclusively on the Father, Son, or Holy Spirit.[44]

As such, trinitarian spirituality attends both to the individual persons in their separate functions and to the perichoretic relationship between the persons of the Trinity. Chan proposes that "[t]he traditional way is to see the perichoretic relationship in terms of the Father by whom the Son is eternally

---

40. Chan, *Spiritual Theology*, 41.

41. Vanhoozer, "Triune Discourse," 25.

42. See Sunquist, *Understanding Christian Mission*, on how the doctrine of the Trinity serves as the foundation for Christian mission. See also Siang-Yang Tan, *Counseling and Psychotherapy*, 325–373, on how Christian theology, in particular the doctrine of the Holy Spirit in the context of Christian spirituality, applies to the ministry of Christian counseling and psychotherapy.

43. Chan, *Spiritual Theology*, 45.

44. Chan, *Spiritual Theology*, 49.

begotten and from whom the Spirit proceeds."[45] While this formula from the Nicene Creed renders the relationships within the Trinity somewhat hierarchical, we are nevertheless reminded that each person of the Trinity is uncreated, one in essence, and equal in power and glory.

A wholesome theology of the Trinity therefore shapes the work of spiritual direction in a rather fundamental way. Significantly, it provides the basis for forging our own mental images of God in Christian experience. Evangelical spiritual director Jeannette Bakke has noted that we all have a mental picture of God and an interpretation of what we think God is like and how God considers us.[46] It is not uncommon that directees come to spiritual direction with faulty images of God (for example, images that are predominantly punitive). Spiritual directors can help directees to reflect on their mental images of God in a manner that is more congruent with the doctrine of the Trinity. We will now consider some of these images as they relate to each Person of the Trinity.

God the Father as Creator and Covenanter

Two dominant images associated with God the Father is that of Creator and Covenanter. Although all three persons of the Trinity participated in the act of creation (see for example, 1 Cor 8:6; Col 1:15–17; Gen 1:2; Job 33:4), the image of God the Father as Creator is often in the foreground in the work of creation (as seen in the Apostles' Creed).[47] Our understanding of the doctrine of God as Creator profoundly shapes how we relate to God and his creation. This doctrine communicates that God not only creates, but he also cares and sustains. He knows how we are formed and accommodates to our limitations (Pss 103 and 139). This doctrine affirms our uniqueness as creatures, guides us on our relationship with God, and guards us against any illusion of immortality. Further, it shapes our understanding of God's providence, and the work of redemption through Jesus Christ.

Consequently, a wholesome understanding of the Creator-creature relationship is essential for life and for the spiritual direction process. Catholic spiritual theologian Henri Nouwen, for example, exposes our propensity toward illusions of our own immortality. When we forget that we are creatures and begin to forge our own idols to feed our need for control, we quickly loose our way. Rather than live in our illusions, Nouwen guides us to move

---

45. Chan, *Spiritual Theology*, 49.

46. Bakke, *Holy Invitations*, 152.

47. See Horton, *The Christian Faith*, 328–31, for a discussion on Creation: God's time for us.

from illusion to prayer. In prayer, we acknowledge our own creatureliness, accord God his rightful place as Creator and begin to relate rightly to God.[48]

Also central to the role of God the Father is the biblical image of God as Covenanter. Covenant refers to the relationship which God has initiated with his people. The covenant was enacted historically, passed on by the Church through tradition, and eternally recorded in the canon of Scripture. Walter Brueggemann describes the covenant as "the deep and pervasive affirmation that our lives in all aspects depend upon our relatedness to this other One who retains initiative in our lives (sovereignty), and who wills more good for us than we do for ourselves (graciousness; cf. Eph 3:20).[49]

"Our understanding of covenant theology, thus, fundamentally shapes our practice of spiritual direction, especially as it pertains to our fundamental identity. As Allen explains, "if covenant indeed means that a person is grounded and finds his or her true identity in that "Other" who is God, then the proper question of "identity," [which is often an issue in spiritual direction,] for us to ask is not only "Who am I?" but "To Whom do I belong?"[50] The challenge that confronts a spiritual director is therefore to help the directee to anchor their identity fundamentally in God. It is when we rest our identity in God that we will discover our true selves—which is so crucial to an experience for freedom and fullness in God.[51] Unfortunately, as Allen laments, the temptation in modern society is to follow the way, not of "God-groundedness," but of "self-groundedness."[52] Consequently, the challenge for both the director and the directee is to keep in central focus the God of the covenant— who is faithful, knows our frame, and invites us to respond to him in faith.

God the Son as Incarnate Word

Integral to the covenant perspective is God the Son as Incarnate Word—for although God effects his covenant as the economic Trinity, it is through the Son that we come to know the Father (John 8:19; 14:7). The Son is the full representation of the Father, and we are reconciled to God through him (Col 1:15–23). It is the Son who was given and broken for us who brought us life. The Christian story of the life, death, resurrection, and ascension

48. Nouwen, *Reaching Out*, 111–60.

49. Quoted in Allen, *Inner Way*, 65.

50. Allen, *Inner Way*, 65.

51. See Mulholland, *The Deeper Journey*; and David Benner, *The Gift of Being Yourself*, for a discussion on the subject.

52. Allen, *Inner Way*, 65.

of Jesus Christ is therefore the foundational story against which we reflect our individual stories. The church's experience of the Word Incarnate and its witness in the Canon of Scripture is the primary reality upon which we receive guidance for our spiritual lives as a derivative and lived reality. As Bakke explains, "we tend to remake God according to a number of distorted images, which is one of the reasons why the incarnation is so important. Only when the Word became human was it possible for us to see a clear view of God "full of grace and truth" (John 1:14)."[53]

Jesuit theologian William Reiser proposes that the incarnation should serve as a starting point for spiritual direction. He reasons that "the incarnation forces us to look at the specific details surrounding the life and ministry of Jesus before we begin contemplating the general and universal relevance of the holy mystery of God inserting itself into the human world and identifying with the human condition."[54] Without the specific details of the story surrounding the life, death, resurrection, and ascension of Jesus, we may be tempted to create all kinds of God-images that appeal to our fancy—or our fears. Reiser emphasizes that "the holy mystery of God, with its excess of presence over the images and words used to name that presence, lies, rather, within the concrete, immediate experience of salvation. For this reason, 'and the Word became flesh' has to be an incontrovertible pre-supposition for the Christian who engages in the practice of spiritual direction."[55]

The Testimony and Authority of Scripture

As such, our attitude toward Scripture—the Eternal Word now speaking as the Written Word through the inspiration of the Holy Spirit—fundamentally shapes our practice of spiritual direction. In Scripture, we find divinely-inspired wisdom that is "profitable for teaching, for reproof, for correction, [and] for training in righteousness" so that we might be "adequate and equipped for every good work" (2 Tim 3:16). While wisdom from the Christian tradition and many contemporary spiritual writers help with spiritual guidance, the Scriptures alone are divinely inspired and so provide the unfailing principles that must govern and guide the work of spiritual direction. As Vanhoozer asserts, the ultimate authority for Christian faith, life, and thought is "the triune God speaking in and through the Scriptures."[56]

---

53. Bakke, *Holy Invitations*, 152–53.

54. Reiser, *Seeking God*, 122.

55. Reiser, *Seeking God*, 125–26.

56. Vanhoozer, "Triune Discourse," 27.

Perhaps that is why Henri Nouwen calls the Bible a spiritual director. He says that people must read the Scriptures for themselves and ask where God speaks to them.[57] As an example, Douglas Webster describes the apostle James as his spiritual guide. He writes, "What a medical doctor does for my physical life, James does for my spiritual life. He is a physician of the soul, a brilliant diagnostician, who detects spiritual disease and accurately prescribes its remedy."[58] While Webster found it helpful to derive guidance from the book of James, it will be more comprehensive to rest our biblical framework for guidance on the entire corpus of Scripture. The entire corpus of Scripture with the whole story of redemption that threading through it must serve as the undergirding and guiding framework for the spiritual director.

While the Scriptures are fundamental to spiritual direction, we discover that different perspectives on the authority of Scripture lead to different approaches to spiritual guidance. There is an apparent difference between Catholic and Protestant perspectives on the authority of Scripture. Bruce Demarest points out that Catholic spiritual writers place church tradition on par with Scripture, which follows the Roman Church's claim to be the definitive interpreter of the Bible.[59] Evangelicals, however, hold that church tradition, while instructive for faith and life must always be verified against the authority of Scripture.[60] This basic difference impacts the way spiritual direction is offered. For the Catholic, authority is vested in the Church as interpreter of both Scripture and tradition,[61] while for the Protestant, church tradition does not receive the same authoritative status as Holy Spirit-inspired Scripture.

Nevertheless, a very helpful connection between Scripture, church tradition, and spiritual direction is prominently seen in the ancient art of *Lectio Divina (Divine Reading)* and the use of the liturgical calendar in the church, including the Divine Hours and the Daily Office.[62] The practice of *Lectio Divina*, through its four movements—*lectio (reading), meditatio (meditating), oratio (praying), contemplatio (contemplating)*—is a means by which the spiritual director can help the directee to listen carefully to God's spoken word through the written word. Through the practice, the Holy Spirit guides the directee to be attentive to particular words or phrases that

---

57. Bakke, *Holy Invitations*, 95.

58. Webster, *Finding Spiritual Direction*, 14.

59. Demarest, "Reading Catholic Spirituality," 120.

60. Demarest, "Reading Catholic Spirituality," 121.

61. See Aumann, *Spiritual Theology*, 26–32.

62. See, for example, Wilson, *Daily Office Readings*.

are especially pertinent to the present moment. The spiritual director then can help the directee to co-discern its meaning or purpose. Following the liturgical calendar, whether it is in the church or in one's personal reading, is a way to systematically cover a large corpus of Scripture and receive its entire counsel. This approach reminds us that we neither read nor pray alone but are part of a larger reality, the universal body of Christ, who are also reading and praying with us. In addition, we are reminded that it is God the Holy Spirit who is also praying in and through us–carrying us in our prayers. Praying the Divine Hours or using the Daily Office is a helpful means for us to develop a rhythm and rule of life—which, to borrow an expression from Eugene Peterson, sustains us in "a long obedience in the same direction."[63]

We are reminded that the Christian life traverses the long haul, with periods of light and periods of darkness—what some spiritual masters refer to as periods of consolation or of desolation. It is part and parcel of our human experience. But it takes on special significance for the spiritual life. For this reason, a significant aspect of Christian spiritual direction is about paying attention to the quality and trajectory of our spiritual affections; or what some simply refer to as the true character of the desires of our hearts.

Susan Philips has pointed out that "much of Scripture and Christian theology is aimed at encouraging us to train our desires toward God."[64] We have just noted that spiritual direction pays close attention to spiritual desires and experiences. Unfortunately, some misunderstand that desires are problematic. But the issue is not with desires per se. The issue, rather, is with unruly desires—motivations and affections that lead us away from God. Consequently, a goal in spiritual direction is to help directees to differentiate (or discern) between authentic and inauthentic desires, and to temper them after the character of Jesus. The proper use of Scriptures helps us in this process. As such, we immerse ourselves in Scripture, with all our heart, soul, mind and strength, so that we may follow after the leading of God—in particular, God the Holy Spirit.

God the Holy Spirit as Guide into all Truth

The mission of the Holy Spirit is to guide us into all truth (John 16:13). Consequently, the Holy Spirit is the true Director in a spiritual direction

---

63. For an example on developing a rule for life, see Chittister, *The Rule of Benedict*. For contemporary examples on the *Lectio Divina*, see Pennington, *Praying the Holy Scriptures;* and Wilhoit and Howard, *Discovering Lectio Divina*.

64. Philips, *Candlelight*, 24.

relationship—for only the Spirit, together with the Living Word, searches deeply into the desires, intents, and motivations of our hearts.[65] When the director and directee meet, their goal is to attend to the voice of the Holy Spirit, ask to hear clearly and follow closely.

The Holy Spirit is the same Spirit testified to in the book of Acts who empowered the early Christians for discipleship and witness as well as the eschatological Spirit who has energized the Christian tradition in the past, does so in the present, and will continue into the future. In the Holy Spirit, we witness God who acted in the past, is presently acting, and will continue to act in the future. By attending and yielding to the Spirit, we close the gap between our conceptions, or misconceptions, of God and our experience of Him as a present reality. Good spiritual direction therefore rests upon a comprehensive theology of the Holy Spirit.

It is here that a Pentecostal perspective of the spirituality of the Spirit is particularly helpful. Looking once more to Chan, he proposes that "if evangelical spirituality is the living out of the supernatural gift of new life in Christ, Pentecostal spirituality further qualifies it as a life of miraculous empowerment."[66] It hones in us "a heightened sense of the divine presence," and reaps in us the fruit of a "deep intimacy" with God and "empowerment for service" with God. The combination of deepen intimacy and empowerment for service, often described as a life of prayer and work, is what Christian spiritual direction strives towards. But, as Chan adds; "At its best, Pentecostal spirituality forces us to recognize that the Christian life is more than just a predictable pattern subject entirely to human control."[67] It anticipates that "God may yet do new things because God is personal and therefore never completely predictable."[68] Apart from celebrating special times of intimacy with God or empowerment for service from God, this Pentecostal framework empowers the spiritual director to guide the directee through puzzling moments in the spiritual journey where all appears unfamiliar with the God one has known till then.

Implications of Trinitarian Spirituality

The importance of trinitarian spirituality to Christian spiritual direction can be further underscored through several of its implications for the spiritual life. First, as the triune God is personal and relational, we also understand

65. See 1 Cor 2:10–13; Ps 139:23–24; Heb 4:12.

66. Chan, *Spiritual Theology*, 47.

67. Chan, *Spiritual Theology*, 48.

68. Chan, *Spiritual Theology*, 48.

our salvation in personal and relational ways. That is, as personal union with God expressed in a living relationship with Him.[69] The goal of the spiritual director is to help the directee to grow through the experience of a deepening communion with God—the imagery of which is drawn from the perichoretic relationship of perfect love within the Trinity.

Bakke explains that the reality of this love that is rooted in God goes beyond our ideas and experiences of human love, and often expresses itself in surprising ways. Sometimes we struggle to differentiate between authentic love from God and counterfeits. But the Holy Spirit helps us to differentiate and to discern.[70] Since our experiences in life or in the Spirit are often incomplete, the spiritual director can draw from the picture of perfect love within the Trinity to help guide a directee toward a more wholesome understanding and experience of the meaning of union and deepening communion with God.

A second implication from the perichoretic relationship within the Trinity is that we begin to understand that "spiritual life is essentially relational without ceasing to be particular."[71] In other words, we are included in a relational context within the holy catholic church as members of the body of Christ, and yet retain our personal identities as children of God. This is rather clearly seen in the biblical teaching of being baptized into the body of Christ, while remaining individually gifted yet, nevertheless, mutually dependent as members of the same body (1 Cor 12). Sometimes, the knowledge of this truth and our experience in practice do not commensurate. But it is here that the spiritual director draws an understanding from the life within the Trinity to guide the directee. As Chan points out, the perichoresis of the Trinity characterized by the distinct persons-in-relation offers a pattern for human relationship. Far from being just a model, "perichoresis is the effective means by which the life of particularity-in-relationality can be realized."[72]

Several things may be realized when a spiritual director brings such a framework to the spiritual direction relationship. First, it helps the directee to cultivate a balance that, on the one hand, develops one's spiritual growth in all its particularity and, on the other hand, to relate as a member of the faith community to which one belongs. This balanced perspective prevents spiritual direction from slipping into an individualistic form of spiritual care, divorced from mainstream of corporate spirituality. Secondly, it helps

69. Chan, *Spiritual Theology*, 52.
70. Bakke, *Holy Invitations*, 163.
71. Chan, *Spiritual Theology*, 53.
72. Chan, *Spiritual Theology*, 53.

the directee to see the interconnectedness of life, and teaches the person to affirm how all of life can come together to celebrate the life in God without losing one's particular distinctiveness or personality. This fine balance that embraces both the personal and corporate experience, and personal and corporate rules of prayer, is an important attribute of spiritual maturity and wholeness.

Thirdly, trinitarian spirituality implies that we participate in God's mission just as we participate in God's life. Chan notes that the Catholic and Orthodox traditions see the mission of the church in terms of participation in the trinitarian mission, in which the Father sent the Son and Spirit into the world. Hence, the Christian's movement to Christ at baptism is inextricably linked to his movement into the world at confirmation.[73] This implies that, in our understanding of the spiritual life, we avoid the artificial separation of life in God with life in the world. New life in Christ implies both the reception of the Holy Spirit and the sending into the world as God's witnesses. Our lives are to be intentionally lived in the Son through the indwelling power of the Spirit as tangible witness in worship to God and acts of service to humanity. Who we are and how we live should reflect the reality of the triune God in us.

For example, Scott Sunquist also draws his understanding of mission from trinitarian theology. He explains that "missiology is first concerned with thinking correctly about the Triune God–the God who by his very nature is a sending God–rather than with particular practices or programs."[74] This explains why the study of missiology must have as its first and final word life in the Triune God.[75] Sunquist's perspective calls to mind our concern that many contemporary spiritual direction training programs often embark first upon a set of practices rather than a robust theology of the spiritual life. A comprehensive understanding of trinitarian spirituality serves as a much-needed corrective.

When a spiritual director brings the insights of trinitarian spirituality to the spiritual direction conversation, she is then able to guide the directee on the implications of how life in the Son is lived in tandem with life in the Spirit as participation in the mission of the triune God. It is not always easy. But there are no other options that are foundational faithful to a Christian understanding of God. Lisa Myers shows how vital trinitarian theology is to the Christian community when she observed that "[in] the shared reflection on experience, when the most familiar metaphors and models for Christian

73. Chan, *Spiritual Theology*, 54.

74. Sunquist, *Understanding Christian Mission*, 2.

75. Sunquist, *Understanding Christian Mission*, 396.

community have begun to fall short, a trinitarian perspective has provided the language and meaning needed to enable the community to continue to recognize and receive the gift that is being offered and to take the personal risks that are necessary to deepen the reality of intimate communion that they share."[76]

Sin and Human Nature

Along with the doctrine of the triune God, Christian spiritual direction must also guide out of a robust theology of sin and human nature. A basic understanding is that, due to the Fall,[77] the human person while still possessing the image of God suffers from it being terribly marred by sin.[78] However, through regeneration and the indwelling Spirit, new life in Christ is birthed and can now be nurtured toward fullness in Christ. Nevertheless, there is an ongoing battle between the flesh and the spirit. The goal of the spiritual life is to resist the flesh and yield to the Holy Spirit.[79] Some have described this process as abandoning the false self (so impacted sin) and embracing the true self in Christ—which will be complete in the beatific vision.[80]

Consequently, Christian spiritual directors need a holistic view of the human person to guide well. Chan explains that "human acts cannot be isolated into purely physical, psychological or spiritual categories" for the human person is really "a functional trichotomy"—consisting of body, soul, and spirit.[81] Willard describes the person as the integration of mind, heart (also called the spirit or will), and body in relation to one's social context, with the soul referring to the inner most part as well as all of one's being.[82] In this regard, Bakke observes that we "experience and relate to God as whole persons involving all our faculties: intellect, will, imagination, emotions, memory, and bodily responses."[83] The work Christian spiritual direction must therefore possess a comprehensive theology of the human person

---

76. Myers, "From a Graceful Center," 90.

77. See Gen 1–3.

78. Major differences between Catholic and Protestant conceptions of sin are discussed in the ensuing paragraphs.

79. See Rom 8:1–17.

80. See Mulholland, *The Deeper Journey*; and Benner, *The Gift of Being Yourself*.

81. Chan, *Spiritual Theology*, 57–58.

82. Willard, *Renovation of the Heart*.

83. Bakke, *Holy Invitations*, 152.

in order to guide well. Otherwise, there is a danger of falling prey to various forms of reductionism of human nature.

Chan proposes that there are three forms of reductionism—materialism, psychologism, and spiritualistic reductionism. "Materialism is the belief that everything about human nature can be reduced to some aspect of the physical world," while "psychologism seeks ultimate explanations in the psychological dimension."[84] It is not uncommon for us to encounter these forms of reductionism among those who are either content to be purely materialistic or have a psychological explanation for virtually everything. In religious circles, however, we encounter the phenomenon of spiritualistic reductionism, which offers a spiritual explanation for every problem. It is important that both the spiritual director and the directee be aware of these forms of reductionism so that they consciously embrace a balanced view of human nature that seeks wholeness in all aspects of life—body, soul, and spirit. As Chan asserts, true Christian spirituality is determined by what becomes of the whole person and not just the various physical, psychological or spiritual components.[85]

As we embrace a holistic view of the human person, one's understanding of sin becomes more comprehensive too. Sin is not treated only in ontological terms (as acts of isolated individuals or isolated acts of individuals) but also in relational terms (sin damages our relationship with God and with others).[86] Sin manifests itself as both interpersonal and structural evil. Such an awareness of the destructive power of sin prevents spiritual direction from becoming concerned only with personal wellness. Instead, it addresses one's relationship with God, others and the society at large. Clearly, our theology of sin and human nature will influence our practice of spiritual direction.

Here again, we are confronted with theological differences between Catholic and Protestant conceptions of sin—resulting in different ways of dealing with sin. The Catholic perspective sees that we are "wounded in our very nature" as a result of original sin. This predisposition to moral evil inclines us to sin; but we must resist it and harness our wills to cultivate the love of God that leads to perfection and sanctification.[87] The Protestant perspective, in particular the Reformed tradition, however, understands the will to be held in bondage as a result of original sin. It is totally incapacitated. One is unable to love God unless one's will is first regenerated by God.

84. Chan, *Spiritual Theology*, 57.
85. Chan, *Spiritual Theology*, 58.
86. Chan, *Spiritual Theology*, 57.
87. Aumann, *Spiritual Theology*, 148.

As Chan observed, the Catholic doctrine of grace working in nature and uplifting it means that sin is not understood in all its radicalness.[88] "The Reformation doctrine of sin, in contrast, recovers the Augustinian and Anselmic concepts, which understand sin in relational terms as well as in all its radicalness. For Augustine, sin has completely disabled the human will. For Anselm, sin is an infinite affront against God."[89] Metaphorically, the Catholic view sees the heart as a garden that is overgrown with weeds. It needs to be weeded and the work of rooting out the weeds is part of the larger work of cultivating a better heart that is more responsive to God. In Protestantism, however, the heart is a wilderness that needs to be radically transformed before cultivation can begin. Spiritual conversion is required before spiritual formation can begin.[90]

These divergent perspectives lead to quite different methods of guiding the soul. Catholic spiritual theologies, resting upon its theology of sanctifying grace bestowed at baptism, often embark on a well-developed structure for the ascetical life aimed at attaining union with God, while Protestant theologies often focuses first on the foundational doctrine of justification, resting on prevenient grace, before going on to discuss sanctification. One's theology of sin and human nature will therefore shape one's practice of spiritual direction. An adequate understanding of this doctrine is fundamental to the practice of spiritual direction, especially in an ecumenical context.

Salvation and Progress in the Spiritual Life

Intimately linked to a theology of sin and human nature is a theology of salvation and progress in the spiritual life. As spiritual direction is fundamentally about spiritual growth, a theological understanding of God's work in salvation, and the issue of grace and human effort for progress in the spiritual life is essential to the task of spiritual direction.

We have already noted that Christian spirituality partakes of the specific story of the life, death and resurrection of Jesus Christ. This is central to our understanding of God's redemptive action in the world. However, as Chan reminds us, "the Christian story is not primarily about how God in Jesus came to rescue sinners from some impending disaster. It is about God's work of initiating us into a fellowship and making us true conversational partners with the Father and the Son through the Spirit, and hence, with

88. Chan, *Spiritual Theology*, 59.
89. Chan, *Spiritual Theology*, 61.
90. Chan, *Spiritual Theology*, 61.

each other (1 Jn 1:1–4)."[91] Consequently, spiritual direction is the sacred work of accompanying a directee's growth in this divine fellowship. It reverentially explores the impact that the Christian story has on the directee's own story as it unfolds in spiritual growth as life in the triune God. In other words, the spiritual director keeps in constant view how the historical realities of the Christian story impacts the historical realities of the directee to bring about transformation in the freedom that God has ushered into the directee's life—a freedom of life in-relation to God and his world.

Consequently, the wholeness that we explore is very different from the wholeness of the gnostic religions, which are so prevalent among the Eastern and New Age spiritualities today. Gnostic tendencies seek a wholeness that is "essentially an ontological freedom that dissolves the self into some larger eternal reality." However, the wholeness that Christian spiritual direction seeks "is an existential freedom understood strictly in personal terms: communion, love and fellowship."[92] A Christian spiritual director must, therefore, be careful and deliberate to take this latter perspective as he guides the directee into deeper communion with God in a distinctively Christian way.

In addition, spiritual directors are often confronted with the paradox of grace and human effort in the pursuit of the spiritual life. How is one to keep in tension the perspective that spiritual growth stems from God's grace but also involves the diligent effort of the disciple? Here, we again find discontinuities between Catholic and Protestant conceptions of grace and human effort. Stemming from its understanding of salvation and progress in the spiritual life, the Catholic perspective emphasizes meritorious works in cooperation with grace as the exercise of the will in pursuit of union with God. The Protestant perspective, however, with its theology of salvation founded on justification by grace through faith, emphasizes works as evidence of the presence of faith empowered by grace.

Nevertheless, the conceptions of grace and human effort remain a persistent issue in Protestantism. Chan points out that there appears to be three common possibilities to the conceptions. The first is that one only acts when moved by felt "new dynamics." This seems to be most represented by different enthusiastic movements. The second is described as "God's-action-in-our-action"—perhaps best represented by John Calvin. That is, we need to act as proof that God is acting in us. A third conception is that "the imperative could be seen as God's appointed means of furthering the life of faith." This is best exemplified by the Puritans, who developed "guides to

---

91. Chan, *Spiritual Theology*, 78.
92. Chan, *Spiritual Theology*, 78.

godliness" that are acted on by faith. From these perspectives, it is quite evident that how a spiritual director guides, and a directee responds, is shaped by their understanding of grace and human effort.

In this regard, Chan emphasizes that a spiritual theology must keep the two understandings of grace together—that is, grace as *God's* unmerited favor along with grace as an empowering gift. The first reminds us that we grow spiritually only by God's grace; while the second reminds us that God has granted the grace (both preveniently and concomitantly) and has thus enabled us to respond to him willingly and diligently. Taken together, growth in the spiritual life can then be seen essentially as a work of grace—in whichever way it comes. Such a conception of grace spurs both the director and directee toward growth and yet keeps both of them humble; as growth is always a fruit of God's grace at work.[93]

Ecclesial Foundations for Spiritual Direction

We now turn to explain why ecclesial foundations are important for the practice of spiritual direction. There are two interconnected reasons. Firstly, as we observed in the previous chapter, this unique ministry is a ministry of the church; and so spiritual direction derives its vision and purpose from the church, especially of the church as a worshipping community. Secondly, the liturgy, as the embodiment of primary theology, serves as a framework that guides the practice of spiritual direction. I will explain why these are so. But first, I make an observation on a present danger that confronts contemporary spiritual direction.

Contemporary spiritual direction is at risk on becoming so individually focused that it loses its connection with the church—from which it receives its legitimacy and vitality as a ministry. It is hard to comprehend how a Christian can grow holistically without being connected with a church and participating in acts of worship with a community of faith. We are reminded that the purpose of Christian spiritual formation is to develop certain qualities "that enable us to live responsibly within the community that we have been baptized into."[94] As the spiritual life is "essentially life-in-relation patterned after and sustained by the Trinity that assumes a definite shape within the church created by Christ, a theology of the visible church becomes crucial for understanding such a life."[95] Christian spiritual direc-

---

93. See Chan, *Spiritual Theology*, 79–84.

94. Chan, *Spiritual Theology*, 103.

95. Chan, *Spiritual Theology*, 103.

tion, as a ministry that nurtures such a life, must be founded upon a theology of the church and its life of worship.

A brief explication of the ecclesial life will illumine how it provides the vision for spiritual direction. As Chan explains, the nature of ecclesial life is, first, a life created by God in Christ, and second, a sacramental life. As life created by God in Christ, our fellowship is always "in Christ." This is the context for our prayers—and all our efforts at making progress in the spiritual life. Our prayers are never just private prayer—""since *all* prayer is but part of the total prayer of the Church" because of the sheer fact of our incorporation into Christ."[96] Since Christian spiritual direction is primarily set in a context of prayer, its legitimacy is derived from the vision of this aspect of ecclesial life. In Christian spiritual direction, we return again and again to this foundational vision as we seek to participation in the life of God in Christ through the Spirit.

Secondly, ecclesial life is a sacramental life. This means that we share the marks of a sacramental community, which include baptism and the Lord's Supper. This vision of a sacramental life in Christ fundamentally shapes the vision of spiritual direction because it provides the most essential marks that remind us of our life in God.[97] Consequently, it is profitable in spiritual direction, especially with a gathered community, for example in a spiritual retreat, to celebrate the Lord's Supper; for it serves as a reminder that we are not individual pilgrims but part of a redeemed community who are together taken up into the life of God in Christ.

Hence, fundamentally, spiritual direction draws its wisdom from the collective wisdom of the church. As Chan argues, "no matter how individually customized the direction may be, it also presupposes a shared life in a community. Our own personal stories as Christians make sense only as part of the larger Christian story."[98] While one of the basic assumptions in contemporary spiritual direction is that God addresses us and reveals himself to us in and through our experience, Lonsdale reminds us that "we belong to a community of faith to whose members God has previously revealed who God is and who they are in relation to God. Both Scripture and the Christian tradition are a record of a community's experience of God and further reflection on that experience."[99] Consequently, we begin to understand why individual spiritual direction flows out of corporate spiritual direction—where the enactments of the gathered community serve to direct

96. Chan, *Spiritual Theology*, 109–10.

97. See Billings, *Calvin, Participation, and the Gift*, 105–43.

98. Chan, *Spiritual Theology*, 235.

99. Lonsdale, "Traditions of Spiritual Guidance," 317.

us in God's primal relationship with his church. We receive direction from the shared ecclesial memory when we gather with the faith community to hear God's Word and recount its history, before this shared memory begins to impact our individual memory and point us in the way forward. It is vital that spiritual direction retains its connection with its ecclesial history and theology.

Unfortunately, much of contemporary spiritual direction tends to reflect on experience too individualistically. When, however, we begin to understand how intimately linked spiritual direction is to the life of the worshipping community, we take care to reflect the individual experience against the larger communal or ecclesial experience. Turning once more to Lonsdale, he points out that the community's experience interacts with the individual experience in two formative ways.

> On the one hand an individual's experience of God is mediated by the community's experience, in the sense that the biblical texts, the traditions, the liturgy and the sacred symbols of the community speak to the individual of God. On the other hand, the community's experience also helps the task of interpretation by either supporting that of the individual or by challenging it. In either case, the community's traditions and life act as a touchstone by which its individual members' experience may be understood and evaluated in direction with a view to shaping the future.[100]

It helps to look at some biblical images of the church for specific ways on how the ecclesial life can shape the individual life. Chan uses three biblical images to describe the church's ontological relationship with the triune God—the people of God, body of Christ, and the temple of the Holy Spirit—all of which help to explain how we can grow in an ecclesial context.[101]

First, the biblical image of the church as the people of God defines our corporate identity in historical perspective. "To call the church the people of God is to recognize that it exists in continuity with the ancient covenant people of God, the people of Israel . . . It is from the church's continuity with Israel as the chosen people of God that we understand the church's own election as people of God."[102] This perspective emphasizes the historical continuity of the church through time. The practice of spiritual direction draws from this historical perspective for a healthy diachronic perspective of the church that helps both director and directee to cultivate a more

---

100. Lonsdale, "Traditions of Spiritual Guidance," 317.

101. Chan, *Liturgical Theology*.

102. Chan, *Liturgical Theology*, 24–25.

comprehensive perspective of the Christian journey. It shapes their identities as people of God and serves to guard against any tendency to interpret Christian religious experience in a myopic way as the broader historical vision will bring perspective to their evaluation of their present experience.

This is further elaborated through an understanding of the church as the body of Christ. The biblical image of the body of Christ tells us that "the church is the divine-humanity by virtue of its being the body of Christ . . . It is an ontological reality, as Christ is ontologically real."[103] This image has two implications. The first is the way communion is understood and the second, the way to understand the Christian tradition.

In the first, Chan observes that "the church is a communion because members are incorporated into the body of Christ; and the church becomes the one body of Christ by eating and drinking the body and the blood of Christ."[104] In this light, Chan explains that "ecclesial communion is first and foremost an essentially Eucharistic communion."[105] In other words, the communion that members share in as an ecclesia is most in focus when they share in the Eucharist. Therefore, participation in the Eucharist directs our spiritual focus by traditioning us in the reality that we are mystically joined to Christ and so receive the necessary food for spiritual growth from him. The implications that this understanding brings to the practice of spiritual direction is that healthy Christian spiritual direction always keeps an eye to the mystical union we have in Christ–and this is most in focus when we participate in the Eucharist. As a practice of the church, Christian spiritual direction must return again and again to this most essential communion.

In the second, tradition is viewed as an ongoing dynamic process that shapes the church's identity and collective memory. "Like a person whose history and memory shape his or her identity, the church as the body of Christ cannot be understood apart from its history and collective memory of Jesus Christ. Tradition is the means by which the church understands its true identity. We can make sense of what the church is now only because it exists in *historical* continuity with the church then."[106] As I mentioned earlier, this diachronic vision of Christian Tradition provides the long-ranging perspective that must undergird the practice of spiritual direction. It is the historical vision that prevents the practice of spiritual direction from becoming short-sighted—looking only at the present experience of the individual without reference to a much longer ecclesial history. The

103. Chan, *Liturgical Theology*, 27.

104. Chan, *Liturgical Theology*, 29.

105. Chan, *Liturgical Theology*, 29.

106. Chan, *Liturgical Theology*, 30–31.

expansive backdrop of ecclesial memory, on the other hand, helps us to gain a clearer understanding of our present experience. Dreyer and Burrows have observed that "worship is a vast repository of this memory. It is the fundamental context in which memory becomes identity through the retrieval of the ancient witness of God's acts, from creation, through the historical narrative of Israel, to the emergence of Jesus and the communities gathered in his name."[107]

A third image of the church is that it is the temple of the Holy Spirit. The image of the church as the temple of the Holy Spirit completes the other two images of the church as the people of God and body of Christ. To speak of the church as the temple of the Spirit is to recognize "its essentially eschatological character, since the Spirit is the Spirit of the 'last days.'"[108] Chan explains that "this construction of the Sprit's role in the church is extremely crucial, because it not only reveals the distinctiveness of the Spirit as Third Person but also reveals the intimate connection between the Spirit and the church. It is in relation to the church as *totus Christus* that the Spirit as Third Person comes to his own."[109]

Chan elaborates that the understanding of the intimate connection between the Spirit and the church expands our understanding of three major interconnected motifs of the Christian life with respect to the Church: Pentecost, the living Christian Tradition, and the eschatological tension within which we dwell. First, Pentecost marks the birth of the church as the body of Christ and the temple of the Holy Spirit; the missionary agency through which God will use as witness to the nations. The Holy Spirit is seen as "subjective embodiment of the way, the truth and the life in the church which is the embodied Christ."[110] This is to see the Church "as the living Tradition [that] embodies a living and developing dogma" that follows the trajectory set by the gospel events: Christ's life, death, resurrection, ascension, Pentecost and the second coming of Christ. In other words, the story of the church is part of the story of God's action in the world. The sending of the Spirit is God's action in the story that is centered in the Third Person of the Trinity.[111] The implications that these insights bring to spiritual direction is that the conversation revolving around the personal story of the directee must be evaluated against the larger Christian story—the living Christian Tradition—to which the church belongs and through which the

107. Dreyer and Burrows, *Minding the Spirit*, 153.
108. Chan, *Liturgical Theology*, 32.
109. Chan, *Liturgical Theology*, 33.
110. Chan, *Liturgical Theology*, 35.
111. Chan, *Liturgical Theology*, 35.

Spirit speaks as a continuing witness to God's missionary and redemptive action in the world.

From this births an understanding of the eschatological tension in our present experience. Chan explains that the intimate connection between the Spirit and the church is seen in the manner in which the Spirit sustains the church within the eschatological tension. While Christ is not physically present between the ascension and the parousia, he is "present eucharistically through the presence of the Spirit. This is the unique ministry of the Spirit in the church age. The church at present is sustained by this Eucharistic presence of Christ. This is why the Eucharist is so central to the liturgy of the church and the invocation of the Spirit is most particularly connected with the celebration of the Eucharist."[112]

Once more, this understanding has implications for the ministry of spiritual direction for, in the same way that the invocation of the Spirit is most particularly connected to the celebration of the Eucharist, the presence of Christ sought during a time in spiritual direction is most particularly connected to the invocation of the Spirit for that time. For this reason, it must always be foremost in the consciousness of the spiritual director that the true Director is the Holy Spirit. For then, the spiritual director is reminded that it is the Spirit who directs and sustains, rather than him. The Spirit who guides in spiritual direction is the same Spirit who is invoked in the celebration of the Eucharist in the gathered community.

Consequently, Christian spiritual direction, which is ultimately about guiding one into a deeper communion with Christ, must derive its theology from a theology of ecclesial communion which, at its heart, is a Eucharistic communion. This Eucharistic communion comforts, strengthens, and sustains in the face of life's difficulties, pain and suffering. Participating regularly in the Eucharist both reminds and shapes our understanding of our spiritual union with Christ. For this reason, a spiritual directee must always be guided as a member of the ecclesia and in the participation in the Eucharist.

Recognizing the church's identity and collective memory in the Christian tradition implies that spiritual direction must ultimately draw its wisdom for guiding an individual's spiritual journey from the funded wisdom of the living Christian tradition. It may be that a directee belongs to a particular Christian tradition and interprets the experience from that orientation, but seen from a larger perspective, the collective threads that run through the unfolding Christian tradition will shed light on one experience's wherever they belong. Once more, we are reminded that the diachronic and

112. Chan, *Liturgical Theology*, 37.

synchronic perspectives of the Christian tradition work together to provide a more comprehensive picture God's action among his people. Spiritual direction must draw from this collective historical wisdom.

THE LITURGY AS PRIMARY THEOLOGICAL STRUCTURE FOR SPIRITUAL DIRECTION

Having laid an ecclesial foundation for the practice of spiritual direction, I now discuss why the liturgy serves as a framework that guides the work of spiritual direction. While the liturgy serves as a coherent structure through which we are holistically formed as a worshipping community, we also derive from it a theology of practice that gives spiritual direction its significance as an ecclesial practice. This is evident in two ways. First, it addresses the problem of spiritual direction becoming an individualistic practice that is divorced from the church. Second, it both anchors the practice in the church and draws its coherence from the *ordo* of the liturgy itself.

Chan explains that "the deep structure underlying the church's liturgy conveys a primary theology that gives the practice of the liturgy its inner coherence and shapes the church into a coherent community. It is from this coherent liturgy that other secondary practices derive their significance as Christian practice."[113] The basic shape of the liturgy is an integrative framework through which to bring coherence to our fragmented religious experience. Consequently, spiritual direction as a derived (or secondary) practice of the church receives its significance and coherence from the basic shape of the liturgy.

Chan explains that there are basically two kinds of practices of the church–those belonging to the *esse* of the church and those belonging to the *bene esse*. Practices of the first kind may be called essential practices. That is, they constitute the church as church. These include the Word and the Sacraments. "To identify Word and sacraments as marks of the church is to say that they are the determinative means by which the Spirit constitutes the church as one holy, catholic and apostolic church."[114] As such, they are essential means that witness to the mission of God in the world.

The church also has *bene esse* practices; which are derived practices. "Practices belonging to the *bene esse* operate somewhat differently. They too are the works of the Spirit and constitutive of the church, but in a different way. Their Christian status depends on how well they are coherently linked to the essential practices and the Christian belief system, and their ability to

113. Chan, *Liturgical Theology*, 87.
114. Chan, *Liturgical Theology*, 88.

form individual Christians depends on how they are personally appropriated through right understanding and intention."[115] Spiritual direction is a derived practice of the church and, as such, draws its criteria from the essential practices of the church—some of which were discussed above. Here, however, the point is made that as a derived practice, it draws its coherence from the coherence within the primary theology of the liturgy. In addition, spiritual direction derives its reason-to-be and foundational criteria from the doctrines we discussed above—the doctrines of the triune God, of sin and human nature, of salvation and progress in the spiritual life, and the community of saints—all of which are enacted in a focused way in the liturgy. Arising from this, spiritual direction must recognize that it also possesses a distinct missionary thrust so coherently expressed in the liturgy of a missionary church.[116]

The Basic *Ordo* of the Liturgy

A brief overview of the basic *ordo* of the liturgy will help us to see why it serves as a foundation for an adequate theology of practice, and hence for the practice of spiritual direction. The liturgy is described as "embodied worship" with a basic shape or *ordo*. As "a consistent whole," it reveals "a whole way of life of the ecclesial community." As Chan explains, participating in a "normative liturgy is [thus] the true way of becoming church."[117] This basic *ordo* consists of two parts: Word and sacrament, which Chan explores through four perspectives:

> [Both] have their basis in the *incarnation*, the Word becoming flesh (Jn 1:14). Thus Christ could be called the "primordial Sacrament." So all true worship is fundamentally sacramental. Second, within the sacramental framework, the Eucharist holds a special place as the "sacrament of sacraments." It is from the Eucharist that we come to a better understanding of the church as essentially communion. The liturgy, therefore, has a *eucharistic* orientation. Third, the Eucharist, which communicates the eternal reality, is always celebrated in time, in daily, weekly and yearly cycles. This means that within the liturgy, eternity and time, the "already and not yet," are set in an *eschatological* tension, giving to the liturgy its *eschatological* orientation. Fourth,

115. Chan, *Liturgical Theology*, 88.

116. See Hauerwas and Wells, *The Blackwell Companion to Christian Ethics*, 7, for a similar connection between worship and liturgy in Christian Ethics.

117. Chan, *Liturgical Theology*, 42.

the liturgy of Word and sacrament is set within two other essential acts: the gathering for worship and the sending forth into the world. This pattern reveals its *missiological* orientation.[118]

I wish to propose that the basic *ordo* and its four orientations both serves as a primary framework for the formation of ecclesial experience— "a whole way of life of the ecclesial community"—and, as a derivative, the practice of Christian spiritual direction. As our spiritual experiences are often fragmentary, we need to evaluate them against a coherent structure. The basic *ordo* of the liturgy, and the four orientations through which it is explored, is such a coherent structure. Ecclesial experience founded upon this coherent framework will help both the spiritual director and directee to reflect upon their Christian experience in a more comprehensive manner. Let us consider how each of the orientations in the basic *ordo* help to guide spiritual direction.

The incarnational orientation reminds us that God has come near— that God has revealed himself to us in Christ Jesus (Col 1:19, 2:9; Heb 1:1–3). In the self-revelation of God in Christ Jesus, we learn the right way to relate to the triune God. When we bring this orientation to the practice of spiritual direction, we remember, first of all, that God has taken the first initiative in reaching out to us, and that the way to God is through his Son, Jesus the Christ. Then, we dispose of all our idols and abandon all illusory forms of living to embrace the One True God in Jesus—full of grace and truth (John 1:14). It sets for us a fundamental direction for life.

The Eucharistic orientation of the liturgy reminds us that God has given himself fully for us. As Chan points out, the Eucharist is not only the culmination of the liturgy, "it is also the sacrament by which Christ gives wholly of himself to the whole church."[119] In Christ, we have a Redeemer, High Priest and Shepherd—who "has been tested in every way" and yet without sin. He is the good Shepherd who lays down his life for his sheep and now continues to shepherd them through his indwelling Spirit (Heb 4:15, John 10:11–16). In thinking about the Eucharist as communion, our participation in it deepens our experience of God given and present with us through his Spirit. In this regard, the Eucharistic orientation deepens our understanding of communion with God in Christ through the Spirit in prayer and in life— and the practice of spiritual direction.

As we consider the eschatological orientation of the liturgy, we note that "the very structure of the liturgy expresses the eschatological tension: the church is in the world and yet not of the world. It is grasped by the eternal

118. Chan, *Liturgical Theology*, 63.
119. Chan, *Liturgical Theology*, 70.

Truth that is Christ, yet it exists in a world of change, a world in which ordinary things (bread and wine) and acts (eating and drinking) carried out in ordinary time are somehow "transfigured" and made the occasions for the transformation of our mortal bodies into the likeness of Christ's glorious body (Phil 3:21)."[120] The eschatological tension in the liturgy tempers a perspective that helps us to cope with the tensions we experience in life. It trains our vision on the eschatological hope in the light of God's pervading grace and redemptive mission as we struggle with, what Hernandez describes as, our psychological, ministerial and theological tensions. The eschatological orientation brings us hope as we wrestle with the polarities between suffering and glory, present and future, and life and death.[121]

Finally, the eschatological orientation reminds us of the missiological orientation. For, as Chan explains, "eschatology sustains the mission of the church. The moment it resolves the tension either by becoming totally immersed in this world or by divorcing itself from the world, it ceases to be the true hope of the world, even when it is involved in all sorts of "mission" activities and programs."[122] The practice of the liturgy reminds us that we, as the church, "straddles the kingdom and the world and maintains its dual orientation toward both."[123] We are priests in God's kingdom but also servants in God's world. The missiological orientation helps to shape the missiological implication of spiritual direction. As both director and directee reflect upon their prayer and life in this light, they begin to discern how their prayer relates to the needs of the world and participation in God's mission.

In summary, the liturgy as a coherent structure not only forms the church comprehensively through its basic *ordo* and four fundamental orientations, it also, by implication, forms the practice of spiritual direction. Because the liturgy is "determinative of ecclesial formation," it provides a *pattern* for understanding practice and a *means* of establishing other secondary practices as ecclesial practices—of which spiritual direction is one.[124]

---

120. Chan, *Liturgical Theology*, 80.

121. See Hernandez, *Henri Nouwen and Spiritual Polarities*, for a good discussion of living with our psychological, ministerial and theological tensions.

122. Chan, *Liturgical Theology*, 83.

123. Chan, *Liturgical Theology*, 83.

124. Chan, *Liturgical Theology*, 90–92.

MISSIOLOGICAL AND ESCHATOLOGICAL
IMPLICATIONS FOR SPIRITUAL DIRECTION

Against this backdrop, we conclude this chapter with several missiological and eschatological perspectives that provides a broader horizon for the practice of spiritual direction. Lonsdale reminds us that "one of the fundamental theological factors that shapes Christian spiritual guidance is the belief that a God of unconditional love invites us, individually and collectively, to live and to act in partnership with God and with another to bring about the reign of God."[125] This missiological perspective guards the practice of spiritual direction from slipping into a matter of colloquial interest but instead lifts it up to participate in God's kingdom mission.

The reign of God is a reality that encompasses every dimension of life. It penetrates the inner and outer spheres of our existences, including the personal and the social-structural. It engenders personal growth into the kinds of people God desires us to be and also engages the struggle to create a society that is more humane and consistent with God's desires.[126] In fact, it is a reality that gives the ministry of spiritual direction its foundational impetus, without which spiritual direction will be reduced to merely personal interests. Its eschatological implications for spiritual direction are so pertinent that it bears quoting Lonsdale in full here:

> Taking part in the struggle to make the reign of God a living reality obviously has an eschatological dimension, which gives Christian spiritual direction its particular perspective on the past, the present and the future. In the life, death and resurrection of Jesus and the revelation of the outpouring of the Spirit, we have an assertion that God's victory over evil is already won, once and for all. This serves to give us confidence that the reign of God, the personal and social transformations which we work for in and through spiritual guidance are in fact possible, and that the primary agent of this process is the Spirit who has already been poured out upon us. This eschatological context in which spiritual direction takes place, however, also gives us a perspective on the future. The belief that the reign of God, while already present, finds its fulfillment in the future life assures us that the work of empowering and liberating that goes on here and now has eternal value and will eventually be brought to completion.[127]

125. Lonsdale, "Traditions of Spiritual Guidance," 313.
126. Lonsdale, "Traditions of Spiritual Guidance," 313.
127. Lonsdale, "Traditions of Spiritual Guidance," 314.

Philip Sheldrake has noted that the divorce of theology and spirituality has led to the danger of separating contemplation from action.[128] However, when spiritual direction is shaped by Christian faith and theology, it has a very different and far broader horizon.[129] This different and far broader horizon is the missiological and eschatological perspectives that must undergird the practice. They are the impetus that bridges contemplation and action. They nurture the life of prayer in the directee through both the prayerful inward communion with God and the prayerful outward participation in the reign of God. They attend to both the commandments to love the Lord our God with all our heart, soul, mind, and strength, and to love our neighbor as ourselves. As Reiser has argued, "the focus question "Where is God in your life?" remains incomplete without "Where are God's people?" The question "What is God like for you?" needs as a follow-up "Who exactly are the people you allow to step into your soul?" "The Spirit of Jesus orients us toward the people of God–which may account for why someone who has learned Jesus' name would want to drive out demons from societies, neighborhoods, and individual lives."[130]

Our missiological engagement is nevertheless guided by our eschatological vision. We hold in tension the "already and not yet." While God's eschatological Spirit has already inaugurated his kingdom, yet there is a future consummation that awaits its fulfillment. We live between these twin realities. Jesus has drunk the cup and given the Spirit; but he awaits the day when he will drink it again in the Father's presence. When we are able to hold this in tension, then we will be more able to embrace the pain and suffering and the mysteries of life. This is an important posture that the spiritual director must help the directee to embrace.

Such a foundational perspective not only serves to undergird the immensely challenging task of serving as a spiritual director, it also helps the directee to look beyond merely personal needs to a much larger horizon with all its missiological implications. They remind us that spiritual direction must not be seen as just another means for personal healing and growth. Nor should it be concerned only with the "inner life" of prayer and personal piety. On the contrary, the practice of spiritual direction must be guided by both the missiological and the eschatological dimensions of being a disciple of Jesus.

When spiritual direction retains the missiological and eschatological perspectives, they serve as a counter-balance against the danger of reducing

128. Sheldrake, *Spirituality and Theology*.

129. Lonsdale, "Traditions of Spiritual Guidance," 314.

130. Reiser, *Seeking God*, 151.

spiritual direction to being merely concerned with personal health and wholeness. On the contrary, "when one's practice of spiritual direction is shaped by a fuller understanding of the mystery of the Incarnation and of the reign of God . . . God invites each person to discover and explore appropriate ways of allowing the reign of God to enter into every dimension of life, social as well as personal, and exploring this is an integral part of the spiritual direction process."[131]

CONCLUSION

Our consideration of the missiological and eschatological dimensions of spiritual direction brings our discussion of the theological component of spiritual direction to a conclusion. While we emphasized the theological perspective in this chapter, I have sought to develop a tri-perspectival framework for the ministry of spiritual direction in the past three chapters. When we begin to see, and retain, the connections between the history, theology and practice of a tradition, we will be better placed to reach across the traditions in a more informed and, hence potentially, helpful way. Arguably, the continuities and discontinuities between the Ignatian and Reformed traditions represent some of the issues involved in reaching across the traditions in an ecumenical setting. It is to a faithful retrieval and analysis of these two great traditions that we turn.

131. Lonsdale, "Traditions of Spiritual Guidance," 314–15.

4

The Historical and Theological Context of Ignatian Spiritual Direction

THE HISTORICAL AND THEOLOGICAL considerations of spiritual direction over the past two chapters were intended to emphasize that the retrieval of a tradition's practice of spiritual direction entails a faithful rendering of its particular history and theology. I attend to the same emphasis as I set out, over the next two chapters; to demonstrate how Ignatius's historical experience influenced his particular theology of spiritual direction which in turn was translated into his method as seen in the *Spiritual Exercises*.[1] I will examine the contextual and personal experiences that shaped his theology of the spiritual life, and demonstrate how these theological constructs in turned influenced his method of spiritual direction. We will find that Ignatius's theology and practice of spiritual direction are inseparable; but for the sake of analysis, this chapter focuses on his theological criteria of direction, and the next chapter on his method of direction.

Apart from utilizing Sandra Schneiders's hermeneutical approach[2] and James Bradley's historical-critical analysis,[3] this chapter also utilizes two hermeneutical keys, by Jesuit theologians Gilles Cusson,[4] and George

---

1. Ignatius and Puhl, *The Spiritual Exercises of St. Ignatius*. References to the *Spiritual Exercises* will simply indicate the standard paragraph number with square brackets (for example [23]).

2. Schneiders, "A Hermenuetical Approach to the Study of Christian Spirituality," 49–64.

3. Bradley and Muller, *Church History*.

4. Cusson, *Biblical Theology and the Spiritual Exercises*.

Ganss,[5] that attends to Ignatius's spiritual worldview. Objectively, Ignatius's spiritual worldview revolves around his understanding of God's plan
in creation, redemption through Christ, and glorification of free human beings in the beatific vision; and subjectively, his understanding of the role we
can play as the history of salvation unfolds.[6] I also pay particular attention
to Ignatius's use of ends and means in the *Spiritual Exercises*. In particular,
he describes our chief end to be living for the greater glory of God (*ad majorem Dei gloriam*), and that we must use all appropriate means to serve this
ultimate end [23].

There is significant consensus among Ignatian scholars that among
the contextual and personal factors that influenced the formulation of the
Exercises, the primary force was Ignatius's own spiritual experience of God's
grace.[7] As John O'Malley puts it succinctly, the *Exercises* "originated in
religious experience, first the author's and then others."[8] Consequently,
we pay particular attention to Ignatius's personal experience in this study—
first, as seen in the nature of his interior life, and second, in his activity of
forming and directing others as seen in the text of the *Spiritual Exercises*.[9]

HISTORICAL FACTORS THAT SHAPED IGNATIUS'S THEOLOGY OF SPIRITUAL DIRECTION

Ignatius's experiences fall naturally into two parts: first, there is the period
from his birth till his conversion, in which I pay particular attention to the
influence of the *vita Christi* (*Life of Christ*), and *Flos Sanctorum* (*The Lives of
the Saints;* also known as *The Golden Legend*); and second, the period from
the beginning of his pilgrimage at Montserrat to the formation of the Society of Jesus. This part of the chapter examines Ignatius's life chronologically,
noting the experiences from his childhood, youth, and adult years, and the
social-cultural and religious influences. I also attend to his ascetic practices
and mystical experiences which, together with the historical-cultural factors, collectively shaped his theological perspective on spiritual direction.

Ignatius grew up, on the one hand, with an unquestioned Catholic
faith; but on the other hand, embracing all the cultural norms of his day.

---

5. Ignatius and Ganss, *Ignatius of Loyola*.

6. Ignatius and Ganss, *Ignatius of Loyola*, 60.

7. Guibert, *The Jesuits*, 10–12, 21–73; Cusson, *Biblical Theology and the Spiritual Exercises*, 1–131; Meissner, *Ignatius of Loyola*, 87–108; and Dalmases, *Ignatius of
Loyola*, 66.

8. O'Malley, *The First Jesuits*, 42.

9. Guibert, *The Jesuits*, 12.

Íñigo López de Loyola, as he was named at birth (1491), was the youngest of thirteen children born to Beltrán Ibañez de Oñaz y Loyola and Marina Sanchez de Licona in the parish of Azpeitia in the Basque province of Guipúzcoa in northern Spain. Basque society was thoroughly Catholic, though feuding and illicit marital unions were common.[10] His father apparently possessed a robust Catholic faith and yet fathered two illegitimate children. His mother was equally pious and had Ignatius tonsured at an early age.[11]

At about fifteen years, Ignatius was sent to the household of his father's friend, Juan Velázquez de Cuéllar, to be educated as a courtier. There, under the influence of court nobility and the tutelage of Pedro Martir de Angleria, Ignatius learnt the skills of warfare, dancing, music, poetry and calligraphy. Ignatius seemed to have excelled particularly in penmanship. However, he was quickly overtaken by vainglory and began to imbibe some of the less desirable cultural norms as he sought to win the favorable notice of Spanish nobility. He became rather reckless in gambling, in his dealings with women, in quarreling and with the sword. He did not keep his faith or himself from sin, and made it clear that he had no intention of becoming a priest.[12]

Ignatius's training as a courtier, however, came to an abrupt end with Velázquez's death in 1516. The next year, with a gift of five hundred coins and two horses from Velázquez's widow Maria, Ignatius entered into the service of Don Antionio Manrique de Lara as a gentleman-at-arms. This move to Najera led to a defining moment in Ignatius's life, which marked the beginning of a journey in his spiritual transformation.[13]

On May 17, 1521, Ignatius was defending the city of Pamplona against an invading French army. His small garrison of fighters was clearly outnumbered by the advancing French troops, but Ignatius, the gallant fighter that he was, refused to surrender. In the fierce bombardment, a cannon ball from the French artillery breached the fortress and "struck [him] on one leg, shattering it completely," and injuring the other severely.[14] With him, the city of Pamplona fell to the invading French army. However, the French soldiers took pity on him and treated him kindly. After giving him first aid, they put him on a litter and took him to his home in Loyola. It was at Loyola that the initial seeds of Ignatius's theology for spiritual direction were sown.

Due to the poor first aid he received from the French doctors and the long journey home, his badly injured leg did not heal well and had to be

10. Puhl, *The Spiritual Exercises of St. Ignatius*, xxv.
11. Caraman, *Ignatius Loyola*, 7–8.
12. Caraman, *Ignatius Loyola*, 11–13.
13. Dalmases, *Ignatius of Loyola*, 28–38.
14. *Autobiography*, #1.

reset. His condition, however, worsened and he was near death. The doctors were not confident that he would recover and advised him to confess and to receive the sacraments. But Ignatius miraculously recovered.[15]

The poorly-reset leg, however, had a protruding bone. Ignatius, still absorbed by his dreams of knightly valor, decided to have the excess flesh and bone removed to save his looks. His willingness to endure such gruesome pain was reflective of his determination—a quality which though is now given over to vanities of this world, the Lord would in time redeem for the purposes of his kingdom.

The Initial Seeds for the Spiritual Exercises

As he was largely confined to bed during the early part of his convalescence, Ignatius asked for books to read; especially books on chivalrous romances. But there were none in the house except for two books, which were the Spanish translations of *The Life of Christ* by the German Carthusian Ludolph of Saxony and the popular collection of the lives of the saints, *The Golden Legend (or Flos Sanctorum)*.[16]

As he read, he daydreamed. At times, he fantasized about returning to life in court and being in the service of a most noble lady. At other times, he imagined following in the footsteps of St. Dominic and St. Francis in their exploits. So he found his imagination oscillating between these two sets of daydreams.[17]

Then Ignatius noticed a difference on how the two sets of daydreams impacted his affections. While his imagination of serving the noble lady and of enjoying the pleasures of worldly things initially brought him "much delight," they eventually left him "dry and dissatisfied." On the other hand, his dreams of following in the footsteps of the saints—of going to Jerusalem, of eating nothing but plain vegetables, and of practicing all the rigors that he saw in the saints—not only brought him much consolation but even after he had put them aside, he found that he remained "satisfied and joyful."[18] So he began to notice that some thoughts left him sad while others left him joyful.

Gradually, Ignatius began to differentiate between the sources of his thoughts. He deduced that some were from the devil and others from God. So, Ignatius began to discern the "diversity of spirits" that was influencing

15. *Autobiography*, #2–3.

16. Guibert, *The Jesuits*, 22–27; *Autobiography*, #5.

17. *Autobiography*, #6–7.

18. *Autobiography*, #8.

him.[19] Later Ignatius drew from these experiences to describe the character of consolation and desolation as criteria for establishing God's guidance through knowledge of interior affections.[20]

The *Spiritual Exercises* thus found its roots in Ignatius's convalescence at Loyola. Ignatius would continue to note and test his thoughts and affective experiences and write them down in simple notes. In the process, he gained deeper insights on interior affections and how one ought to respond to them. His experience of the diversity of spirits at Loyola shaped his theology for discernment.

These insights led to his conversion. He loathed his past life and felt an intense need to do penance for it. He greatly desired to imitate the saints, to go on a pilgrimage to Jerusalem, and to observe the fasts and the disciplines as a generous soul would express his love to God. He described how one night he had a vision of the Virgin Mary with the holy Child Jesus and was greatly consoled. That spurred him all the more to leave his past life and pursue with great vigor a new life of constant penance. At one point he considered entering the Carthusian monastery, but the desire to do penance as he went about the world was stronger and so he committed himself to it.[21]

Influences from the *Flos Sanctorum* and the *Life of Christ*

It is well established that Ignatius appropriated the *Flos Sanctorum* and the *Life of Christ* in his theology of spiritual direction.[22] The *Flos Sanctorum* is

19. Ignatius was describing the influence of different "spirits" on his thoughts and affections. In the *Spiritual Exercises*, "thoughts" are not simply abstract ideas but are instead "different movements produced in the soul" by different "spirits" [313]. They involve our imagination and affections and tend toward actions, either interior or exterior. The "spirits" can be a good spirit [that is, God or his angels], an evil spirit [Satan and his demons] or the influence of our flesh [fallen nature]. "Thoughts brought about by the spirits are thoughts, good or bad, in so far as they come unbidden and, as it were, from 'outside' of ourselves (cf. [32,347])." See Ivens, *Understanding the Spiritual Exercises*, 1.

Jules Toner clarifies that what Ignatius refers to as movements produced in the soul is "the flux of thoughts (such as judgments about God, self, the world, plans, lines of reasoning, lines of association, or imaginings), and of affective acts (such as love, hate, desire, or fear), and of affective feelings (such as peace, warmth, coldness, sweetness, bitterness, buoyancy, or depression)." See Toner, *A Commentary*, 37. The practice of Ignatian discernment involves the noticing of these movements in the souls, to understand their nature and source, and to admit or reject them.

20. Rahner and Loose, *Ignatius of Loyola*, 50–51.

21. *Autobiography*, #9–12.

22. See Ganss, *Ignatius of Loyola*, 15–26; Cusson, *Biblical Theology and the Spiritual Exercises*, 8–22; O'Malley, *The First Jesuits*, 24, 46, 264; and Rahner, *The Spirituality of*

replete with tales of the saints, many of its etymologies are fanciful and yet it appealed to Ignatius because it spoke to the need for penances and value of pilgrimages. At this stage of his growth, Ignatius's desire to imitate the saints was still driven more by his human effort and will power than by a profound and interior attachment to the Lord.[23]

Ludolph's *Life of Christ*, however, shaped Ignatius work on the *Exercises* more directly.[24] Of the identifiable sources that influenced the *Spiritual Exercises*, the *Life of Christ* was "without doubt the most important."[25] Its succession of ideas as well as its structure significantly influenced Ignatius's own spirituality and the way he structured the *Exercises*.[26] As Ganss points out, a comparison between the *Life of Christ* and Ignatius's *Exercises* revealed striking similarities between their structure and contents, including core meditations and contemplations. A major difference, however, was that Ludolph adopted a narrative approach and expounded each topic at length, while Ignatius "gives only brief points . . . for an exercitant to expand on his own contemplation, according to his own needs and graces from God."[27] This distinctive was a mark of Ignatius's originality in his composition of the *Exercises*.

It may, therefore, be said that the *Life of Christ* provided the initial spiritual theology for the *Spiritual Exercises*. It introduced Ignatius to the biblical character of the spiritual world and many of its expressions were incorporated into the *Exercises*, including similar ways of interpreting the Gospel scenes.[28] It laid the basis for a spiritual life that was "solidly struc-

---

St. Ignatius, 24–35 on how the *Golden Legend* by the Dominican Jacobus de Voragine (d.1298) and the *Life of Christ* (*Vita Jesu Christi* by the Carthusian Ludolph of Saxony) influenced Ignatius and his composition of the *Spiritual Exercises*. Ignatius read the Spanish versions of these two books. See also, Shore, *The Vita Christi of Ludolph of Saxony and Its Influence on the Spiritual Exercises of Ignatius of Loyola*.

23. Ganss, *Ignatius of Loyola*, 13–26; see also Cusson, *Biblical Theology and the Spiritual Exercises*.

24. Ganss, *Ignatius of Loyola*, 16–19.

25. O'Malley, *The First Jesuits*, 46.

26. It is beyond the scope of this work to detail the contents of the *Life of Christ* and its corresponding influence on the *Exercises*. It has 181 chapters. In Part I (92 chapters), Ludolph devotes his introduction to explaining methods for contemplating the events in Christ's life, followed by contents on the Trinity and the Word, God's plan of salvation for fallen humanity, the Annunciation, the Circumcision, the Flight, and the Hidden Life. Following these (in Parts I and II) are 127 chapters on the Public life, 18 chapters on the Passion, and 12 chapters on the Risen Life and the Ascension. The final 7 chapters are dedicated to the Pentecost, the Praise of God, the Last Judgment, and Heavenly Glory–see Ganss, *Ignatius of Loyola*.

27. Ganss, *Ignatius of Loyola*, 20.

28. Cusson, *Biblical Theology and the Spiritual Exercises*.

tured around three principal realities: the Trinity, Christ, and our condition as creatures."[29] This explains why the meditations and contemplations of the *Exercises* are so centrally focused on the life, death, and resurrection of Christ.

Ludolph's twin emphases on Christ as "the foundation of salvation" and sinful humanity's "radical powerlessness" to effect its own salvation, issues in the call to the sinner in "two complimentary stages;" first of purification, and also of commitment to following Christ as the only way of salvation.[30] The first reflects the sinner's "profound contrition" and "zealous proposal always to refrain from evil and to do good;" while the second "emphasizes the personal, intelligent adhesion of the faithful person to his Lord."[31] The former expresses the sinner's utter dependence upon Christ while the latter the sinner's sole desire to imitate Christ.

Up to this point, we identified two major historical influences that shaped Ignatius's theology of spiritual direction. The first was his awareness of the diversity of spirits in his daydreams. Ignatius's perception of the influences of the spirits upon the affections laid the initial seeds for a theology of the discernment of spirits. The second was the profound influence of the *Life of Christ* on his theology of salvation and progress in the spiritual life. Like the *Life of Christ*, his spiritual views are profoundly trinitarian, distinctively christological; addressing the problem of sin and evil, and embracing the way of salvation in Christ.

Nevertheless, at this stage of his life, he was still a pilgrim enamored with imitating the life of the saints by sheer self-effort. God would continue to work in the life of this pilgrim to further guide him in the way of discernment–the experiences to which we continue to examine.

Movement and Self-Discovery from Montserrat to Jerusalem (1522–1523)

As we examine how his experiences on the road shaped his understanding of spiritual direction, two incidents stood out as he was traveling to Montserrat. In the first incident, he was enraged by a Moor's rude remarks concerning Mary's virginity. Ignatius possessed a particularly strong devotion to the Virgin Mary. Unable to discern his interior movements, he resorted to letting his mule decide whether he should stab the Moor or not, depending on which road the mule would take at a fork. The incident revealed that he

29. Cusson, *Biblical Theology and the Spiritual Exercises,* 10.
30. Cusson, *Biblical Theology and the Spiritual Exercises,* 12.
31. Cusson, *Biblical Theology and the Spiritual Exercises,* 12.

was still driven by his lopsided zeal and disordered interiority, and it served as a glaring example of how not to do spiritual discernment. The other was his decision to firmly put his past behind and follow Christ in the way of the pilgrim. He gave his fine clothes to a beggar and donned a pilgrim's tunic made of hemp-linen. He spent three days in confession and a whole night in prayer at the shrine of the Black Virgin at Montserrat in February 1522. Ignatius would incorporate such an attitude of resolve and determination into the *Spiritual Exercises* and the Society of Jesus.[32]

Ignatius's experiences at Manresa from March 1522 to February 1523 marked a major turning point in his spiritual pilgrimage. The experiences significantly honed his theological understanding of the interior life, which is an aspect that is so fundamental to spiritual direction. Initially, he was still given to extremes as he fasted for long periods and let his hair and nails grow unattended. In that unstable condition, Ignatius saw a beautiful serpent entice him; and he responded with both emotions of delight and disgust. Ignatius would confess in his autobiography that he was still without much knowledge of interior things at this time. But the episodes with the serpent began to teach him what false consolations are. Later, the serpent would tempt him into thoughts of desolation. Recognizing that they were temptations from the enemy, Ignatius rejected the desolate thoughts and committed himself to the grace of God. These were important lessons in noticing and understanding the diverse affections of our soul.

Despite his three-day confession at Montserrat, Ignatius struggled with scruples during this time. Fasting and praying did not help. He was so terribly tormented that he contemplated suicide. Fortunately, a wise confessor instructed him to stop his fasts and not to confess anymore. This counsel of wisdom helped him to receive God's grace and deepened his insights on the discernment of spirits.[33]

Ignatius said that during this time "God treated him . . . just as a schoolmaster treats a child whom he is teaching."[34] He had given himself to extremes but slowly God gave him more insights into his interiority and gradually guided him into a more balanced way. Ignatius's ascetic practices and mystical experiences over the course of the year at Manresa deepened his understanding of the spiritual life. The notes he took of these experiences became the core of the *Spiritual Exercises*.

32. *Autobiography*, #14–17; Dalmases, *Ignatius of Loyola*, 49–53.
33. *Autobiography*, #19–25; Dalmases, *Ignatius of Loyola*, 54–70.
34. *Autobiography*, #27.

Ignatius related in his autobiography that his spiritual understanding was deepened in five major aspects during this time.[35] They pertained to the Trinity, creation, Christ's presence in the Eucharist, the humanity of Christ and the Virgin Mary. One day, while he was reciting the Hours of our Lady at the Dominican church, "his understanding was raised on high, so as to see the Most Holy Trinity under the aspect of the three keys on a musical instrument, and as a result he shed many tears and sobbed so strongly that he could not control himself."[36] This experience on the mystery of the Trinity lingered with him for years, bringing him much consolation, and it prompted the attention he gave to the Trinity in the *Spiritual Exercises*.

Ignatius's insight into God's creation also deepened during this time. This too received emphasis in the *Exercises*, especially in the First Principle and Foundation. Ignatius's understanding of the Eucharist was also strengthened as he perceived "with interior eyes" the body of Christ in the Eucharist. Consistent with Catholic sacramental theology, "what he saw clearly with his understanding was how Jesus Christ our Lord was there in the Most Holy Sacrament."[37]

Then Ignatius also reported visions of many apparitions both of the humanity of Christ and of Mary. As it appears, these special graces were rather unique to Ignatius, and he did not suggest that they were meant for everyone. While these sightings certainly enriched his spiritual experience, he did not seem to accord them a central role in the practice of spiritual direction.

The climactic moment of his experience at Manresa was the unique illumination at Cardoner that brought him such "a great clarity in his understanding" that it is "as if he were another man with another mind."[38] It significantly transformed his spiritual consciousness. As he puts it, there "the eyes of his understanding began to be opened; not that he saw any vision, but he understood and learnt many things, both spiritual matters and matters of faith and scholarship, and this with so great an enlightenment that everything seemed new to him."[39]

Ignatius's spiritual experiences at Manresa therefore significantly influenced his theology of spiritual guidance. The graces that he received fundamentally influenced his understanding of God and his creation, Christ and the plan of salvation, and humanity and the created world. It also illumined

---

35. *Autobiography*, #28–30.

36. *Autobiography*, #28.

37. *Autobiography*, #29.

38. *Autobiography*, #30.

39. *Autobiography*, #30.

his understanding into the mysteries of the Christian faith as well as insights into the interior movements of the soul.[40] It was as if Ignatius himself was "the first exercitant" and the *Exercises* that he wrote were the fruit of his personal experiences at Manresa.[41] Ignatius would continue to develop these exercises during his years as a pilgrim from Manresa to Paris before they were published in their definitive form twenty-six years later in 1548.

The next major episode that connects Ignatius's own spiritual progress to his theology of spiritual direction was his pilgrimage to Jerusalem in 1523. The pilgrimage exercised his faith and foreshadowed the initial seeds of the later apostolic endeavor of the Jesuits. Challenged by the rough passages at sea and dangers from unruly elements on the road, his ill-health and the absence of financial means for the journey, Ignatius relied on God for all he needed. He learnt humility through begging and generosity through sharing the little that he had with other beggars. Yet in the midst of the ups and downs, he experienced "great assurance in his soul that God would provide a way for him to go to Jerusalem."[42] He recounted that the "Lord appeared to him often, giving him great consolation and determination" during this time.[43] These experiences shaped the *Exercises*' emphasis on persevering in faith, hope, and love, the theological virtues that fundamentally defined what consolation is.

Ignatius had planned to remain in Jerusalem and devote himself to converting the Muslims but given the tense situation between the Christians and the Turks, the Franciscan superior who had authority over him advised him against it. Discerning that it was not God's will for him to remain, Ignatius decided that he should give his time to the study of grammar and theology in order to better help souls and engage in the apostolic mission; and so he headed for Barcelona.

The Student Years at Barcelona, Alcala, Salamanca, and Paris (1523–1535)

Arriving at Barcelona, he embarked on learning basic grammar. But he would often be distracted by "new insights into spiritual matters" that hindered his learning. When he began to discern that they were in fact temptations from the devil, he told his master teacher that he would devote himself

---

40. Cusson, *Biblical Theology and the Spiritual Exercises*, 31.
41. Dalmases, *Ignatius of Loyola*, 66.
42. *Autobiography*, #42.
43. *Autobiography*, #44.

to the studies and not be waylaid by the distractions. This experience taught him how to discern false consolations.

His good progress in grammar secured him a place to study liberal arts at Alcala. For the next year and a half, Ignatius mastered Peter Lombard's *Sentences* among other subjects. During this time, he also "engaged in giving spiritual exercises and teaching Christian doctrine and this bore fruit for the glory of God."[44] He experienced the joy of seeing many persons come to "a deep understanding and relish of spiritual things,"[45] a way of interior formation that became the hallmark of Ignatian spirituality.

During this time, however, the Inquisition probed into his activities of helping souls and despite finding no fault in his teaching imprisoned him for forty-two days. The inquisitors warned him not to instruct or speak to anyone about the faith until he received four more years of theological education. Although falsely accused and imprisoned, Ignatius counted it an honor to suffer for the Lord. With the help of the archbishop of Toledo, he headed to Salamanca for further studies.[46]

More trouble awaited him at Salamanca. There the authorities questioned him on theological matters, such as his understanding of the Trinity, the Eucharist, his differentiation between venial and mortal sins, but ultimately, the question came down to whether he thought he taught under the inspiration of the Holy Spirit. Sensing that their line of questioning revolved around the heresy of illuminism, Ignatius did his best to dodge the questions, and he was ultimately successful. But with options at Salamanca closed, he left for the University of Paris.

The years at the University of Paris provided for a deeper grounding in the humanities and theology. He first enrolled in the College de Montiagu to strengthen his Latin grammar.[47] He had no means of support and had to beg alms. He sought employment but did not find any and his poverty clearly hindered his studies. Eventually, he spent two months each year in Flanders begging alms and what he collected there was able to sustain him for the rest of the year. Through this means, Ignatius was able to give more

44. *Autobiography*, #57.

45. *Autobiography*, #57.

46. *Autobiography*, #57–62.

47. Ignatius came into contact with the profound influence of the Brethren of the Common Life at the College of Montaigu. It explains why the Imitation of Christ (*Imitatio Christi*) held such an influence on him beginning from Montserrat through to his death. However, it is beyond the scope of this work for an in-depth investigation into the influences that arose from his contact with the Brethren of the Common Life. For more information see, Van Engen, *Sisters and Brothers of the Common Life*, 317–319. See also Van Engen, *Devotio Moderna: Basic Writings*.

attention to his studies. The experience of poverty and alms begging significantly shaped his understanding of the meaning of identifying with Christ as poor and humble, and the theme became a major feature in the *Exercises*.

While at Paris, Ignatius began giving the *Exercises* to more people, at one point three people simultaneously. The transformations he witnessed through these helping relationships encouraged them all. However, he soon came under the scrutiny of the Inquisition once again. Wanting to clear his name once and for all, Ignatius went to see the inquisitor, the Dominican Valentin Liévin. Liévin told him of their awareness of his activities and requested to see the writings of the *Exercises*. The inquisitor found the *Exercises* highly praiseworthy and requested a copy. From that point on, Ignatius received the freedom to circulate the *Exercises* and to focus on his studies. He completed the Licentiate in the Arts on March 13, 1533, and the Master of Arts degree a year later on March 14, 1534.[48]

Ignatius's years of study at the universities of Alcala and Paris help account for his grounding in traditional Catholic theology. Major interpreters of Ignatian spirituality have all noted the influence of Peter Lombard and Thomas Aquinas on Ignatius's thinking.[49] Scholars identify a "harmony of thought" between Peter Lombard's writings on God and his work in creation and Ignatius's Principle and Foundation.[50] They also notice the similar emphases found in Ignatius's Foundation and Aquinas' comprehensive view of God's plan of creation and redemption.[51] Nevertheless, one cannot be certain whether Ignatius *intentionally* drew from Lombard, Aquinas, or in our earlier consideration, from Ludolph's *Life of Christ*—or for that matter, from the *Imitation of Christ*, a book that held a profound influence on Ignatius and the Jesuits.[52] What matters here, as Ganss notes, is that the ideas of Lombard and Aquinas "are part of [Ignatius's] personalized concept of God's plan of creation and redemption, and are therefore keys to our deeper understanding and correct interpretation of his writing."[53]

48. Dalmases, *Ignatius of Loyola*, 106–26.

49. See, for example, Rahner, *The Spirituality of St. Ignatius*, 94; Guibert, *The Jesuits*; Ganss, *Ignatius of Loyola*, 35–40; O'Malley, *The First Jesuits*, 243–253.

50. Ganss, *Ignatius of Loyola*, 38–39.

51. Ganss, *Ignatius of Loyola*, 39.

52. See Von Habsburg, *Catholic and Protestant Translations of the Imitatio Christi*, for insights on the influence of the *Imitatio Christi* on St. Ignatius and the Jesuits.

53. Ganss, *Ignatius of Loyola*, 40.

Formation of the Society of Jesus (1535–1556)

In 1534, Ignatius gave the *Exercises* to several people, among whom were Pierre Favre and Francis Xavier.[54] It was at this time that Ignatius forged several close friendships that were dedicated to the purpose of glorify God through helping souls that served as the initial seeds for the formation of the Society of Jesus. As O'Malley notes, these friends came from different nations and different social classes, and their ages ranged from nineteen to about forty-three. Their common bonds where their friendship, their study at the University of Paris, and most deeply their experience of the *Exercises* under the guidance of Ignatius and their shared desire to glorify God through apostolic endeavors.[55]

On a summer day, August 15, 1534, on the feast of the Assumption of Our Lady, Ignatius and his six friends bound themselves to a life dedicated to the good of souls and to keeping the vows of poverty, chastity, and obedience to the Pope. Thus was birthed an apostolic mission concerned immediately for the good of souls and ultimately for the greater glory of God (*ad majorem Dei gloriam*).

In the spring of 1535, on his doctor's advice, Ignatius left Paris for his home in Spain to recuperate from recurring stomach ailments which turned out to be chronic cystitis associated with gallstones.[56] Before he left, his friends and he agreed that they would re-gather in Venice about a year later to make a pilgrimage to the Holy Land. Ignatius rejoined his six friends in Venice the next year. As a war with Turkey was looming on the horizon, they could not find any ship that would sail to Palestine, so they decided to wait. Ignatius and his friends were ordained to the priesthood on June 24, 1537.[57] Leaving Venice they "dispersed in groups of twos and threes to Verona, Vicenza, Monselice, Bassano, and Treviso, where they first spend forty days in seclusion and prayer and then engaged principally in street preaching. . . ."[58] These early expressions of apostolic activity were characteristic of Ignatian spirituality.

Ignatius's time at Vicenza turned out to be rather like a second Manresa.[59] There "he received many spiritual visions and many rather ordinary consolations, but especially when he began to prepare for his ordination

---

54. *Autobiography*, #82.
55. O'Malley, *The First Jesuits*, 32.
56. Puhl, *The Spiritual Exercises of St. Ignatius*, xxxv.
57. O'Malley, *The First Jesuits*, 33.
58. O'Malley, *The First Jesuits*, 33.
59. Ganss, *Ignatius of Loyola*, 41.

. . . and when he was getting ready to celebrate Mass."[60] It appeared that in contrast to his time in Paris, when he was given to academic work, he could now devote himself more fully to prayer and so enjoyed these rather profound experiences.

After a year, as there was still no passage available to the Holy Land, Ignatius and his companions decided that they would go to Rome and offer their services to the Pope.[61] Along the way, Ignatius received a special vision at *La Storta*. There, while he was praying at a church, he "experienced such a change in his soul and saw so clearly that God the Father placed him [Ignatius] with Christ his Son that he would not dare to doubt it.[62] Hence, at La Storta, Ignatius felt so deeply affirmed that Christ was with him and he with Christ that the "with Christ" principle would dominate his worldview from then on.

Ignatius eventually arrived in Rome in mid-November, 1537. From then till his death on July 31, 1556, Ignatius and his friends served Jesus. The ministry of the Society was distinctively Christ-centered and trinitarian, and decisively aimed at what brings greater glory to God. As Ganss notes, "the Christ who appeared to him at La Storta was the glorified Christ who was still living and functioning in and through the Church, his mystical body, and specially through his vicar, the pope."[63] For Ignatius and his fellow Christ-followers, their special devotion would be to this "whole Christ" and to do whatever is helpful to souls and to God's glory.

Toward this end, the apostolic work through ministries, both local and foreign, bore witness to their commitment to Christ and its missionary zeal in his name. As O'Malley notes, the pastoral ideals and practice of the Society of Jesus is definitively expressed in the original version of the Formula: for "the progress of souls in Christian life and doctrine and for the propagation of the faith."[64] This twofold goal is clearly achieved when one examines the list of ministries that the Society engaged. These included the preaching and teaching of the Word, especially in the giving of the *Exercises*; ministries in the Church through the Sacraments, worship and prayer, ministries of mercy that included the establishment of hospitals and aid to prisoners, to the dying, the prostitutes and the orphans. They developed the work of education and established numerous schools and universities, and promoted the work of theological education as well as the teaching of the laity. Indeed,

60. *Autobiography*, #95.
61. *Autobiography*, #96.
62. *Autobiography*, #96.
63. Ganss, *Ignatius of Loyola*, 43.
64. O'Malley, *The First Jesuits*, 69–70.

through these diverse means, Ignatius and his friends displayed a love for Jesus, deep and far reaching enough that virtually no plausible initiatives were overlooked for what would offer help to souls and bring greater glory to God, their sole and ultimate end in a Christ-centered life.

The preceding survey of the core historical influences on and personal experiences of Ignatius suggest the following key sources of his theology of spiritual direction.

First, Ignatius's experiences shaped a theology that is focused on the greater glory of God. His orthodox Catholic faith nurtured his deep devotion to the Holy Trinity and the Virgin Mary as mediatrix before God. This was evident in his vision at Cardoner. For Ignatius, his chief end was to glorify God, and the means was to imitate Christ. Hence his theology was also distinctively Christo-centric. The Holy Spirit was present in his experience, but Ignatius avoided overt mention of the Third Person of the Trinity due to his troubles with the *alumbrados*.

Second, Ignatius's shame over his past and his struggles with sin shaped a theology of sin that is deeply conscious of the depravity of human nature and the wiles of the enemy. Sin is an affront to God and sabotages spiritual progress, and it must be dealt with decisively and persistently through the practice of penance. His deliverance from scruples taught him that God was merciful and grants the grace one needs to pursue spiritual growth and salvation in Christ, and hence motivates people to submit to God and to cooperate with grace that they may eventually attain to salvation.

Third, Ignatius's experience of interior movements of the spirits forged his theology of discernments of the spirits. This emphasis is uniquely Ignatian and a very important aspect of Ignatian spiritual direction. These insights uniquely shaped how he structured the *Exercises* and the criteria he used for discernment, which is a central focus in his way of proceeding in direction.

Fourth, Ignatius's experience of God working, and working with God to help souls shaped his theology of expressing our desires to God. The *Exercises* would consistently encourage us to tell God what we want, which not only puts us in touch with our desires but also purifies and shapes them for God's Kingdom purposes.

Finally, Ignatius's knowledge of God's mission and his positive experiences of helping souls, perhaps wrought from his experiences at Jerusalem and throughout his studies, shaped his theology of an active spirituality. For Ignatius, love must be expressed in deeds and apostolic mission. The *Exercises* will nurture in the exercitant a heroic outlook that is expressed in humble service and lived for the greater glory of God.

IGNATIUS'S THEOLOGICAL CRITERIA
OF SPIRITUAL DIRECTION

Having examined how the contextual and personal experiences of Ignatius shaped his theology of spiritual direction, we turn now to the question on how his theology shaped his practice of spiritual direction as seen in the *Spiritual Exercises*. While foundational aspects of this theology were evident from his personal history, they become more evident within the *Exercises* themselves. We keep in focus the two hermeneutical keys that George Ganss and Gilles Cusson proposed.[65]

The first hermeneutical key, the preeminence of God's plan of salvation through Christ, is the objective biblical criterion that guides the subjective experience and response of the exercitant. God, for Ignatius, is Creator and Lord, whom he respectfully addresses in his sixteenth-century context as the "Divine Majesty" [5]. God is the Trinity–Father, Son, and Holy Spirit; the "Three Divine Persons" seated in the heavenly throne of the Divine Majesty [101–109].

For Ignatius, the triune God not only created the heavens and the earth and everything in it, he actively seeks a reciprocal relationship with the human being, who is created in his image. God's good creation was unfortunately damaged by "the sin of Adam and Eve," resulting in "great corruption" on the human race and causing many to be lost in hell [51]. Looking down from heaven upon this grave predicament, the Three Divine Persons decreed that the "Second Person," Jesus Christ, should become man to save the human race [102]. God thus effects a plan of salvation that is accomplished through the incarnation, life, death, resurrection and ascension of Jesus Christ.

This preeminent foundation, the objective criteria, upon which the *Spiritual Exercises* are based therefore, carries a distinct focus on the Trinity and on Christ. Ignatius assumes a loving and merciful God who has both made salvation available and is actively pursuing the sinner through his love.

Following from his objective criteria, Ignatius designed the *Spiritual Exercises* as a text and process to help an exercitant to discover and fit oneself into God's plan of salvation and spiritual growth. Ignatius recognizes that God reaches out to us in love and that we are capable of experiencing the love of God. The *Spiritual Exercises* therefore seek to raise an exercitant's awareness of God's redeeming love and move the will to respond in trust

65. Ganss, *Ignatius of Loyola; and* Cusson, *Biblical Theology and the Spiritual Exercises.*

and total surrender. This is the subjective part of the experiential process in the *Exercises*.

To maximize the potential for spiritual experience and growth, Ignatius urges one to enter upon the *Exercises* "with magnanimity and generosity [of mind, heart, and service] toward his Creator and Lord, and to offer Him his entire will and liberty, that His Divine Majesty may dispose of him and all he possesses according to His most holy will" [5]. Its focus is distinctively Christo-centric and nurtures through prayer the grace to know Christ more intimately, love him more dearly, and follow him more closely. This love and obedience is to be experienced interiorly through the affections and expressed exteriorly in apostolic mission.

As Ganss notes, the subjective experience here is not limited to the experiences one gathers in prayer but includes the opportunities for apostolic service for the advancement of God's kingdom.[66] The "experiential," therefore, includes both the contemplative and the active dimensions of one's life. It is experience that seeks understanding through prayer and expression through service for the greater glory of God.

Ignatius's Concept of Salvation and the Goal for the Exercises

We begin our retrieval and analysis with the "introductory observations" which were intended "to provide some understanding of the spiritual exercises . . . and to serve as a help both for the one who is to give them and for the exercitant." The twenty annotations contain important theological and methodological principles that define the purpose and process of the *Exercises*. Ignatius recommends that the spiritual director familiarizes himself with them before meeting the exercitant. It was Ignatius's practice to explain Annotations 1, 20 (if the *Exercises* were done in a full retreat and 18 or 19, as they are adapted to the exercitant's life setting), 5 and 4, in that order before giving the Foundation.[67] An analysis of these four annotations–in that order, therefore, reveals important insights on Ignatius's own theological emphasis and method of direction for the *Exercises*.

The first Annotation reveals that Ignatius envisaged a two-pronged purpose for the *Exercises* that first addresses the problem of "inordinate attachments," and "after their removal," of "seeking and finding the will of God in the disposition of our life for the salvation of our soul [1]." Ignatius's theology of sin and salvation shaped this dual purpose for the *Exercises*. Sin must be removed so that God's will may be sought and found. The adherence

66. Ganss, *Ignatius of Loyola*.
67. Palmer, *On Giving the Spiritual Exercises*, 21.

to God's will then leads to the salvation of our soul. The means to achieve this dual purpose included "every method of examination of conscience, of contemplation, of vocal and mental prayer, and of other spiritual activities" as proposed in the *Exercises* [1]. This arrangement echoes Ignatius's own experience and understanding in the context of the sixteenth century, as the following note from the Official Directory attests: "A means of salvation—Among other instruments which God in his goodness has deigned to bestow upon our Society of Jesus for procuring both our own and our neighbors' salvation and perfection, not the least is the Spiritual Exercises."[68]

Since salvation is so central to Ignatius's theological assumptions, it is important to understand what salvation means in Catholic theology. In his commentary on the *Exercises*, Ganss explains that the phrase "to save one's soul" means "to save and perfect or develop one's whole self into the eternal life (John 17:3) of the beatific vision (1 Cor. 13:12; 1 John 3:21)." There is, hence, a dual meaning to the phrase "to save one's soul." It refers not only to one's salvation per se but also one's spiritual growth—onward into the eventual beatific vision. "From parallel passages," Ganss elaborates, "we know that by "salvation" Ignatius meant also continual spiritual progress; e.g., 20 "as much progress as possible"; 135 "to arrive at perfection"; *Cons*, 3: to labor for "the salvation and perfection" of one's neighbors; 813: "to reach their ultimate and supernatural end." This theological understanding fundamentally shaped the text of *Spiritual Exercises* and the process of direction.[69]

Before Ignatius goes on to explain how this theological construct shapes the structure of the text, however, he would brief the exercitant on two other important dispositional criteria as part of the preparation for the *Exercises*. Ignatius envisaged that the *Exercises* are ideally practiced in "as great privacy as possible" so that distractions are lessened and the exercitant can give full attention to the Lord [20]. This does not imply living in seclusion in a monastery, as some might interpret it from a contemporary perspective. Ignatius simply meant that a separate room or house that provided for the maximum privacy would serve the purpose [20]. He then articulated three important theological impetuses: First, by withdrawing from "numerous friends and acquaintances and from many occupations not undertaken with a pure intention," an exercitant "gains no little merit before the Divine Majesty" in order to "serve and praise God our Lord." Ignatius regards the intentional withdrawing into seclusion to seek God as meritorious before God. Second, "in this seclusion the mind is not engaged in many things, but can give its whole attention to one single interest, that is, to the service of its

68. Palmer, *On Giving the Spiritual Exercises*, 290.
69. See Ganss, *Ignatius of Loyola*, 391–94.

Creator and its spiritual progress. Thus it is more free to use its natural powers to seek diligently what it so much desires." Two theological emphases
are evident here: first that one may give singular focus to the service of God
and spiritual progress, and second, that one may work deeply with what one
desires.[70] Third, "the more the soul is in solitude and seclusion, the more
fit it renders itself to approach and be united with its Creator and Lord;
and the more closely it is united with Him, the more it disposes itself to
receive graces and gifts from the infinite goodness of its God" [20]. Ignatius
perceives that total attention in seclusion will better facilitate a closer union
with God and that it brings the needed graces and gifts from a good God.
While Ignatius uses the language of merit, it is important to note here that it
is God who gives the graces and gifts out of his goodness.

He then goes on to annotation 5, which I will elaborate in greater detail later, and so touch on briefly here. Its main thrust is to urge the exercitant to enter into the *Exercises* with "magnanimity and generosity" of spirit
toward his Creator and Lord, and "to offer Him his entire will and liberty,
that His Divine Majesty may dispose of him and all he possesses according to His most holy will" [20]. It is quite unmistakable that the emphasis
on magnanimity and generosity arose from Ignatius's culture of chivalry
and knighthood. Yet it communicates a central thrust in Ignatius's theology and method of spiritual direction. The exercitant is urged to pursue the
magis, the more, expressing greater love for Jesus and greater service to one's
neighbor for the greater glory of God.[71]

With these foundational attitudes and horizons in mind, Ignatius then
proceeds to explain how the focused-retreat might rollout over thirty days
[4]. Though structured into four parts that stretches over four "Weeks," they
do not necessarily correspond to the calendar week. Each is instead a time
with a specific focus. The main idea is to work for the fruit sought for that
period so that further progress can be made.

The Design of the *Spiritual Exercises*: A Text and Process

Hence the *Spiritual Exercises* were intentionally structured into Four Weeks
that mirrors the Roman Catholic three-fold order of salvation: purgation,
illumination, union [4, 10].[72] The First Week was "devoted to the consider-

---

70. Aschenbrenner, *Stretched for Greater Glory*, 33.

71. Aschenbrenner, *Stretched for Greater Glory*, 16–17.

72. According to Greg Peters, the presence of the triple way was a "sine qua non
of mystical theologies" and "retained its place in the writings of the greatest Catholic
Reformation spiritual authors of the sixteenth century, such as St. John of the Cross (d.

ation and contemplation of sin" and corresponds to the emphasis on purgation [4]. The Second Week, "which is taken up with the life of Christ our Lord up to Palm Sunday inclusive," corresponds to the illuminative way, while the Third and Fourth Weeks that corresponds to the passion of Christ our Lord, and his Resurrection and Ascension mirror the unitive way [4]. In this arrangement, the Catholic order of salvation renders the *Spiritual Exercises* as a text and process for guiding one's journey toward salvation and perfection in the beatific vision.

This fundamental theological premise is again taken up in Annotation 21[73] and applied to the practice of penance.[74] Efforts at self-mastery may reflect the context of Spanish chivalry in which Ignatius crafted the *Exercises* but also his understanding of penance, to which he gave himself to in extreme at the early stages of his spiritual pilgrimage.[75] Apart from overcoming oneself, the Catholic understanding of penance embraces the idea of making satisfaction for sins and of earning merit for the graces that one desires. The idea of meritorious works as contributing to spiritual progress is captured in the *Exercises* [see 20]. However, grace is equally emphasized and ultimately recognized as a gift of God [see 46]. While the appropriate use of penance finds its way into the text, the exercising of one's will in cooperation with grace is significantly more emphasized throughout the *Exercises*. For this reason, many recent authors have appealed for a more balanced assessment of Ignatius's intent for the *Exercises*:

> the wording in itself can sound Pelagian or semi-Pelagian, as if one sought and found God's will on one's own, apart from the action of grace. Some early commentaries on the *Exercises* by

1591) and St. Teresa of Avila (d. 1582), and even continued past the era of the Catholic Reformation and into the twentieth century." However, it fell out of favor in Roman Catholic circles after being seriously questioned by the Jesuit theologian Karl Rahner (d. 1984). See Peters, *On Spiritual Theology: A Primer.*

73. The *Spiritual Exercises*, "which have as their purpose the conquest of self and the regulation of one's life in such a way that no decision is made under the influence of any inordinate attachment" [21].

74. Ignatius gives three reasons for exterior penance, and it is here that the Pelagian tendencies are most apparent. The principal reason for performing exterior penance, he writes, is to secure three effects [87]:
"To make satisfaction for past sins;
To overcome oneself, that is, to make our sensual nature obey reason, and to bring all our lower faculties into greater subjection to the higher;
To obtain some grace or gift that one earnestly desires. Thus it may be that one wants a deep sorrow for sin, or tears, either because of his sins or because of the pains and sufferings of Christ our Lord; or he may want the solution of some doubt that is in his mind."

75. *Autobiography,* #12, 14, 55, 74.

Polanco and others, though they generally insist on the necessity of grace in every stage of the process, at times sound this
way. However, the most basic premise of the book taken in its
entirety, other writings in the Ignatian *corpus*, as well as other
commentaries on the *Exercises*, especially those by Nadal, indicates an orthodox meaning. Indeed, the fundamental premise
of the *Exercises* is the continuous action of God in the whole
process . . .[76]

Idigoras similarly appeals to a consideration of the entire Ignatian *cor-*
pus, especially his *Spiritual Diary*, for a balanced view on this matter. "With
this *Dairy*, the stereotyped image of Ignatius as a wooden ascetic, a volun-
tarist, even to the point of being a Pelagian, a man of action with military
panache, fades away, or at least, in order for the picture to be complete, must
be seen alongside the view of Ignatius the mystic, with infused contemplation, with a total passivity of his knowledge and love . . ."[77]

A balanced assessment appears that we must keep in view not only
Ignatius's practice of penance in the context of the sixteenth-century Roman
Church but also in the overall light of his entire spiritual pilgrimage: his experiences, writings, and commentaries. The Pelagian tendency was indeed
present, but so was the emphasis on grace. As we recall, he learnt much from
his struggles with scruples at Manresa. As he said, the Lord "mercifully . . .
delivered him" when he obeyed the counsel of his confessor to stop his fast,
and he gained freedom to stop confessing anything from the past.[78]

Functioning from within the Roman Catholic Church in the sixteenth
century, Ignatius would have embraced the Church's understanding of salvation. It meant embracing salvation through the washing of regeneration
at baptism and the notion of continual growth toward spiritual perfection
and ultimately into the beatific vision. While Christ is the Redeemer and
Mediator between God and humankind, the "attainment" of salvation is
also linked to one's spiritual progress through moving the will to cooperate
with grace in response to God's mercy. Such a perspective within the ecclesial and theological milieu to which he belonged thus explains why Ignatius
would use the language of salvation the way he did.

We gather from these perspectives that an Ignatian understanding of
"to save one's soul" would mean an understanding of God's salvation plan as
seen in God's creation, redemption in Christ, and the continuing spiritual
growth toward its full realization in the beatific vision. Consequently, as

---

76. O'Malley, *The First Jesuits*, 38.

77. José Ignacio Tellechea Idígoras, *Ignatius of Loyola*, 481.

78. *Autobiography*, #25.

Cusson states, the *Exercises'* purpose is "to foster in others a similar itinerary of purification and of appreciative attachment to the powerfully efficacious light of God's plan for salvation and spiritual growth."[79] This was Ignatius's chief presupposition for the *Exercises* in concord with his Catholic spiritual worldview.

THEOLOGICAL CRITERIA
IN THE "INTRODUCTORY OBSERVATIONS"

The theological criteria that shaped Ignatius's method of direction are found in the "Introductory Observations." Ignatius's theology of deep interior transformation, reflective of his experience at Loyola and Manresa, is reflected in annotation two: "it is not much knowledge that fills and satisfies the soul but the intimate understanding and relish of the truth" [2]. This is a "key phrase for understanding the spirituality of the Exercises"[80] for it reflects the Ignatian principle of *non multa sed multum* (not many things but much).[81] Hence one reaps "greater spiritual relish and fruit" by going over the prayer material and reflecting deeply upon them for oneself [2]. The aim is not to get through a mass of material but to "grasp profoundly whatever we pray about."[82]

The spiritual director is instructed to limit the narration of the facts for contemplation or meditation but "point out a vein which the exercitant can then mine for himself."[83] In the process, the exercitant might discover an insight and understand a truth which comes "either from his own reasoning or from the grace of God enlightening his mind" [2]. This is why Aschenbrenner observes that "in making the *Exercises* [one is] taught by God much more than by the one who gives the *Exercises*."[84]

The criterion of "intimate understanding and relish of the truth" distinguishes between general knowledge that fills the mind and felt knowledge that shapes the affections of the heart, and is a critical principle in the Ignatian way of spiritual direction. The *Spiritual Exercises* calls the latter "inner knowledge" [63, 104, 333] for it penetrates beyond the surface into the depths of the mystery or truth.[85] It indicates "a personal assimilation of

79. Cusson, *Biblical Theology and the Spiritual Exercises*, 39.

80. Ivens, *Understanding the Spiritual Exercises*, 4.

81. English, *Spiritual Freedom*, 45.

82. English, *Spiritual Freedom*, 45.

83. Palmer, *On Giving the Spiritual Exercises*, 303.

84. Aschenbrenner, *Stretched for Greater Glory*, 13.

85. Ivens, *Understanding the Spiritual Exercises*, 4.

the truth."[86] Ignatius does not belittle the intellect but emphasizes the use of both the intellect and the will in the making of the *Exercises* [3], for they, together with the memory, form the faculties of the soul [45, 50].

This theological criterion complements annotation fifteen where the spiritual director is advised to "permit the Creator to deal directly with the creature, and the creature with his Creator and Lord" [15]. Ignatian spiritual direction seeks to nurture one's ability to recognize God's voice and this must happen through depth of personal relationship with God. The spiritual director serves as a spiritual companion and co-discerner and must work at "a balance at equilibrium" and not get in the way of God's work in the exercitant's life.

The reference to God communicating directly with the exercitant was not a popular idea in Ignatius's sixteenth-century context because it seemed to imply the heresy of illuminism. Perhaps that is why, with the exception of one reference in the "Rules for thinking with the Church" [365], Ignatius refrained from overt mention of the Holy Spirit in the *Exercises*. There, Ignatius states that the same Holy Spirit who gave the Ten Commandments now governs the Church and rules for the salvation of our souls. For Ignatius, the Holy Spirit is our True Teacher who speaks the truth into the depths of our hearts in concord with the teachings of the Church. So the action of the Holy Spirit on the exercitant is assumed, and it is central to the *Exercises*.

The emphasis on God's direct engagement with the exercitant may render Ignatian direction rather individualistic, and for good reasons, for no one else can decide for the exercitant concerning the matter of obedience to God's will. God's direct engagement with the exercitant is a form of personalized guidance. Nevertheless, when it is viewed within the context of the Church with the director serving as a guide, the element of community remains and serves as a counterbalance against any form of individualism.

To encourage greater responsiveness to God, Ignatius urges the exercitant to embrace the spirit of the "more" (*magis*) in spiritual direction. Ignatius recognizes that "it will be very profitable for the one who is to go through the *Exercises* to enter upon them with magnanimity and generosity toward his Creator and Lord" [5]. Ivens describes this attitude as "the quintessential spirit of the *Exercises*, and anticipates in specific detail the language of the prayer of the Contemplation to Attain Love, in which one offers one's liberty and all one possess to be disposed of according to God' will [234]."[87] As the Foundation (which possess the core theological criterion) and the

---

86. Aschenbrenner, *Stretched for Greater Glory*, 13.
87. Ivens, *Understanding the Spiritual Exercises*, 7.

Contemplation to Attain Love bookends the *Exercises*, this foundational attitude facilitates the maximum transformation in the exercitant.

Collectively, theological criteria in annotations two, three, fifteen, and five significantly shape the Ignatian way of proceeding in spiritual direction. Spiritual direction is received through an intimate understanding and relish of the truth, with mind and heart, in a direct Creator-creature relationship, entered into firstly by God's free initiative, and responded to with a magnanimous and generous spirit in the directee. It is facilitated within the context of the Church through the help of a spiritual guide.

We note that annotations two and three explain how the faculties of the soul are engaged in the process. The intellect (or mind) is engaged in acts of reasoning and the will (or heart) in acts of manifesting our love. Classical spiritual literature in Ignatius's time uses the intellect and mind, and likewise the will and heart, interchangeably.[88] This double aspect reflects the Ignatian emphasis that combines firm and lucid reasoning with loving submission to God's grace.[89] Ignatian prayer also uses the faculty of memory, especially in its imaginative prayer. Hence, these three powers together move the soul, and they reflect the "contemplative character of the Exercises."[90] This emphasis ensures that the process of guidance does not become a mere intellectual accumulation of information but remains a formational integration of truth in the depths of one's mind and heart.

The contemplative character of the *Exercises* leads to the attention given to the interior movements of the spirits. Ignatius's own experience of the diversity of spirits taught him to anticipate them during a time in prayer. He crafted two sets of rules (or principles) for understanding and responding to these diverse spirits–described as consolations and desolations [313–327, 328–336], and they serve as a "theology" of Ignatian discernment, which is so central to Ignatian spiritual direction. I will elaborate more on the rules when I explain how they work with the prayer exercises of the First and Second Weeks.

Here, Ignatius offers several principles to guide the director [6–10]. Firstly, the director is to be watchful for the absence of these movements in the directee [6]. If nothing seems to happen in prayer, the director is to enquire how the directee observed the prayer methods and to guide from there. If, however, the director observes that the directee is in desolation, he must gently encourage her, explain to her the wiles of the enemy and prepare her for a coming consolation [7]. Should the director perceive, from

88. Ivens, *Understanding the Spiritual Exercises*.
89. Guibert, *The Jesuits*, 134.
90. Ivens, *Understanding the Spiritual Exercises*, 3.

the directee's experiences of desolations and consolations, that she has need for understanding them, he should explain the rules of discernment to her [8]. However, care must be taken in employing them. The first set of rules will enlighten the experiences of the First Week (when the directee is exercising in the purgative way), and the second set in the Second Week (which is more aligned to the illuminative way). It is unwise to give the second set for the First Week's exercitant as they contain more subtle insights into the diversity of affections and may confuse the directee [9]. However, when the director perceives that the directee is assailed by false consolations, he should guide her using the rules for the Second Week [10]. These guiding principles explain how spiritual direction is to be practiced in the Ignatian way, and they derive their theological insights from Ignatius's own experience in practicing them.

Annotations eleven to thirteen explain why it is prudent to abide by the design of the *Exercises*. As each Week serves a specific purpose, the directee is to give dedicated focus to that Week and not get ahead of herself [11]. In the same spirit, the directee should take care to persevere in the *Exercises* according to its intended purpose or duration especially during a time of desolation [12–13]. These principles apply because the Ignatian way of direction utilizes precise prayer methods (even though there is flexibility with the content) and are effective only when they are carefully observed.[91] Sometimes, "to run ahead of grace is not generosity but foolishness."[92]

Annotation fourteen also works together with annotations fifteen and sixteen, especially during a time of decision making. Here, Ignatius cautions the director against the temptation to influence the directee one way or the other. Instead, as we have noted earlier, the director should strive to be at an equilibrium and let God deal directly with the directee. The directee should also exercise the posture of indifference and not give in to any inordinate attachment, but rather choose that which tends to "the service, honor, and glory of the Divine Majesty" [16].

Given the anticipated presence of desolations and consolations while engaging in the *Exercises*, Ignatius recommends that the director be "kept faithfully informed about the various disturbances and thoughts caused by the action of different spirits" [17]. As these thoughts "involve imagination and feeling, and . . . tend towards actions, either interior or exterior," they must be carefully discerned.[93] It is therefore prudent for the directee to share them with the director. This is an important dynamic between the directee

91. Guibert, *The Jesuits*, 133.
92. Aschenbrenner, *Stretched for Greater Glory*, 23.
93. Ivens, *Understanding the Spiritual Exercises*, 17.

and director that contributes to greater effectiveness in the discernment process.

Through this brief review of annotations six through seventeen, we observe that a major focus in Ignatian spiritual direction is the attention given to the experiences of desolations and consolations. It is through the awareness of these movements of the spirits that one begins to discern what is of God or not of God. Knowledge of how the good spirit and the evil spirit works (Rules for Discernment) thus provide clues on how to respond well. Through time and practice, a directee gradually gathers a deepening knowledge of God and of self, and what makes for a good and wise response. The outcome is a more discerning self that knows how to follow the voice of God.

Annotations eighteen to twenty convey the principle that the *Exercises* must be adapted to the life-setting and capability of the exercitant. This criterion works in tandem with the Ignatian emphasis on discernment in the present. The *Exercises* are a means to discern the movements of God in the present, within the limits of the exercitant and in the present life-setting. Consequently, annotation eighteen guides the director on how to adapt the *Exercises* to those who do not have the capacity to make the entire set of *Exercises*, while annotation nineteen provides for those whose life-setting prevents them from taking time off for an extended retreat. Annotation twenty lists the advantages for those who can make the *Exercises* in a thirty-day retreat in "solitude and seclusion."

In summary, we note that the spiritual director's chief concern is the exercitant's experience of the movements of the spirits in prayer. As discernment is an "affectively-rich act of knowing," the director co-discerns with the directee the "quality and trajectory" of these affections.[94] As discernment presents important implications for the direction of one's life and spiritual destiny, Ignatius urges that an exercitant come to God with a freely disposed intellect and will, and carefully gathers a deep understanding and relish of the truth during the time in prayer. The knowledge of these movements of the spirit then serves as the material for discernment in the exercitant's pilgrimage toward a deeper knowledge of God and of self.

The important point here is that the theological criterion for Ignatian spiritual direction lies in a felt-knowledge ("*sentir*") of one's interiority. It is the ability to discern where these diverse movements of the spirit come from and where they are headed that serves as the central task of spiritual direction. The ultimate end is a life that is fully disposed to the will of God and lived only for the greater glory of God. The means is the ability to

94. Howard, *Affirming the Touch of God.*

discern the movements of the spirits to recognize those that are of God, to admit them, and those that are not, to reject them. The exercitant hones this ability through utilizing the three powers of the soul to gather a deep interior knowledge of the truth, by the grace of God through the guidance of the Holy Spirit.

5

The Ignatian Method
of Spiritual Direction

As we turn to examine Ignatius's method of spiritual direction, we begin with an analysis of the First Principle and Foundation before going on to the *Exercises* for the First Week. The First Principle and Foundation is crucial to Ignatian spiritual direction for it rehearses the basic theological framework and sets the direction for the *Exercises*. It has been described as "the groundwork of the whole moral and spiritual edifice" of the *Spiritual Exercises*.[1] Contemplating this core theological criterion in Ignatian spirituality thus serves as the first exercise in his method. It states (hereafter referred to simply as Foundation):

> Man is created to praise, reverence, and serve God our Lord, and by this means to save his soul.
>
> The other things on the face of the earth are created for man to help him in attaining the end for which he is created.
>
> Hence, man is to make use of them in as far as they help him in the attainment of his end, and he must rid himself of them in as far as they prove a hindrance to him.
>
> Therefore, we must make ourselves indifferent to all created things, as far as we are allowed free choice and are not under any prohibition. Consequently, as far as we are concerned, we should not prefer health to sickness, riches to poverty, honor to dishonor, a long life to a short life. The same holds for all other things.

1. Palmer, *On Giving the Spiritual Exercises*, 311.

Our one desire and choice should be what is more conducive to the end for which we are created. [23]

As Ignatius utilizes the constructs of means and ends in the *Exercises*,
the Official Directory dissects the Foundation into three parts: (1) the end
for which man is created, (2) the means for attaining this end, and (3) the
difficulty of choosing the right means, given that what is most conducive to
the attainment of this end is unknown to us.[2] Ignatius urges an exercitant
to choose the "praise, reverence, and service" of our Creator God and Lord
as the chief end in one's life. In order to choose well, however, an exercitant
must possess the quality of indifference–"that a person must place himself
in a state of entire indifference and equilibrium"—so that one is free to
choose whatever would serve the greater glory of God.[3] Ignatian indifference, as a critical theological criterion in the process of spiritual direction,
thus receives critical attention along with the Foundation in his method.

The notion of indifference is easily misunderstood. It has to do with
the ordering of desire rather than the eradication of desire. In the light of
the opposing pulls of the movements of the spirits, the *Spiritual Exercises*
identifies the problem of inordinate desires as a chief obstacle to the development of indifference. Consequently, Ignatian spiritual guidance is significantly concerned with the ordering of desires, so that "no decision is made
under the influence of any inordinate attachment" [21].

Methodologically, the Foundation serves as an exercise to chart a fundamental direction for the exercitant. She should head only towards the end
for which she is created and not allow any inordinate attachments to derail
her. She should make herself indifferent to all created things and utilize them
only to the extent that they will help her to attain her end. The meditations
relating to the Foundation thus fundamentally etch two theological criteria
in the heart of the exercitant: first, to "praise, reverence, and serve" God for
his greater glory; and second, to be indifferent to all created things, desiring
and choosing only what is more conducive to this end. The attainment of
salvation is the eventual fruit in the beatific vision. In terms of method, the
Foundation serves as "a basic point of reference" throughout the *Exercises*
and throughout life.[4]

2. Palmer, *On Giving the Spiritual Exercises*, 311–12.

3. Palmer, *On Giving the Spiritual Exercises*, 312.

4. Ivens, *Understanding the Spiritual Exercises*, 26.

THE PURGATIVE WAY OF THE FIRST WEEK

With the laying of the Foundation, the Ignatian *Exercises* then progresses to the First Week. The problem of inordinate attachments receives attention in the First Week with its devotion "to the consideration and contemplation of sin" [4], and which corresponds to the purgative way of the Catholic *ordo salutis* [10]. The 1599 Official Directory describes the Week's focus as a "reflection upon sins with a view to reaching knowledge and genuine detestation of their foulness, along with appropriate sorrow and satisfaction."[5] Cusson observes that it is "an experience of repentance and conversion" and "becomes the point at which one gets a first grip on the genuine experience of Christian salvation."[6]

The method guides the exercitant into a two-fold knowledge. First, on the objective level, there is the knowledge of the reality and awfulness of sin, but also of God's mercy and love. Second, on the subjective level, we find an experience of deep sorrow for ones sin and spiritual poverty but also of the Christian hope.[7] Two forms of examinations, the Daily Particular Examination of Conscience [24–31] and the General Examination of Conscience [32–44], and five meditations on sin and hell [45–71] facilitate the method. Additional directions also help to make the exercises and the practice of penance better [72–90].

The two Examens, as they are commonly called, are intended as resources for arresting sinful tendencies in one's life. The Particular Examen, intended to uproot "bad weeds and thistles" before good seeds are sown, guides the exercitant through three different times of the day (morning, midday, evening) and each day of the week to pay particular attention to a sin that persistently poses as a hindrance to spiritual growth.[8] Progress is monitored in a dairy [31]. The General Examen is designed to heighten one's awareness of sins so as to make a better confession. It examines one's thoughts, word, and deeds, identifies where one has sinned, and then asks God for pardon and resolve to amend with God's grace [32–43]. It utilizes five points that includes giving thanks to God for favor received; asking for the specific grace in that exercise; the actual exercise that examines thoughts, words, and deeds; asks God for pardon; and finally resolves to amend with the grace of God [43].

---

5. Palmer, *On Giving the Spiritual Exercises*, 310.
6. Cusson, *Biblical Theology and the Spiritual Exercises*, 137–38.
7. Palmer, *On Giving the Spiritual Exercises*, 309.
8. Palmer, *On Giving the Spiritual Exercises*, 22.

On the surface, the Examen appears to be rather negatively focused on the subject of sin. The experience in the exercise, however, extols the mercy of God and the forgiveness of sins [50, 53, 60, 61]. It thus both registers the problem of sin but also the mercy and grace of God. It "helps keep the person open to the action of the Spirit" [and] "facilitates the process of liberation" as it works "the graces of the Exercises into the events and relationships and personal growth-situations of daily life."[9] This, apparently, was Ignatius's experience.[10]

Ignatius's Theology of Sin and Its Resolution

In Ignatius's context, all pre-baptismal sins have been expiated through baptism. Therefore the concern here is with post-baptismal sins. The Catholic Catechism identifies them as venial and mortal sins. Mortal sin destroys charity in the heart by a grave violation of God's law and robs ones of habitual grace, which is so essential to the supernatural life of the soul. Venial sins are acts of unloving attitudes that hurt others and, while they do not destroy the state of grace, they do nevertheless violate God's law. The way to atone for both mortal and venial sins is through the practice of penance.[11]

Ignatius adopts this traditional view of sin and its resolution and aligns the *Exercises* in its practice. Consequently, the general and daily examinations of conscience, confession, and practice of penance are features in Ignatian spiritual direction as they are found in the First Week. Having said that, contemporary practitioners of Ignatian spirituality have significantly adjusted these practices to today's context and emphasized more God's unconditional love and saving grace.[12] One Ignatian scholar has also directed the focus to an examination of consciousness that sought to notice the Lord's presence in the course of a day.[13]

I wish to highlight several major features in Ignatius's way of direction in the prayer exercises of the First Week. The first is the construct of the preparatory prayer and the grace that is sought in it [46]. Included in every meditation and contemplation throughout the *Exercises* is a preparatory prayer through which an exercitant asks God for the specific grace intended for that meditation or contemplation [see, for example 55, 62, 91, 101, and

---

9. Ivens, *Understanding the Spiritual Exercises*, 33.

10. Guibert, *The Jesuits*, 66–68.

11. Tanquerey and Branderis, *The Spiritual Life*, 340–61.

12. English, *Spiritual Freedom*, 48–51; Lonsdale, *Eyes to See, Ears to Hear*, 132.

13. See Aschenbrenner, "A Check on Our Availability."

so forth]. Ignatius embraces the Thomistic (and Tridentine) understanding of nature and grace and so applies it in his method.[14]

This emphasis on grace is very significant as, more often than not, Ignatian spirituality has been perceived as placing a greater emphasis on human effort rather than grace. Cusson observes that while "Ignatius calls for all the personal effort which the retreatant can furnish . . . in reality he counts only on God's grace."[15] It will become clear that Ignatius emphasizes the priority of grace as we examine the preparatory prayer in the text of the *Spiritual Exercises* in this chapter. Ignatius embraces the paradox of human effort and grace working together.

As mentioned earlier, in Catholic theology, sin damages one's cooperation with habitual or sanctifying grace, which is so necessary for obedience to God and spiritual progress. Acts of penance are, therefore, efforts at obtaining grace that one desires for the purpose of rectifying past sins and making spiritual progress [87]. This involves actual grace, which is needed to lift up nature and move the will.[16] A primary concern in Ignatian spiritual guidance is, therefore, on guiding an exercitant to cooperate with actual grace.

The preparatory prayer, "which is never changed," therefore guides the exercitant to ask for the grace desired so that the will is moved to cooperate with God [43, 48, 55, 65]. Ignatius's basic assumption of the compatibility between grace and human nature meant that they not only rely upon God's grace but also strove to use all "human means" at their disposal. This basic assumption is reflected in the Society's Constitutions.[17] The Thomistic principle that "grace perfects nature" meant the acceptance of the exercise of free will in human activity under the influence of grace. "In this view, the will [though] wounded and enfeebled by Original Sin, [is] not vitiated or destroyed. Grace, always the primary factor, allowed the will to "cooperate" with it, so that in some mysterious way human responsibility played its part in the process of salvation."[18] In this regard, Ignatian spirituality affirms the paradox that spiritual progress is made wholly on personal effort and wholly on grace.

14. O'Malley, *The First Jesuits*, 265.

15. Cusson, *Biblical Theology and the Spiritual Exercises*, 111.

16. Tanquerey and Branderis, *The Spiritual Life*.

17. Ignatius, *Constitutions*, para 147–62.

18. O'Malley, *The First Jesuits*, 249.

"What I Want"—The Dynamism of Desire

Linked to the preparatory prayer's petition for grace, is giving attention to "what I want and desire"–another central motif in Ignatius's use of petition as preparation for prayer [48]. Michael Ivens makes this important comment:

> Petition is a central motif in the Exercises and takes a number of forms. Essential to the Exercises as a personal faith-venture are the wholly spontaneous petitions (cf. [54], [109]). But together with these, and especially characteristic of the Exercises, there are the forms of "given" petition (such as the Preparatory Prayer above, the petitions of the Triple Colloquy [63, 147], and the series of eleven petitions included in the preludes to meditation and contemplation[19]).[20]

The important function that these petitions serve is that they put us in touch with our desires. As we already noticed in the introductory observations, the theme of desire is a major one in Ignatian spirituality. However, the problem of inordinate desire is real. Hence, the ordering of desire becomes a continuing theme through the Exercises. As a preparation for prayer, Ignatius's exhortation to the exercitant to ask for the desired grace specific to a meditation or contemplation becomes a means for developing an awareness of, and the purification of, desires.

The dynamism of desire in the Exercises is carried over from Ignatius's own pilgrimage experience. From the time he left Loyola, he was filled with "new and intense desires for the service of God."[21] However, these desires, though efficacious, were tainted by human ambition and needed to be purified. After the time of purification and illumination at Manresa, Ignatius's desires became more "matured and solidly rooted in God's plan of creation, salvation, spiritual growth, and ultimate beatitude."[22] For Ignatius, spiritual desire, therefore, became a divine gift; one that has God as its ultimate object. It is God's love that "engenders and nourishes this desire, while the desire itself seeks the perfection of love in the praise and service of God."[23]

Ignatius's famous letter to Teresa Rejadell clearly expresses that authentic desires come from God:

19. See annotations [48, 55, 65, 91, 104, 139, 152, 193, 203, 221, 233]
20. Ivens, Understanding the Spiritual Exercises, 48.
21. Cusson, Biblical Theology and the Spiritual Exercises, 120–21.
22. Cusson, Biblical Theology and the Spiritual Exercises, 121.
23. Cusson, Biblical Theology and the Spiritual Exercises, 122.

If you look closely, you understand that these desires of serving
Christ our Lord are not your own, but come to you from our
Lord. If you were to say that our Lord gives you great desires of
serving Him, you would be giving praise to the same Lord because you are making known His gift, and you glory in Him, not
in yourself, because you do not attribute that grace to yourself.[24]

When understood in this light, every preparatory prayer's expression
of "what I want and desire" becomes an opportunity to experience the ordering of desire from God's perspective. Hence in the meditations on sin
in the First Week, for example, petitioning the grace desired becomes an
opportunity to see sin for what it really is from God's perspective, and from
that a true sorrow for sin in my life. The outcome is a transformation of my
attitude toward sin and the aligning of my desire with God.

Hence, in asking for what I want and desire, I am in fact disposing
myself to God's purifying grace and transforming love. In my prayerful expression of my desire, I open myself to God's grace that purifies and leads
me into the light. The expression of my desire transforms what appears to
be an "exterior and voluntaristic" involvement in the *Exercises* into one that
truly expresses a felt need "in the depths of my being."[25] "It is the route of a
desire that progressively mounts, through purification, toward full indifference, and then the radical choice in favor of the crucified Christ; of Christ
as the Savior."[26]

The expression of what I want and desire, this "response to an interior
need," is a first step toward reaping the fruit of indifference; for, as Cusson
explains, indifference "is not the extinction of desire" but "is desire in its
purified form, allowing it to rise to a higher level where ardor and discreet
charity are paramount."[27] Within this "dynamic forward thrust," one gradually "no longer desire anything except, under the movement of the Spirit," to
praise, reverence, and serve the Lord.[28] This is the outcome of learning to
ask for what I want and desire under the banner of God's guidance.

Ignatian Meditation—Engaging "The Three Powers of the Soul"

Ignatius guides the exercitant to use "the three powers of the soul" in Ignatian prayer [50–51]. The memory, the understanding, and the will are

24. Ignatius and Young, *Letters*, 20. Letter to Teresa Rejadell.
25. Cusson, *Biblical Theology and the Spiritual Exercises*, 128.
26. Cusson, *Biblical Theology and the Spiritual Exercises*, 128.
27. Cusson, *Biblical Theology and the Spiritual Exercises*, 128.
28. Cusson, *Biblical Theology and the Spiritual Exercises*, 130.

utilized in discursive meditation. I have already made reference to Ignatius's use of the understanding and the will in my brief comment on annotation three. Here, I wish to elaborate on the critical role that these "faculties of the soul," as they were called in classical spirituality, play in Ignatian meditative prayer.

Keeping in mind the hermeneutical key proposed by Cusson, we note how Ignatius guides the exercitant from an objective understanding of God's plan of creation and salvation in Christ (universal) to the subjective aspect of the exercitant's personal experience and response (particular).[29] These dimensions constantly interact with each other. As Cusson explains, "the universal enlightens the personal, and the particular, touching on what is most personal, is seen against a background which includes God's total, expansive truth."[30] This "dialectic interaction" between the universal and the particular, necessarily involve the understanding and the will. It is for this purpose that Ignatius employs the three powers of the soul in prayer.

Ivens notes that there is a three-stage sequence in the specific use of the three powers in this first exercise [50]. First, there is "a summoning to consciousness of truth already held in the memory;" second, "a process of exploring this content with the mind," and third, a "response of the affections (or of the 'heart')."[31] These are the devices in Ignatius's use of discursive prayer in the *Exercises*. As I noted in my comments on annotation two, the thinking function of the mind does not necessarily refer to the accumulation of much knowledge. Rather, what is sought by the mind is a deep understanding and spiritual relish of the truth. It is this interior knowledge that moves the will to action in response to God.

Consequently, the employment of the memory, intellect and will serve a rather important function in the Ignatian method of prayer. The memory recalls what has been retained from Scripture and past experiences in prayer. The intellect does the work of reflection, asking God for light through Scripture meditation and gathers spiritual understanding. The fruit of the intellect then passes on to impact the will. The affections of the heart are moved by the deep relish of God's truth, and so the will is drawn toward God by his redeeming grace, and learns to act in accordance with God's revealed truth and good will.

While the three powers of the soul function together as a unit, the ultimate focus is upon the heart. We have already emphasized that it is not the aim of the mind to amass much information but to gather spiritual

29. Cusson, *Biblical Theology and the Spiritual Exercises*.
30. Cusson, *Biblical Theology and the Spiritual Exercises*, 98.
31. Ivens, *Understanding the Spiritual Exercises*, 46.

understanding. This in turn impacts the heart to respond, by the grace of God, in generosity and magnanimity toward God and humankind. The pivotal point in spiritual transformation therefore lies in the heart. For as Nadal, one of Ignatius's closest associates, writes, "It is in the heart that we find the beginning of every grace and of every spiritual understanding."[32]

The Colloquy—Imaginative Conversation

Another element in Ignatius method of prayer is the use of the colloquy. Simply put, a colloquy is a conversation between friends or master and servant [54]. Strategically placed at the end of a prayer exercise, Ignatius intends for it as a culmination to prayer marked by the "personal and spontaneous quality of conversation between friends."[33] The colloquy can also arise at any point in prayer as the exercitant grows in intimacy with God, including them as expressions of interior affections in a time of prayer.[34]

For example, in the Colloquy in annotation fifty-three, the exercitant is asked to reverentially "imagine Christ our Lord present before you upon the cross, and begin to speak with him, asking how it is that though He is the Creator, He has stooped to become man, and to pass from eternal life to death here in time, that thus He might die for our sins" [53]. Because of its use of the imagination, the colloquy is sometimes referred to by Ignatian scholars as "imaginative contemplation."[35] As a familiar, yet reverential, conversation, this becomes the highpoint of the first exercise in the First Week.

Annotation fifty-three goes on to ask: "What have I done for Christ?" "What am I doing for Christ?" "What ought I do for Christ?" An important observation here is that it is typical in Ignatian spirituality to move the exercitant's response "from the affective to the effective, from the response of the heart to, eventually, the response of 'doing.'"[36] This is the apostolic focus in Ignatian spirituality, for as he said, "love ought to manifest itself in deeds rather than in words" [230].

Ignatius's typically concludes the colloquy with the Lord's Prayer—the "Our Father." It is another motif that Ignatius utilizes to direct the affections of the exercitant to God. When prayed with both mind and heart, it

32. Quoted in Cusson, *Biblical Theology and the Spiritual Exercises*, 106.

33. Ivens, *Understanding the Spiritual Exercises*, 53.

34. Palmer, *On Giving the Spiritual Exercises*, 316.

35. Ivens, *Understanding the Spiritual Exercises*, 53.

36. Ivens, *Understanding the Spiritual Exercises*, 54.

engenders a full-hearted surrender, guiding the soul to rest in reverence and freedom in God.

Ignatius also utilizes a Triple Colloquy that reflects his Catholic devotion. They are shared respectively with our Blessed Lady, Mary, the Mother of Jesus; with the Son, Jesus the Christ; and with the Father, the eternal Lord. Ignatius follows this sequence in the triple colloquies and urges the exercitant first to petition Mary, our Lady, to obtain grace from her Son, concluding with a "Hail Mary"; then the same petitions are made to her Son to obtain graces from the Father, concluding with the "Soul of Christ" ; and finally, the same requests are made directly to the Father, closing with "Our Father." As Ignatius has a very high regard for the Virgin Mary, it was his particular practice to appeal to the Blessed Lady to petition for grace on his behalf. The appeal to the Son is made not with reference to Jesus as the Risen Christ but as one who has become man for us, our mediator and advocate.[37] Ignatius consistently utilizes the triple colloquies in the Second, Third, and Fourth Weeks.

The Application of the Senses—Another Ignatian Prayer Method

Ignatius's insight on the human as an integrated being of mind, body and spirit finds yet another expression in his method of guidance: the application of the senses [65–70]. It utilizes the five senses: sight, sound, smell, taste and touch to maximize the experience in some prayer exercises. Hence, for example, in the meditation on hell, to see "the vast fires," hear "the wailing," smell "the smoke," taste "the bitterness of tears," and touch "to feel the flames." This utility is not the same as the meditations, which are discursive. They are instead non-discursive and are meant for another aspect of spiritual profit. They assist those who struggle with the intellect in meditation to gradually lift them up to discursive meditation. They also help those who reap much from discursive mediations to descend into contemplating the sensible things and find "in each one of them nourishment, consolation, and fruit because of the abundance of its love which makes even the slightest detail and tiniest gesture assume great importance and afford matter for love and consolation."[38]

The preceding constructs thus represent Ignatius's method of guidance in prayer. "The grace I seek" works together with the "what I want" in every preparatory exercise to express the *iq quod volo* (the dynamism of desire)– that element of intentionality that is so foundational to Ignatian prayer and

37. Palmer, *On Giving the Spiritual Exercises*, 316.
38. Palmer, *On Giving the Spiritual Exercises*, 322–23.

reflective of Ignatius's emphasis of human effort cooperating with grace. It featured significantly in Ignatius's own experience, and he now seeks to engender it in the exercitant. Though initially tainted by inordinate desires, it nevertheless gives rise to prayerful search and is gradually purified over time. A gift and a grace from God, spiritual desire is "the dynamism or synthesizing force" that draws together the many elements in Ignatian spirituality toward spiritual growth.[39]

The three powers of the soul are used to heighten one's awareness of the affections and to guide them to cooperate with God. Ignatian prayer emphasizes the importance of engaging the imagination, mind, and heart to work together in soul care. Their deployment throughout the *Exercises* renders them a major means through which Ignatius achieves his goal of guidance. The application of the senses further emphasize the engagement of the entire person, body, mind and heart in the act of prayer. Finally, the colloquy emphasizes the intimate conversation that must characterize genuine prayer, and so renders it as a major construct in his method.

First Steps in Discernment:
The Rules of Discernment for the First Week

As I continue chronologically, I will now examine the first set of rules of the discernment of spirits which are more suited to the exercises of the First Week. As we have noted, a primary subject matter in spiritual direction is the directee's experience of interior movements of the spirits. I have already discussed Ignatius own experience at Loyola and Manresa, and that he anticipates an exercitant's experience of them during prayer [6] and advices a director on how to respond [7–10]. The rules of discernment are not a method of prayer but they accompany the prayerful and attentive work of the mind (intellect) and heart (will) and help an exercitant to recognize and follow God's voice.[40] The goal is to examine the "quality and trajectory"[41] of these affections and to identify whether they are from God or from the evil one and the flesh. Overtime, the spiritual acumen developed through the process of discernment is spontaneously applied to all of life.

The first set of rules contains theological criteria that fundamentally differentiate between consolations and desolations. These are more suited to the experiences of the exercitant in the First Week; and Ignatius provides guidance on how to use them. He also cautions to not mix them with the

---

39. Cusson, *Biblical Theology and the Spiritual Exercises*, 118–31.

40. Smith, *Listening to God*.

41. Howard, *Affirming the Touch of God*.

second set of rules, which are more suited for the Second Week [9]. The rules are related to one's fundamental direction in life. For those who "go from one mortal sin to another," Ignatius says, the enemy, that is the evil one or our flesh, is "ordinarily accustomed to proposed apparent pleasures" [314] in order to keep that person in that path of destruction—and not know it. Hence, the enemy will promote apparently soothing affections, "sensual delights" and the like, that are aimed at keeping that person in that direction. The good spirit, however, will attempt to do the reverse. He will "rouse the sting of conscience and fill them with remorse" [314], and seek to turn them to God.

However, for those headed to life—those that "go on earnestly striving to cleanse their souls from sin and who seek to rise in the service of God our Lord to greater perfection"— the evil spirit will seek to "harass with anxiety, to afflict with sadness, to raise obstacles backed by fallacious reasonings that disturb the soul," in order to "prevent the soul from advancing" [315]. The good spirit, however, will seek to "give courage and strength, consolations, tears, inspirations, and peace," and that the soul can keep going forward in doing good [315].

Ignatius, thus, offers definitions of consolation and desolation with reference to one's direction in life. Ignatius calls consolation "an interior movement [that is] aroused in the soul, by which it is inflamed with love of its Creator and Lord, and as a consequence, can love no creature on the face of the earth for its own sake, but only in the Creator of them all" [316]. We noticed an immediate affinity with the Foundation; which called one to live only for the love, worship and service of our Creator and Lord. The first character quality of a consolation has fundamentally to do with the direction of the movement in one's soul. A consolation is fundamentally about the soul being drawn by God's love toward God, with the outcome that it loves all others with the love of God. Ivens emphasizes that "such a love is one of the major keys to Ignatian spirituality. The goal and high-point of that spirituality is a love defined not only in terms of God himself, but a love of God in which all other loves are included."[42]

We must be careful to note that not every emotional feeling of love constitutes a consolation, for one may love out of selfish and inordinate reasons. Hence, one must honestly examine the deeper motivations for one's affections to determine if they are in fact connected to God and not merely to the flesh. As English points us, "it is the beginning of spiritual consolation only when that human love is directly related to the love of God."[43]

42. Ivens, *Understanding the Spiritual Exercises*, 215.
43. English, *Spiritual Freedom*, 115.

Consequently, a central characteristic of Ignatian consolation is that it is a quality of love that has its source in God and is in turn expressed as love for God and for others in service. This is a core theological criterion in Ignatian spiritual guidance; one that is consistent with Scripture's emphasis on the two most important commandments. It expresses the apostolic mission of Ignatian spirituality.

But there is more to consolation. Ignatius goes on to elaborate that it "is likewise consolation when one sheds tears that move to the love of God, whether it be because of sorrow for sins, or because of the sufferings of Christ our Lord, or for any other reason that is immediately directed to the praise and service of God" [316]. The key phrase that serves as a determinant is "immediately directed to the praise and service of God." Here, again, we observe its relationship to the Foundation. Hence, it is not just tears per se, but tears that move to the love of God. Consolation can and does include tears. The exercitant will be encouraged to know that the experience of tears, though sometimes disruptive and tiring in the spiritual life–and may on the surface appear no different from a desolation to others–is in fact a consolation when they are intimately connected to the praise and service of God.

Finally, Ignatius defines consolation as "every increase of faith, hope, and love, and all interior joy that invites and attracts to what is heavenly and to the salvation of one's soul by filling it with peace and quiet in its Creator and Lord" [316]. This description, with its reference to the three theological virtues, fundamentally defines what consolation is. In a consolation, the increase of faith, hope, and love leads to all interior joy that comes from an attentive gaze on God and his plan of salvation in Christ. This fundamental confidence in God and his way of salvation leaves the soul peaceful and quiet, resting securely in God. The relational component in this criterion is fundamental, for it is only in God that there will be an increase in faith, hope, and love.[44]

Appreciating the quality and trajectory of spiritual consolation, therefore, is an important feature in the Ignatian way of spiritual direction; for it is spiritual consolation that will move the soul in the way and character of God. So to notice and embrace it keeps one connected to God and his love. Equally important is the skill at noticing the presence of desolation, for it threatens to pull one away from God. Hence, Ignatius describes spiritual desolation as "what is entirely the opposite" of spiritual consolation. Spiritual desolation is described as

> darkness of soul, turmoil of spirit, inclination to what is low
> and earthly, restlessness rising from many disturbances and

44. Ivens, *Understanding the Spiritual Exercises*, 216.

temptations which lead to want of faith, want of hope, want of love. The soul is wholly slothful, tepid, sad, and separated, as it were, from its Creator and Lord. For just as consolation is the opposite of desolation, so the thoughts that spring from consolation are the opposite of those that spring from desolation. [317]

Here, as in the discernment of consolation, it is not sufficient just to notice the presence of such "darkness of soul" and assume that one is headed in the wrong direction. As we saw earlier, sometimes one can be assailed by the evil one when desiring to love and follow God. The important clue here is to note both the "quality and trajectory" of the affection. Here, desolation is both "darkness of soul, turmoil of spirit" and the like, and leads to want of faith, hope, and love. When the movement of the spirit is headed in that direction, it reveals itself as desolation. It drags one away from God. Another important clue is the thoughts that spring from the affections of the heart. Ivens' notes that the concluding reference to thoughts "is evidence of the importance of the implicit or explicit "thoughts" which interact with feelings in the total experience of consolation and desolation."[45] Hence we are reminded that the mind (intellect) and the heart (will) work together in discernment as it does in the exercise of prayer. Indeed, these two most basic components of the human being, what classical spirituality refers to as the faculties of the soul, are to be most eminently attended to for life and health.

With a basic grasp of what consolations and desolations are, Ignatius guides the exercitant on a right response during a time in desolation. Four rules counsel an exercitant on what to do during a time in desolation [318–321]. First, in time of desolation one must never change a decision that was made during a preceding consolation but "remain firm and constant" in that resolution. For Ignatius explains, "just as in consolation the good spirit guides and counsels us, so in desolation the evil spirit guides and counsels. Following his counsels we can never find the way to a right decision" [318]. Second, "it will be very advantageous to intensify our activity against the desolation" [319]. Here, Ignatius recommends persevering in prayer, meditation, the Examen, and penance. As we noted from his autobiography, Ignatius found this to be helpful in his own life. English makes this remark: "It is truly remarkable what penance can achieve when we are in desolation. Often it can knock us out of a desolate condition by giving a sort of jolt to our woeful spirit."[46] However, one must also guard against any Pelagian

---

45. Ivens, *Understanding the Spiritual Exercises*, 217.

46. English, *Spiritual Freedom*, 118.

tendency toward mere effort for overcoming temptation, for it is always God's grace that triumphs rather than our self-efforts. Consequently, the third advice follows. Though one may feel left to one's "natural powers" to fend for oneself, Ignatius reminds that God's help and grace is always available [320, 322]. Hence, fourthly, one must "persevere in patience" and use the means of help mentioned earlier, trusting that consolation will return [321, 319]. The principles we observe from the preceding advice are that, when in desolation, one must not change a decision made during a time in consolation, but with the grace of God, persevere in prayer. For the Lord will sustain one through that time and will offer consolation again.

Ignatius then offers three reasons why we suffer from desolations. First, because we have been lazy or negligent in our exercises of piety; second, because God wishes to try us and see what is truly within us; third, because "God wishes to give us a true knowledge and understanding of ourselves, so that we may have an intimate perception of the fact that it is not within our power to acquire and attain great devotion, intense love, tears, or any other spiritual consolation; but that all this is the gift and grace of God our Lord" [322]. These perhaps are the common experiences in one's spiritual pilgrimage. We can sometimes be lazy and neglect the regular practice of the Examen, for example, and that can render us less sensitive to impending desolations. Or one might be in spiritual fervor and God allows the evil one to test us to reveal the true quality of our professed love for God. By far, however, it is the third reason that offers a rather important theological principle. That is, it is always a "gift and grace of God" that we make progress in the spiritual life. As English says, "God may allow us to be desolate at times in order to impress upon us the fact of our Pelagianism, our desire to control God. God want us to abandon the mistaken notion that we can command consolation to come and desolation to go by an act of will."[47]

Hence, the following two rules counsel an exercitant to anticipate the ebb and flow of times in desolation and consolation. This appears to be the normal pattern in life. It is therefore important that when one is in consolation, to take care to remain humble and recall how little he is able to do in time of desolation. Likewise, when in desolation, to remember that he can find his strength in his Creator and Lord, and that God offers sufficient grace to overcome [323–324].

To these, Ignatius offers advice on the typical ways the enemy conducts himself. Ignatius says that sometimes the enemy might conduct himself "as a woman" [325]. That is, "he is a weakling before a show of strength, and a tyrant if he has his will." As Ignatius elaborates, the principle is that when

47. English, *Spiritual Freedom*, 121.

tempted, one must not be afraid and give in; but, by God's grace, coura-geously resist the devil and he will flee (James 4:7). Next, Ignatius adds that the enemy may conduct himself like "a false lover" [326]. The devil's trickery here is to suggest to the exercitant that the temptations one experiences in the soul "be received secretly and kept secret." When so seduced, an exerci-tant must expose the devious temptations to a trustworthy and reliable di-rector (James 5:16). Finally, Ignatius adds, the enemy might conduct himself like a military commander laying siege upon a stronghold. He will encamp around it, explore it, and attack at the weakest point [327]. Likewise, our enemy will seek to attack us at our weakest point. Perhaps, the point to note in these descriptions is that one must not only be aware of the typical ways the enemy operates but also of one's own vulnerability. Is it timidity of spirit, naivety of mind, or total lack of self-knowledge? As English notes: "One of the purposes of the First Week of the *Exercises* is for retreatants to discover their own strong and weak points so that they are conscious of where the Enemy will attack."[48]

The first set of rules of discernment therefore work together with the prayer exercises of the First Week to develop three foundational insights in the exercitant; the knowledge of self, the knowledge of the enemy, and the knowledge of God. Ignatius designed the exercises, based on a deep under-standing of God's truth, to draw attention to the affective movements within the soul both during prayer and beyond. As the exercitant notice these af-fective experiences, he learns to discern the nature of these movements of the spirits; whether they are consolations or desolations. The practice of the Examen, in particular, serves to heighten the awareness of these movements and to recognize them for what they are. This leads to a deep knowledge of self in the light of God's revealing truth. Concurrently, Ignatius's rules work together with Scripture to assist the exercitant to gather an understanding of how the enemy works. As we noted earlier, the First Week's exercises help an exercitant to identify one's areas of vulnerability, and to be especially guard-ed against the tactics of the evil one. Through these prayer exercises and affective experiences, the exercitant reaps the fruit of a deep knowledge of God's unconditional love [53] and all-sufficient grace [322]; God's free gifts and graces in his plan of salvation in Christ Jesus. Hence, through the deep experiences of God's purgative work within the soul, an exercitant begins to abandon more and more the sinful tendencies and yearns more and more to be more yielded to God. This is the initial fruit through the First Week.

48. English, *Spiritual Freedom*, 124.

A PIVOTAL EXERCISE:
CONTEMPLATION ON THE KINGDOM OF CHRIST
AS A TRANSITION TO THE SECOND WEEK

When the exercitant has gained sufficient insight on consolations and desolations, he is then guided into a pivotal exercise that serves as a transition between the First and the Second Weeks: the contemplation on the Kingdom of Christ. It is a key transition point that calls the exercitant to choose Christ and serve Him generously. Here, it is helpful to reprise the focus of the preparatory prayer, which as we were reminded is prayed at the beginning of every meditation and contemplation. It calls us to beg God for the grace "that all my intentions, actions, and operations may be directed purely to the praise and service of His Divine Majesty" [46]. The contemplation on the Kingdom echoes the core theological criterion found in the Foundation and is itself a foundation for the exercises in the ensuing Weeks.

The grace desired here is to hear the call of Christ the King and be "prompt and diligent to accomplish His most holy will" [91]. To accomplish this, Ignatius divides this contemplation into two parts—first, the imaginary call of an earthly king; and second, the actual call of Christ our King—to elicit in the exercitant a decisive act of will to follow Christ. Having dealt with the inordinate desires that hinder such a response in the First Week, and anticipating the grace to follow Christ closely in the ensuing three Weeks, this contemplation becomes a pivotal exercise that seals in the directee a fundamental decision to be resolute in serving Christ the King.

It is important to note the "two poles of the Ignatian dialectical interaction," which Cusson renders as "contemplation" and "offering."[49] The exercitant is called to contemplate the call of the King in the light of God's universal plan of salvation, and respond with generosity in a personal expression of one's particular vocation in Christ. To be sure, the problem of inordinate desires will never be totally eradicated in one's life. It will have to be confronted again and again in the course of following Christ. Fundamentally, however, this exercise serves as a major step to reaffirm the exercitant's decision to choose life with Christ over death in sin.

Once more we note Ignatius's use of imaginative prayer. In the first part, Ignatius harkens to his sixteenth-century context and his previous career as a noble knight to paint the picture of a noble king calling his subjects to join in his mission to conquer the world for God. Through this imagery, Ignatius encourages the exercitant to imagine one's right response to the call of such a noble earthly king.

---

49. Cusson, *Biblical Theology and the Spiritual Exercises*, 172.

Then in the second part, Ignatius adds that if we respond with generosity to the call of an earthly king, "how much more worthy of consideration is [the call of] Christ our Lord, the Eternal King, before whom is assembled the whole world" [95]. Here, Ignatius seeks to move the exercitant to make a resolute commitment before embarking on the exercises of the Second Week. A firm commitment is needed in order to reap the most benefit in the ensuing Weeks, during which one hones the desire to see Jesus more clearly, to love him more dearly, and to follow him more closely. It also embraces the apostolic ideal of sharing in Christ's mission, which in the Ignatian vision is always contemplation translated into action.

At this point, then, the theological criterion is one of expressing whole-hearted commitment in response to the call of Christ. To seal this commitment, Ignatius crafted the following prayer:

> Eternal Lord of all things, in the presence of Thy infinite goodness, and of Thy glorious mother, and of all the saints of Thy heavenly court, this is the offering of myself which I make with Thy favor and help. I protest that it is my earnest and my deliberate choice, provided only it is for Thy greater service and praise, to imitate Thee in bearing all wrongs and all abuse and all poverty, both actual and spiritual, should Thy most holy majesty deign to choose and admit me to such a state and way of life [98].

THE ILLUMINATIVE WAY OF THE SECOND WEEK— CONTEMPLATING CHRIST

The Call of Christ the King launches the exercitant into the Second Week in a spirit of commitment and generosity. The exercitant's self-image as a loved and forgiven sinner will be gradually transformed into one who is continually drawn by God's love to follow Christ lovingly and closely. The Week's exercises focus on contemplations of the life of Christ, beginning with the Incarnation through to the events on Palm Sunday.

The contemplations of the Second Week are partitioned into "three time-periods."[50] The first time-period is devoted to contemplating the mysteries of Christ's infancy and the "hidden" life. It may take three days, with two mysteries contemplated on each day. The second time-period (fourth day) begins with an Introduction to the making of an election or "The Making of a Choice of a Way of Life [135]. On this day, the exercitant

---

50. Cusson, *Biblical Theology and the Spiritual Exercises*, 243–77.

contemplates the Two Standards, Three Classes of Men, and Three Kinds of Humility. These are key contemplations in the Ignatian way because of their decisive impact. The third time-period focuses on the public life of Christ and stretches from the fifth day of the Week till its completion, which can take up eight days or more. Once again, it is important to keep in focus the hermeneutical keys as we analyze how these contemplations guide the directee.

First Time-Period: Contemplations on Christ's Hidden Life

The first time-period involves the contemplation of six mysteries. Ignatius utilizes the same method as the First Week by beginning with the usual preparatory prayer and preludes before the actual contemplation. Here again, Ignatius appeals to the use of the three powers of the soul, paying special attention to the intellect and the will. Hence, in this first contemplation of the first day, the first and second prelude ask the directee to imagine the memory of the biblical teaching on God's salvation plan in Christ and the annunciation to Mary in the gospel of Luke [102–3, 262].[51] The third prelude guides the exercitant to ask for "what I desire." This format is retained for the rest of the Week's exercises and applied to each contemplation.

Here, it is useful to highlight the difference between a meditation and contemplation as they are utilized in the *Exercises*. While both of them use the mind and heart, meditation tends to be more discursive and contemplation more affective. In meditation, one thinks over the subject matter more with the mind, while in contemplation, one seeks a heart-felt and devout experience.[52] Nevertheless, Ivens warns against drawing the distinction too exclusively in the *Exercises*. He notes that discursive elements come into the later "contemplations," and if "meditation" begins with the intellect, it is itself a movement toward the level of the affections.[53] In contemplating the Gospels' stories during the Second Week, one seeks to relive them and engage with the subjects in the story, principally toward a more heartfelt unity to Christ. As English notes, "the act of presence is basic to contemplation. It is an attempt to be present with Christ in a given mystery."[54]

51. We note Ignatius's word of caution not to overextend in the attempt to use the imagination. Those who struggle with the use of the imagination need not spend too much time on it. As Ignatius clarifies, the composition of the place is not the primary fruit of the meditation but only a way and an instrument toward it. See Palmer, *On Giving the Spiritual Exercises*, 315.

52. Ivens, *Understanding the Spiritual Exercises*, 46, 90.

53. Ivens, *Understanding the Spiritual Exercises*, 46n49.

54. English, *Spiritual Freedom*, 131.

The first day's contemplation reflects Ignatius's spiritual worldview. For Ignatius, God is the Trinity, who is intimately concerned about the decadent state of humanity that is headed toward hell. The Trinity decreed that Jesus, the Second Person, should become man to save the human race, and sends the Angel Gabriel to announce the plan to our Lady—the mystery of the gospel according to the Scriptures [102]. The mystery of the gospel is the objective criteria that undergird Ignatius's theology for the *Spiritual Exercises*. The contemplation, thus, serves as Ignatius's method of assisting the exercitant to experience its mystery and implications in one's life, which is the subjective component of the *Exercises*.

At this point, it is appropriate to add a word concerning the role of the Holy Spirit in the *Spiritual Exercises*. As we noted earlier, Ignatius refrained from direct references to the Holy Spirit except for one instance in the Rules for Thinking with the Church. The reason could be due to the heresy of illuminism in his day. However, Ignatius significantly assumes the presence and guidance of the Holy Spirit throughout the *Exercises*, as the Official Directory affirms.[55] From our hermeneutical perspective, then, it is "the action of the Holy Spirit in the exercitant's soul" that moves her to respond to Christ's bidding to participate in his Kingdom mission. For Ignatius, it is the Holy Spirit who works the grace of God into the life of the exercitant. Thus, as Cusson argues, "the unity of God's plan of salvation and sanctification is brought about by the Holy Spirit." Ignatius's own language in the *Exercises*, however, lacks specific reference to the Holy Spirit, choosing instead to address the "Three Divine Persons." Nevertheless, where there are specific references to the Holy Spirit in the gospel contemplations, Ignatius retains that precision.[56]

Hence, in the three points of the first exercises, Ignatius proposes that the exercitant use the imagination to see, hear, and consider the terrible state on the face of the earth and how the Three Divine Persons are determined to work for its salvation. Then the same devices are utilized in the second contemplation, which is on the nativity. The third and fourth contemplations consist in repeating the first and second exercises. The fifth contemplation applies the five senses to the first and second contemplations. The colloquy is again deployed at the end of each contemplation.

Here we notice again some of Ignatius's methods for contemplation; namely, the use of the imagination, intellect, and will; the use of repetition and review of prayer; and the use of the colloquy. All these are intended to help the exercitant to deeply consider and contemplate the mysteries and

---

55. Palmer, *On Giving the Spiritual Exercises*, 290 and 348.
56. Cusson, *Biblical Theology and the Spiritual Exercises*, 235–43.

experience the presence of desolations and consolations. Then, through the awareness and understanding of these interior affections, receive the grace of God to follow and imitate Jesus more closely.

These same elements and motifs for prayer are applied and adapted to the remaining Weeks and serve as a consistent format and process for the exercitant [127–134]. As the exercitant becomes more and more familiar with them, she can then attend to the spirit of the exercises and become very aware of the movements of the spirits. For Ignatius, this awareness honed by the discernment of spirits in the Second Week is God's way of guidance through his Holy Spirit. The regular practice of the Examen–at mid-day and in the evening–becomes a way of life and further nurtures the exercitant's awareness of the affections and engenders responsiveness to the Lord's presence, so that the exercitant might follow with generosity and love. Gradually, prayer become simpler as the exercitant becomes more and more familiar with the flow of the exercises.

Second Time-Period: Pivotal Exercises in the Second Week

Here at the beginning of the second time-period, Ignatius transitions the exercitant into this Week's exercises with the Introduction to the Consideration of Different States of Life [135]. The exercitant is invited to ask "in what kind of life or in what state His Divine Majesty wishes to make use of us" [135]. This is an important transition wherein the exercitant begins to contemplate how she might better follow and serve Christ in her unique personal vocation.

The first meditation is The Two Standards. It is important to note the third prelude in order to grasp the purpose of this meditation. It is to "ask for a knowledge of the deceits of the rebel chief and help to guard myself against them; and also to ask for a knowledge of the true life exemplified in the sovereign and true Commander, and the grace to imitate Him" [139]. We recall that a fundamental decision has already been made in the Foundation to choose Christ and bring glory to God. Hence, the objective of this mediation is not to make a choice. Rather, it is to expose the tactics of the enemy and guard ourselves against them; and to meditate over how we might be able to better follow Christ and imitate Him.[57]

Hence, the first part is committed to gaining insights on the Standard of Satan and his antics. Satan is exposed as one brazen enemy, who stands on "the vast plain" of Babylon and inspires "horror and terror," who scatters

---

57. Ivens, *Understanding the Spiritual Exercises*, 105–13; English, *Spiritual Freedom*, 145–60; Aschenbrenner, *Stretched for Greater Glory*, 87–99.

his demons all over the world and lays "snares for men and bind them with chains." His primary tactics is to lure with riches, empty honors, and overweening pride [142]. From these three primary vices, the evil one lures all to the other vices.

The Standard of Christ is the total opposite. Christ stands on "a lowly place," "chooses so many persons" and "sends them throughout the whole to spread His sacred doctrine among all men." For Christ, his virtues are spiritual and actual poverty instead of pride, insults and contempt instead of the honor of this world, and humility as opposed to pride [146]. These three beginning virtues then lead to all other virtues.

The contrast is stark. Hence, Ignatius urges the exercitant to follow the Standard of Christ—and through the triple colloquy ask our Lady, her Son, and the Father for grace to imitate Christ and share his virtues. This is the way to life under the banner of Christ.

A second important meditation on this fourth day of the Second Week is the Three Classes of Men. Here, Ignatius presents to the exercitant three classes of men, each of whom have acquired ten thousand ducats in not an entirely appropriate or upright way. However, they wish to save their souls and find peace in God by ridding themselves of the burden arising from the attachment to this sum of money [150]. Hence, the exercitant is invited to picture herself standing before God and choose what is more pleasing to His Divine Goodness [151].

All three classes of men would like to rid themselves of the attachment so as to find peace in God and assure their salvation. The first class of men, however, dies before they did so. David Fleming calls them the ones who have "a lot of talk, but no action."[58] The second class of men wants to be free of the attachment but not get rid of the money. They want both God and the money. Fleming calls them the "to do everything, but the one thing necessary" type. They wish to negotiate with God, and may do many good "spiritual" things, but refuse to face the real issue and give up the very thing that causes the inordinate attachment.

The third class of men want to rid themselves of the attachment, "but they wish to do so in such a way that they desire neither to retain nor to relinquish the sum acquired. They seek only to will and not will as God our Lord inspires them, and as seems better for the service and praise of the Divine Majesty" [155]. This group, Fleming calls, the "to do God's will is my desire" type. Hence, "they will make efforts neither to want that, nor anything else, unless the service of God our Lord alone move them to do

---

58. Fleming, *Draw Me into Your Friendship*, 117.

so. As a result, the desire to be better able to serve God our Lord will be the cause of their accepting anything or relinquishing it" [155].

This group gets to the point of Ignatius's aim in this meditation: to develop the virtue of indifference. This was the point in the third prelude; "to ask for the grace to choose what is more for the glory of His Divine Majesty and the salvation of my soul" [152], and the triple colloquy aids its quest. This harks back to the First Principle and Foundation. The theological principle that this meditation emphasizes is the ultimate aim of living only for the greater glory of God. The posture of indifference is a supporting means toward this end.

Third Time-Period: Contemplations on the Public Life of Christ and Discernment for the Making of an Election

The contemplations on the life of Christ resume on the fifth day and continues for as many days as the director and the directee agree on. Ignatius makes provisions for this flexibility in accordance with what the directee deems best for a time in the Second Week [158–164]. During this time, the directee also has the freedom to make a choice of a way of life. The second set of rules for the discernment of spirits are suited to this time, and they work together with all that the directee has experienced up to this point, along with the following meditation on humility.

A third significant meditation in the Second Week is Three Kinds of Humility [165–168]. Annotation 164 explains that this meditation can serve as an entry point into the time when the Choice of a Way of Life is made. Hence, this meditation of the three kinds of humility can be thought over from time to time during the day to probe the exercitant's interior motivation.

The three kinds of humility can be described as three degrees of humility. The first appears to be the least in degree and seeks not to commit any mortal sin, not even if one is made lord of all creation, so as to obey God in all things in order to save one's soul. The second moves one notch up, "more perfect than the first," and seeks not to commit any venial sin but rather seek to be indifferent to riches or poverty, honor or dishonor, a long life or a short life, "provided only in either alternative I would promote equally the service of God our Lord and the salvation of my soul" [166]. The third goes even further, "the most perfect," and seeks to imitate Christ more closely by desiring and choosing "poverty with Christ poor, rather than riches; insults with Christ loaded with them, rather than honors; . . . to be accounted as worthless and a fool for Christ, rather than to be esteemed as wise and prudent in this world" [167].

The aim of this meditation is to move the exercitant to choose the third kind of humility. If an exercitant chooses to do so, then she could use the three colloquies in the previous meditation to help her. We note here that while Ignatius emphasizes the virtue of indifference in the Foundation and in the second kind of humility, he describes a humility that is even more profound in the third kind and appears to prefer that, calling it the most perfect kind of humility. This being the case, the theological emphasis here is to imitate the self-emptying humility of Christ as found in Philippians 2:1–11. The Ignatian way of spiritual guidance is to imitate Christ with one's entire being.

Deepening in Discernment: The Rules of Discernment for the Second Week

Ignatius anticipates that an exercitant will experience more subtle affective pulls in the Second Week and so provides eight further rules for the discernment of spirits which are more suited to the experiences of this Week. The focus remains on the interior experiences of consolations and desolations in the directee and on discernment as a process. Due to the subtlety of these interior movements, the special concern here is the deception of the evil one in his deployment of false consolations.[59] Hence, this second set of rules help the directee to be more alert in the process of discernment.

Rule 1 is an opening principle that clarifies the characteristic ways in which God and his angels, as opposed to the evil one, move the soul [329]. In principle, the good spirit or good angel acts to give to the soul "true happiness and spiritual joy" and to "abandon all the sadness and disturbances which are caused by the enemy." The evil one, on the contrary, fights against such happiness and consolation "by proposing fallacious reasonings, subtleties, and continual deceptions."

This rule harks back to Rule 2[315] of the First set of rules for the First Week. Hence, the theological principle operating here is that true happiness and spiritual joy are from the good spirit, while sadness and disturbances are from the evil one. However, it should be immediately clarified that not all forms of happiness are true nor all joy spiritual. Neither is sadness necessarily evil. There is therefore an element of subtlety here that must be further discerned. Nevertheless, it is characteristic for the good and evil

---

59. Toner, *A Commentary*.

spirits to act the way they do; for as scripture teaches, a tree reveals its true character by its fruit.

Rule 2 thus clarifies what is the character of a consolation that is solely from God. It is called the Consolation without a preceding cause. Ignatius states that "God alone can give consolation to the soul without any previous cause" [330]. Ganss notes that "consolation without a previous cause is an invasion of God into the soul without any previous use of its own intellectual, volitional, or sense faculties."[60] The meaning and confirmation of this consolation is the subject of much discussion.[61] It is, however, beyond the scope of this work to delve into the details of what a consolation without previous cause is and how it can be confirmed. It is my opinion that Ignatius placed this rule here as a contrast to the following rules which all discuss consolations with a preceding cause, which are quite often the norm in one's experiences, and hence more care is needed in discerning their true character.

Rule 3 therefore provides a principle on how the good and evil spirits typically work in a consolation with a preceding cause. While the first set of rules for discernment describes the evil spirit as bringing desolation, here the evil spirit is described as also being able to console. However, it has a different agenda: "that afterwards he might draw the soul to his own perverse intentions and wickedness" [331]. Here, the theological principle is that one must discern the true character of a consolation.

Rule 4 thus exposes the deceitful schemes of the evil one. Ignatius states it clearly: "It is a mark of the evil spirit to assume the appearance of an angel of light. He begins by suggesting thoughts that are suited to a devout soul, and ends by suggesting his own." The sly action of the evil spirit here is to begin by suggesting what is apparently good. The devil's deceit, however, is that "little by little," almost imperceptibly it draws the soul in a contrary direction into his hidden snares and evil designs [332].

Rule 5, therefore, guides the exercitant to "observe the whole course" of one's thoughts and trace the "beginning, middle, and end" of their trajectory to determine if they truly serve God's purposes. If they do, then it is a sign that they are from the good angel. If they do not, then they are from the evil one. The typical signs of what hinders the progress of the soul are that which are "evil, distracting, or less good than the soul had formerly proposed to do." They tend to weaken the soul and disquiet it or destroy the peace, tranquility, and quiet which it had before. The exercitant is to also

60. Ganss, *Ignatius of Loyola*, 194.

61. See, for example, Toner, *A Commentary*, 291–313 for a discussion of the opinions of Karl Rahner, Harvey Egan, Herve Coathalem, and Daniel Gil.

check whether the trajectory compromises the basic dispositions of indiffer-ence and full commitment to the greater glory of God or any of the postures nurtured in the meditations in the Second Week [333].

Once a false consolation is detected, rule 6 encourages the exercitant to do a review of the whole course of the temptation to learn the "customary deceits of the enemy." The theological principle for guidance here is that of review. We have already mentioned earlier how Ignatius utilizes a review of prayer to gain insights into the significant interior movements one experi-ences during a time in prayer. Here, Ignatius utilizes the same principle to help the exercitant to learn about the tactics of the evil one. The care taken in tracing the quality and trajectory of consolation will reveal if it is of the good spirit or the evil spirit [334].

Here it is useful to note Ivens' remark that while consolations "can mask and even endorse a disordered motivation," we do not have to be overly suspicious of every experience of consolation, for that would work against the nurturing of habitual discernment.[62] As the next rule will show, the good and evil spirits typically work according to their true nature and character.

Rule 7 [335] reiterates the principles of rule 1 and 2 of the First Week [314, 315]. However, it is cast more in the light of subtlety consistent with the mood of the Second Week. All the same, the actions of the good and evil spirits are consistent with their true character. Hence, for one progressing onto greater perfection, the good spirit will leave a "delicate, gentle, [and] delightful" touch, while the evil spirit will come across as "violent, noisy, and disturbing." However, for those going from bad to worse, the actions of the spirits are reversed. According to their true character and objective, the good spirit will guide to freedom and life, and the evil spirit to bondage and death. This rule therefore serves as a general assurance of the reliability of consolations. That said, given our human tendencies, the next rule serves as a final guard against potentially new deception in the experience of an afterglow.

The point of rule 8 [336] is to guard against the tendency to make hasty plans and resolutions in the afterglow of a consolation without previ-ous cause. Ignatius says that during this time, a "soul is still fervent and favored with the grace and aftereffects of the consolation which has passed," but may hastily make decisions that "are not granted directly by God our Lord." Hence, one is to "carefully examine" them and ensure that they are indeed made according to true consolations.

---

62. Ivens, *Understanding the Spiritual Exercises*, 231.

In summary, the main warning here is the deception of the enemy in the form of false consolations. Care must be taken to examine the quality and trajectory of a consolation to determine its true character, especially in the diverse affections that are anticipated in the Second Week. The experience of a consolation without previous cause does not necessary mean that what follows still belong to the intent of the consolation, so careful discernment is again needed during this time in the afterglow. Taken together, these rules help to deepen the awareness of God's leading in the process of discernment.

Making a Choice of a Way of Life[63]

When an exercitant is ready, Ignatius then guides her onto the exercise on Making a Choice of a Way of Life or what is commonly called, the making of an election [169–188]. This is a sacred and climatic moment for those who enter into a focused retreat for this expressed purpose. The introduction is critical here. For in it, Ignatius states in no uncertain terms that we must live only for the end for which we are created. This is the principal theological criterion of the *Exercises*. The introduction thus reprises the First Principle and Foundation: "I must consider only the end for which I am created, that is, for the praise of God our Lord and for the salvation of my soul" [169]. It also echoes the disposition of the Third Class of Men [155] and the second kind of humility [166].

63. All major interpreters of Ignatius's *Exercises* recognizes that there are two major schools of interpretations—the "electionist" and the "perfectionist." The "electionist" assert that Ignatius's major objective in the *Exercises* was to guide the Exercitant toward the election. The "perfectionists," however, argue, especially in light of annotation nineteen, that Ignatius goal was to guide a person to growth in the spiritual life, in which the making of an election is a step in that direction.

Hugo Rahner is electionist in his interpretation of the *Exercises*. He considers as central to the *Exercises* the meditations on The Kingdom of Christ and The Two Standards, which in his opinion, calls one to a fundamental choice between serving Christ or the Evil One. For Rahner, these two meditations serve as the nexus, as everything before and after them lead into this critical making of a choice. Discretion, or familiarity with the diversity of spirits, is therefore foundational to making such a choice. Hence, he argues that the *Exercises* must be made in full to be effective. It was Ignatius's preference that only those who possess the aptitude that the entire *Exercises* are given to them. Otherwise, only the First Week is given. It is only when one is skilled in the discernment of spirits that they are sent into the world to serve Christ our King, to deny the world and live only for Christ the King and on the other hand, to be sent into the world to wrestle it from Satan's hands for Christ. See Rahner, *The spirituality of St. Ignatius*.

However, most commentators today are of the opinion that the two ways of interpretation complement each other. See Ganss, *Ignatius of Loyola*; and Cusson, *Biblical Theology and the Spiritual Exercises*.

For this reason, Ignatius recalls the differentiation between ends and means: "I must not subject and fit the end to the means, but the means to the end" [169]. He explains how many have confused the two, choosing first to marry, which is the means, and then to serve God, which is the end. Likewise, others have confused between the choice of benefices, which is the means, and the service of God, the ultimate end. Ignatius adds that those who confuse the means with the end tend to conform to their inordinate attachments. Consequently, they confuse the two and "what they ought to seek first, they seek last" [169]. Therefore, in this introduction, Ignatius underscores the critical importance of establishing as one's first aim the service of God, the end for which we are created. Then, with this priority established, one can choose the appropriate means for what brings greater glory to God. This introduction is by far the clearest statement on Ignatius's theological criterion in his way of spiritual direction.

Upon this introductory foundation, the exercitant is then guided into a time during which a choice may be made. This time consists of a consideration about matters which a choice should be made, followed by guidance on three times when a correct and good choice of a way of life may be made. The third time in which a choice may be made in turn consists of two ways in which the choice may be made.

The opening set of considerations clarifies for the exercitant what matters are worthy of choice. Ignatius's advice that they must be "indifferent or good in themselves, and such that they are lawful within" the Church and not bad or opposed to her, echoes his theological criteria. Ignatius then goes on to clarify between changeable and unchangeable choices. The priesthood and marriage are two examples of unchangeable choices. For those who have chosen them, there is no apparent need to make another choice so Ignatius says that they should "take care to live well in the life [one] has chosen" and not seek to make a change, even if they felt that they have made the choice poorly—that is under the influence of the flesh or any inordinate attachment. Nevertheless, they can make a choice with regards to spiritual growth, choosing to love Christ more deeply and to serve him more selflessly.

In matters changeable, Ignatius recommends not making a change "if one has made a choice properly," and should "perfect himself as much as possible in the one he had made" [173]. If the choice "has not been made sincerely and with due order," then Ignatius recommends making a change "in the proper way" [174].

Ignatius describes three times for the making of a choice or election [175–177]. These are actually "three spiritual situations, each characterized by a certain kind of evidence of God's will and by a mode of decision-making on our part corresponding to this evidence."[64] Ignatius describes the "First Time" as "When God our Lord so moves and attracts the will that a devout soul without hesitation, or the possibility of hesitation, follows what has been manifested to it. Saint Paul and Saint Matthew acted thus in following Christ our Lord" [175]. Ignatius's point is that there are times, such as those experienced by Saint Paul and Saint Matthew, when God acts in such a way that it is beyond doubt that what is manifested is God's will, and one is simply moved to follow God. In those situations, Ignatius reckons, one simply follows God's call. The main point is that "it is a situation in which the evidence consists in being [manifested], decisively and unambiguously, the course to follow, and the response is one of simple assent."[65]

The second time is "when much light and understanding are derived through the experience of desolations and consolations and discernment of diverse spirits" [176]. This time explains why Ignatius took care to design the exercises of the First and Second Weeks as he did, to instruct the director to attend to the exercitant's experience of diverse affections and to hone the exercitant's acumen through the two sets of rules for the discernment of spirits. Ignatius's way of guidance draws significantly from an interior knowledge of the affections. Consequently, the process of making a decision in the second time is primarily through the theological criteria from the discernment of spirits.

The third time is "a time of tranquility" [177]. That is, when the soul is "not agitated by different spirits, and has free and peaceful use of its natural powers." While the focus in the second time is discernment due to the presence of diverse spirits, the focus in the third time is rational assessment due to the absence of diverse spirits. This does not mean a total absence of spiritual movements, but rather that they are not sufficiently significant to render it as a second time. As Ivens notes, "the criterion [here] is not *movement of the spirit*, but reason."[66] Hence, Ivens argues that "the third time establishes a basic principle that our rational faculties, converted and graced, are still capable by themselves of finding God's will, and to do this is not absolutely necessary to experience movements of the Spirit."[67]

Ignatius then suggests two ways to make a good and correct choice in the third setting. The first way consists of six points of guidance, which I note in summary form [179–183].

64. Ivens, *Understanding the Spiritual Exercises*, 135.

65. Ivens, *Understanding the Spiritual Exercises*, 136.

66. Ivens, *Understanding the Spiritual Exercises*, 138.

67. Ivens, *Understanding the Spiritual Exercises*, 138.

First Point: Place before my mind the object on which a choice is to be made.

Second Point: Affirm my fundamental dispositions as expressed in the Foundation: the posture of indifference, and what is more conducive for the greater glory of God.

Third Point: Petition God to work through my mind and will; the mind to weigh the matter with care and fidelity, and the will to be conformed to God's will.

Fourth Point: Using as criteria my basic disposition in the end for which I am created, I weigh the advantages and disadvantages of each alternative I know.

Fifth Point: Then I evaluate the decisions to see which one is more reasonable, being careful of my sensual inclination.

Sixth Point: Offer the choice to God and ask for confirmation.

The theological criteria we observe at work here are those found in the Foundation and the utilization of the mind and heart. It is hoped that at this time, the exercitant would be able to decide from a posture of indifference. If not, it will not be possible to make a good choice in the third time. When, however, an exercitant is able to deliberate from a posture of indifference and keep in clear focus the end for which one is created and committed to, then the use of one's natural reasoning faculties is not unprofitable. God works through a mind after Christ's own mind and a heart after God's own heart.

Should the first way become inconclusive, Ignatius offers a second way through his imaginative role-play; which I summarize here in point form [184–188].

First Rule: Petition God for an interior sense of love to make a choice only for the sake of God.

Second Rule: Role play on how I would advice another, especially when I wish to see them practice all perfection. Then apply the same advice to myself.

Third Rule: Imagine how I might make the decision at my death's bed. Then adopt the same decision now.

Fourth Rule: Picture making the decision before God on Judgment Day. Then make the same decision now.

Concluding Note: Offer the decision to God and ask for confirmation.

As Ivens notes: "the second way in the Third Time is not a method of obtaining evidence of God's will, but rather a way of testing the quality of a felt inclination that moves us to a particular choice."[68] The logic here is that sound advice given to another in a time of tranquility is certainly usable by God, and hence can be applied to oneself, if the heart is firmly inclined to the love of God and his greater glory. Such a choice offered to God will still be tested through the wisdom of confirmation, but it is one that acknowledges God's good gifts of a sound mind and reverential heart, along with a posture of indifference. In this second way, the theological criteria for a good choice are again the fundamental dispositions of the Foundation and the creative and responsible use of the mind and heart.

THE UNITIVE WAY OF THE THIRD AND FOURTH WEEK

The Third and Fourth Weeks are dedicated to the contemplation of the Passion and Resurrection of the Lord respectively [190–209 with 289–298; and [218–229 with 299–312]. They help with confirming one's decision, especially when self-denial is demanded in the Third Week. Joy, however, follows in the Four Week after one has persevered in following the Lord. The contemplations use the basic structure consistent with the previous exercises so I will not comment on them. I will instead examine Ignatius's theological criteria in his method.

The first observation is that the Third and Fourth Weeks combine with the first two Weeks to form an organic whole; these are intentionally designed, as Ignatius described, in annotation four which is evident through the text and process of the *Exercises* [4]. These Weeks, therefore, continue the "process of contemplative development" which is so central to the intent of the *Exercises*.[69] There is, however, "a certain change of spiritual climate" in that the graces in these two final weeks move from the more "external graces" of knowledge, love and committed discipleship of the first two weeks to the more "immediately participatory sort," that is, "suffering *with* Christ [203], [and] joy *with* Christ [231, cf. 48]."[70] There is, therefore, an emphasis in cultivating the virtue of compassion in the Third Week and celebration in the Fourth Week.

The progression is one of increasing intimacy with Christ, not only as a disciple who longs to see Jesus more clearly, love him more dearly

68. Ivens, *Understanding the Spiritual Exercises*, 142.
69. Ivens, *Understanding the Spiritual Exercises*, 146.
70. Ivens, *Understanding the Spiritual Exercises*, 146.

and follow him more nearly in the Second Week, but now to nurture "a contemplative involvement" with Christ in his passion and resurrection.[71] The exercitant thus seeks to participate with Christ in the whole paschal mystery—rendering these Weeks as more aligned with the unitive way of the Christian pilgrimage.

The theological principle here is, therefore, the "with Christ" principle. "In the Passion . . . to ask for sorrow *with* Christ in sorrow, anguish *with* Christ in anguish, tears and deep grief . . ." [203, emphasis added]. The emphasis is to be with Christ and share in our souls his sorrow, suffering, and anguish. Likewise, in contemplating the resurrection, the purpose is to "be glad and rejoice intensely because of the great joy and the glory of Christ our Lord" [221]. It is the principle of sharing, of being with. This applies not only to the habit of following Christ, but is expressed in the concrete act of Christian spiritual companioning or guidance. Christian spiritual guidance principally embraces the "with Christ" and with one another principle.

Total Surrender in Love: The Contemplation to Attain Love

This overriding principle brings us to the concluding contemplation of the *Exercises*, which, as intended, in turn seals this principle in us: it is the Contemplation to Attain the Love of God. As the title suggests, the focus is on love; God's love for us and our reciprocal love for God. This is not only meant to be the culmination of four weeks of progressive development in following and loving Christ, it is also meant to guide the exercitant into the continuing reality of finding and loving God in all things [233].

Thus, Ignatius makes the point that "love ought to manifest itself in deeds rather than in words" [230]; and that love "consists in a mutual sharing of goods" between one beloved and another [231]. Here, the exercitant is spurred on to reach a love that is concretely expressed in actions as well as experienced in affections. This is the Ignatian ideal of being a contemplative in action. As we witnessed in Ignatius's own life and those of the members of the Society, this way of being is expressed in its mission and apostolic service. It is little wonder that Nadal summarizes the Jesuit way of life as "*spiritu, corde, practice*;" "in the Spirit, from the heart, practically."[72]

In this light and towards this ideal, Ignatius urges the exercitant to express the desire "for an intimate knowledge of the many blessings received, that filled with gratitude for all, [she] may in all things love and serve the Divine Majesty" [233]. This resonates with the disposition asked for in the

71. Ivens, *Understanding the Spiritual Exercises*, 146.
72. O'Malley, *The First Jesuits*, 251.

Foundation, making these two contemplations "book ends" that seal the spirit of the *Exercises*.

The points for contemplation confirms its purpose by focusing the exercitant to "ponder with great affection" on "the blessings of creation and redemption" and "moved by great feeling" to offer oneself entirely to God. Thus the exercitant prays:

> Take, Lord, and Receive (*Suscipe*)
>
> Take, Lord, and receive all my liberty, my memory, my understanding and my entire will, all that I have and possess. Thou hast given all to me. To Thee, O Lord, I return it. All is Thine, dispose of it wholly according to Thy will. Give me Thy love and Thy grace, for this is sufficient for me.

There are few prayers more comprehensive and climactic than this and the one expressed in the Kingdom meditation. One's entire being—memory, understanding, and will—is offered to God as an expression of total abandonment. What is desired is simply God's love and grace—echoing the "with God" principle. Hence the second point in the contemplation ponders deeply God dwelling in all creatures and in me—making me a temple of the Holy Spirit. God in me and I together with God, co-working and co-laboring, first God for me, and then, I as an offering in response. This contemplation plunges the exercitant into an overwhelming realization of all God's blessings and gifts. The only possible outcome of this deep knowledge is one's response of humility and gratitude, expressed concretely in love and action—to God and to our neighbor, for the greater Glory of God. This is the fruit of Ignatian spirituality, rolled out in its way of proceeding through the *Spiritual Exercises* of Saint Ignatius.

CONCLUSION:
THE IGNATIAN WAY IN SPIRITUAL DIRECTION

The main theological thrust of the *Exercises* is the spirit of *magis*, or the more that seeks the greater glory of God. This emphasis, most prominent in the Foundation and the Contemplation to Attain Love, pervades the entire vision of the *Exercises* and the Jesuits as a company of Jesus. All their motivations and decisions must be measured against this ultimate end to ensure that all things are directed solely to the praise, reverence and service of God.

The *Spiritual Exercises*, as a text and process, thus systematically guides an exercitant through the prayer exercises in each Week that progressively works on the purgative, illuminative, and unitive aspects of one's relationship with Jesus. Every method of prayer, whether it is the examination of conscience, a meditation or contemplation, the application of the senses or the colloquies, even the efforts at penance–serve as means to nurture an increasing sensitivity to the voice of the Holy Spirit and of seeking and finding God's will for the ultimate end of serving God's purposes for God's glory.

The Ignatian response to the problem of inordinate attachments is to nurture the virtue of indifference through a deepening awareness of the interior movements of the spirits and cultivating the discipline to choose only what God prefers. The variety of prayer methods deepens the ability to relish the truth and awareness of one's interiority; and the rules for discernment bring light to the process of discernment. Therefore an exercitant learns to ask for the desired grace in every preparatory prayer so that one's intentions, actions, and operations may be brought to cooperate with God's grace. The three powers of the soul are moved together with the application of the senses so that one's entire being is involved in the process. The rules of discernment then illumine the experiences of diverse spirits and clarifies what is of God or not of God. In the process, the exercitant learns to discern and to choose well. This deepening knowledge of the self in relation to God gradually guides the exercitant toward increasing spiritual freedom as one resolves to surrender all of one's will to God.

The subject matter for prayer is the Scriptures, especially the gospels, and several extra biblical meditations. These hark back to Ignatius's own experience. So the Ignatian way of guidance implements this Christo-centric focus. God is first only when Christ is first. The movement through the Weeks, therefore, thoroughly immerses one in the Scriptures and decisively nurtures one to choose Christ. It is in choosing to imitate Christ, that one learns self-abnegation. It is also in choosing to imitate Christ that one prefers to serve another. So the Ignatian method guides one to follow the way of Christ–in love and in action, in suffering and in glory.

One of Ignatius's closest associates, Jeronimo Nadal, sums up Ignatian spirituality with three words: "in the Spirit, from the heart, practically." To emphasize the depths of understanding and relish of the truth, however, it may be elaborated that the Ignatian way of spiritual direction be summed up as: an inner understanding and relish of the truth (that quality of "*sentir*") translated into a way of life in the Spirit, from the heart, practically. This is the essence of what it means to find God in all things and be a contemplative in action through prayer and apostolic service for the greater glory of God.

6

John Calvin's Spiritual Guidance in Historical and Theological Context

WHILE JOHN CALVIN (1509–1564) was widely known as one of the most influential sixteenth-century Protestant reformers and a brilliant theologian, it is perhaps less commonly remembered that he was also a teacher and pastor to numerous exiled French protestants, especially to the infant Protestant churches in Strasbourg, Basel, and Geneva. In fact, as Calvin explained, he wrote the first edition of the *Institutes of the Christian Religion*,[1] published at Basel in 1536, as a teaching aid for those who wished to pursue true godliness.[2] He would, over the next twenty-four years, expand and elaborate on this work, first conceived as a catechism, into a comprehensive guide for the development of genuine piety.[3] Calvin may, therefore, be regarded as

1. References to *the Institutes of the Christian Religion* will hereafter abbreviated as *Institutes*. Citations from the *Institutes* are from 1960 edition, translated by Ford Lewis Battles, and edited by John T McNeill, and follow the conventional way of using three digits to refer to book, chapter, and section.

2. See Calvin, "Prefatory Address to King Francis I of France," in Calvin, *Institutes of the Christian Religion*, 9. 1536 "Prefatory Address to King Francis I of France": "My purpose was solely to transmit certain rudiments by which those who are touched with any zeal for religion might be shaped to true godliness."

See also Calvin, "John Calvin to the Reader" in Calvin, *Institutes of the Christian Religion*, 3—the 1559 Latin version of the *Institutes*: "it has been my purpose in this labor to prepare and instruct candidates in sacred theology for the reading of the divine Word, in order that they may be able both to have easy access to it and to advance in it without stumbling."

3. See Calvin, *Institutes of the Christian Religion* (1536 edition); Battles, *Interpreting John Calvin*, 91–116; and Hesselink, *Calvin's First Catechism*, 42.

a spiritual guide for his life and times—serving his Lord and parishioners untiringly as reformer, theologian, teacher, and pastor in response to the diverse needs of nascent Protestant churches in sixteenth-century Europe.

Calvin's theology of the spiritual life and his method of spiritual guidance were, consequently, forged through his experiences and responses to the confluence of cultural, educational, polemical, and religious factors set within the ferment of the Protestant and Catholic Reformations. A study of his theology and method of spiritual guidance, therefore, requires a careful review of the historical factors that shaped his thought and religious convictions. It must examine the historical context of sixteenth-century Europe and the Roman Church, especially the social locations of France, Germany, and Switzerland, where Calvin devoted considerable amounts of time as a student, and as pastor, teacher, and reformer. It must especially analyze the *Institutes*—widely regarded as "a work of capital importance most valued by Calvin"[4]—along with Calvin's other major works such as the commentaries, catechisms, sermons, tracts and treatises, and letters, for a comprehensive understanding of his theology and approach to the spiritual life.

As I did with Ignatius of Loyola, I will similarly devote two chapters to my study of John Calvin. This chapter will focus on a retrieval of the historical factors that shaped Calvin's religious thought while the next chapter examines his approach to spiritual guidance. In my historical analysis, I first examine the formative impact from his education in humanism and the classics before going on to consider how his interactions with other Protestant reformers and the polemics in the context of the Reformations further shaped his thought on the Christian life, especially as they are evinced in the *Institutes*.

While I continue to use the methods of Sandra Schneiders,[5] and Bradley and Muller[6] for my study, I also attend to Calvin scholars for their advice and methods on Calvin research. For example, Richard Muller warns that Calvin's thought has been deconstructed by nineteenth- and twentieth-century writers in search of a theological ally or historical source for their theological arguments. He warns against the tendency to impose an interpretive grid upon Calvin's text such as those found in some modern critical editions but instead take care to establish the specific sixteenth-century context within which the documents ought to be read.[7] I share Philip Sheldrake's concern that much of contemporary interest in spirituality is happening

---

4. Wendel, *Calvin: Origins*, 111.
5. Schneiders, "A Hermeneutical Approach."
6. Bradley and Muller, *Church History*.
7. Muller, *The Unaccommodated Calvin*, 4.

within a "theological vacuum" and that faithfulness in interpretation entails the understanding that spiritualities must be understood first as historically-located before their relevance is explored across time and space.[8]

Muller's and Sheldrake's warnings are especially pertinent in view of tendencies in contemporary spirituality to borrow from a variety of sources without due consideration for their historical antecedents or theological persuasions. Consequently, I seek to read John Calvin within his historical context and understand the intent and function of his writings as he intended for them in that context before exploring their relevance for today.

HISTORICAL FACTORS THAT SHAPED CALVIN'S THEOLOGY OF THE CHRISTIAN LIFE

Tumultuous Religious Climate

As we embark on an exploration of the historical factors that shaped Calvin's theology of the Christian life, we are met with the tumultuous religious climate that confronted the church in the sixteenth century. The deterioration within the Catholic Church and the winds of change brought on by the Protestant Reformation pervaded the religious climate in Calvin's day. The Roman Church was plagued by spiritual and moral abuses, there was widespread biblical illiteracy, and its clergy was often regarded as incompetent. Calvin complained that "those who were regarded as the leaders of the faith neither understood [God's] Word, nor greatly cared for it. They drove unhappy people to and fro with strange doctrines, and deluded them with I know not what follies."[9] Although the Reformation was already in progress and the printing press in use, the Scriptures were still not readily available in the vernacular and there was a shortage of reliable guides for its study. Randall Zachman aptly sums up the situation as "a time when many Christians, both Roman and evangelical, recognized that the ministry of the church was in crisis [and that] neither bishops nor priests were skilled in the interpretation of Scripture or particularly adept at teaching the summary of the doctrine that leads to genuine piety."[10]

Several decades before Calvin emerged on the Reformation scene, Christian Humanist Desiderius Erasmus (1469–1536) had already birthed a vision and hope for reforming Christendom. "His hope was that through Christian scholarship and wholesome instruction the philosophy of Christ

8. See Sheldrake, *Spirituality and History*.

9. See "The Reply to Sadoleto" in Calvin, *John Calvin: Writings on Pastoral Piety*, 43.

10. Zachman, *John Calvin*, 11.

(*an aspect of piety*) could be so clearly portrayed that plowboys and prel-
ates, citizens and kings would at last understand the meaning of the gospel
and would be moved to revive the whole darkening world."[11] While only
antiquity may judge the outcome of Erasmus's vision, his Christian humanism influenced Calvin's education in a major way. His call to "return to the
sources" [Latin: *Ad fontes*] profoundly shaped Calvin's perspective on reclaiming the Scriptures and the Church Fathers as the foundational sources
for theology and piety.[12]

When Calvin was barely eight years old, Martin Luther (1484–1546)
nailed his ninety-five theses on the door of the Castle church in Wittenberg in protest against the Roman Catholic Church's interpretation of the
sacrament of penance, and for its abuses in the sale of indulgences. Years
later, Calvin would echo these same concerns, and collaborate with Luther
in their efforts at reform. Luther's influence on Calvin was so significant
that Calvin would go on to address him as "the very excellent pastor of the
Christian Church, my much-respected father."[13]

While Luther was leading reforms in Germany, Ulrich Zwingli (1484–
1531) was actively at work in Switzerland. There Zwingli wielded significant
influence as an evangelical theologian and preacher. His sermons ranged
over the whole New Testament in six years and his theological position
on infant baptism and the Lord's Supper were widely known.[14] Zwingli's
contribution, too, would influence Calvin's approach on spiritual guidance,
though differences between them were evident. Such was the religious climate in which Calvin grew as an adolescent and teenager. It was a world
in which the Roman Church was in desperate need of renewal while the
ferment of Protestant reform was spreading rapidly through major cities in
Europe.

Parental Influence

Jean Cauvin, as he was named at birth, was born to Gerard Cauvin and
Jeanne Lefranc in the small French town of Noyon. Calvin had three brothers, Charles, Antonie, and Francois, and two sisters, Marie and another,

---

11. Spitz, "Desiderius Erasmus," 60, italics added.

12. See Lane, *John Calvin*, on Calvin's extensive use of the Church Fathers. Note,
however, Lane's eleven theses which clarified that Calvin's use of a patristic source
should not immediately be assumed as influence on Calvin, for Calvin could have used
it for what was expedient for his purposes. Lane, *John Calvin*, 1–13.

13. Calvin, *Letters of John Calvin*, 1:440.

14. Thompson, "Ulrich Zwingli."

whose name is unknown. His father came from a family of dock workers and coopers in the fishing town of Pont-l'Eveque but later left for Noyon. Gerard Cauvin became a successful lawyer in Noyon and looked after the financial affairs of the church. Due to his connection with the Noyon Cathedral, Gerard procured benefices for Calvin and his brothers, and so he "may have had to commit himself to guide Jean towards the study of theology," which, however, would not be surprising since he was an episcopal official.[15] John Calvin seemed to have been marked for a career in the service of the church from an early age.

John Calvin's mother, Jeanne, died in 1515 when Calvin was only six years old. Little is known about his mother except that she had a reputation for piety. It could be said that Calvin "grew up in an environment of piety" in his early childhood. However, after his mother's death, "the church increasingly became his mother, informing Calvin's later affirmation of the traditional Christian dictum that no one can have God as Father who does not have the church as mother."[16] Such early training explains why Calvin confessed in his *Commentary to the Psalms* of 1557 that until his conversion, he was "obstinately devoted to the superstitions" of the Roman Church. Evidently, Calvin was committed to the Catholic faith from an early age until the "sudden conversion" that subdued his heart and made him teachable.[17]

John Calvin, however, never fulfilled his duties as a chaplain nor undertook any of the ecclesiastical responsibilities that the benefices entailed. Instead, he was thrust into educational pursuits from an early age. At about seven years, his father enrolled him in the School of the Capettes, together with the children of the Hangest family, for Latin studies. Then, in 1523, he and the Hangest children entered the Collège de la Marche in Paris, where they were instructed by a preceptor as day students. From there, Calvin transferred to the Collège de Montaigu, where he completed the philosophical preparatory studies as a baccalaureate, followed by a Master of Arts degree in 1528, at the age of nineteen. On his father's instructions, he then went on to Orleans to study civil law. It was assumed that Calvin studied in Orleans from 1528 to 1532, with a year spent at the University of Bourges (1530–1531) and for Seneca studies in Paris (1531–1532).[18] Through these years, Calvin was nurtured by the best minds in education—and they

15. Wendel, *Calvin: Origins*, 15–17.

16. Selderhuis, *The Calvin Handbook*, 11.

17. Calvin, "The Author's Preface," in *Comm. Ps 30*. "And first, since I was too obstinately devoted to the superstitions of Popery to be easily extricated from so profound an abyss of mire, God by a sudden conversion subdued and brought my mind to a teachable frame."

18. Selderhuis, *The Calvin Handbook*, 24.

contributed significantly to how he emerged as a leading reformer in the Christian church.

Outstanding Educators

Ford Lewis Battles identified six teachers who made a mark in Calvin's education. First, there was Mathurin Cordier, "one of the finest Latinists," from whom Calvin learnt Latin at the University of Paris. Then there were two experts in Roman Law, Pierre de l'Estoile with whom Calvin studied at the University of Orleans (1528; 1532–33), and the "famed Italian juriconsult," Andrea Alciati (autumn 1529–end 1530), under whose tutelage Calvin studied "Roman Law within the broadest understanding of Latin and Greek classical authors and institutions." Further, Calvin received expert guidance in Greek and Classical Literature from Melchior Wolmar (end 1530–end Feb 1531) at Bourges, Guillaume Budé (1531–32) at Paris, and Pierre Danes (late Fall 1531) at the University of Paris. While Calvin studied under most of them for a short time, he did so at a critical time in his own life and history. Almost all these men were educational innovators whose ideas contributed to Calvin's educational philosophy—and, hence, his career as exegete of Scripture, theologian, and reformer.[19]

It was evident that Calvin read Erasmus, Guillaume Budé, Lorenzo Valla, and a number of other French and Italian humanists.[20] He would have learn from Erasmus and Budé the importance of establishing reliable critical editions, and of interpreting texts in light of their literary, linguistic, and cultural contexts, so that their genuine meaning would emerge from that context.[21] It was also evident that Calvin read the Church Fathers, for example St. Augustine, whose City of God, he mentioned fifteen times in his *Commentary on the De Clementia of Seneca*.[22]

Reform Movements

There is little doubt that Calvin's education in humanism, law, and the classics significantly shaped how he organized his thought and writing. Yet there was little evidence that Calvin modified his religious attitude while he was still a student among these great teachers. As he confessed, he remained

19. Battles, *Interpreting John Calvin*, 51–61.
20. Wendel, *Calvin: Origins*, 31.
21. Zachman, *John Calvin*, 16–17.
22. Wendel, *Calvin: Origins*. See also, Lane, *John Calvin*.

a rather staunch Catholic, although he did embrace more and more the humanist ideal.[23] Providentially though, the humanistic education that Calvin received would significantly shape his method of retrieving antique documents and of organizing this thought and arguments, a skill that would become very pertinent to the formulation of his theology of the Christian life. It is quite reasonable to say that Calvin's early education under some of the best minds during this time significantly shaped his intellectual formation, which in turned influenced his approach on guiding the church, especially as seen in his appeal to the Church Fathers and his use of a diverse range of sources for the construction of the *Institutes*.[24]

Apart from the influence of Christian humanism, there was the question on whether Calvin was also influenced by the *Devotio Moderna*—a movement founded by Gerard Groote (1340–1384), that flourished during the fifteenth and sixteenth centuries in the Low Countries and Germany. At the least, Calvin would most likely have met it during his studies at the University of Paris. In his work on the spirituality of John Calvin, Lucien Richard devoted an extended discussion to the influence of the *Devotio Moderna* on the sixteenth-century spiritual climate and examines the extent of its impact on John Calvin's own spirituality. He argues that the *Devotio Moderna* influenced such schools of spirituality as the Erasmian, the Ignatian, and, to a certain degree, the contemporary Protestant spirituality of its time.[25]

In his analysis on the continuities and discontinuities between Calvin's and Groote's piety, Richard observes that the spirituality of John Calvin shows "a remarkable resemblance" to the vocabulary, but to a lesser extent the ideas, in the writings of Gerard Groote, and the *Imitation of Christ* (a work commonly attributed to Thomas à Kempis (c.1380–1471) and who was intimately connected to the *Devotio Moderna*).[26] He observed that Calvin's spirituality followed the same impulse as the *Devotio Moderna* in its emphasis on the transcendence of God, as indicated by his preoccupation with the concepts of election, holiness, and the glory of God. Richard argues that Calvin synthesized these concepts into a spirituality of total self-abnegation and complete consecration in service to the glory of God expressed through worship. He, however, noticed that Calvin's emphasis on the centrality of worship was not strongly defended in the *Devotio Moderna*—giving strong evidence of a discontinuity. Moreover, in his linguistic

---

23. Wendel, *Calvin: Origins*, 23.

24. Lane, *John Calvin*.

25. Richard, *The Spirituality of John Calvin*, 12.

26. See Habsburg, *Catholic and Protestant translations of the Imitatio Christi*, 1–48.

analysis of *devotio* and *pietas*, he notes Calvin's strong dislike for the external forms associated with *devotio* and preference for *pietas* as expressing the interiorization reflective of an authentic spirituality. In the final analysis, Richard concludes that Calvin's spirituality differed radically from that of the *Devotio Moderna*.[27]

Recently, Clive Chin's study concurred with Richard's findings and argues that Calvin was more likely indirectly influenced by the *Devotio Moderna* through the work of Erasmus. Chin posits that Erasmus absorbed and transformed tenets of the *Devotio Moderna* by combining inner spirituality with learning, as is manifested in his concept of the philosophia Christi, and influenced Calvin' integration of piety and doctrine as seen in the epistemological and ontological dimensions of Calvin's spirituality. Chin's dissertation proposes that Calvin's spirituality contains the twin dimensions of *Unio Mystica* and *Imitatio Christi* which reflect Calvin's concept of the two-fold grace of justification and sanctification and a life of discipleship in the pattern of Christ.[28]

Fellow Reformers

Calvin's interaction with fellow reformers certainly contributed to the shaping of his theology of the Christian life. Although there was no record of Luther having spoken directly to Calvin, he nevertheless had a significant influence on Calvin. Calvin was certain that Luther's recovery of the gospel of justification by faith alone apart from meritorious works was the turning point of the controversy with Rome. He believed that such a faith could only be created and sustained by the gospel of free grace and mercy of God in Jesus Christ, through the power of the Holy Spirit.[29]

During his exile to Basel from 1535 to 1536, following the Nicholas Cop incident in Paris, Calvin encountered the teaching and exegesis of the Swiss reformers, especially John Oecolampadius and Ulrich Zwingli. Calvin developed a high regard for Oecolampadius, particularly in the way he recovered for the church the symbolic thinking of the Fathers, especially about the sacraments, over against the language of substance that had dominated the papacy after the Fourth Lateran Council. Calvin was persuaded by Zwingli's claim that the true body of Christ is in heaven but was critical of the way he divorced the elements from the self-offer of Christ, making them

---

27. Richard, *The Spirituality of John Calvin*, 48–129.

28. Chin, *Unio Mystica and Imitatio Christi*.

29. Zachman, *John Calvin*, 18.

empty signs.[30] Calvin pondered at length Luther's and Zwingli's positions on the Lord's Supper and eventually defined his own position in the matter of the Eucharist.[31]

The first edition of the *Institutes*, published in 1536, was the product of his time at Basel. Structured as a booklet of six chapters, it followed the basic plan of Luther's catechism, and elaborated on the law, faith, prayer, true and false sacraments, and Christian freedom.[32] It was designed to serve as a catechism and could be individually read. The two chapters that addressed the issues of false sacraments and Christian freedom, and his letter to the French King, however, gave it an apologetic tone, and necessarily so given the prevalence of erroneous doctrines. It is from his letter to King Francis I that we learned of Calvin's intent, even at this early stage of his career, for the *Institutes* to be a means for the development of piety:

> When I first set my hand to this work, nothing was farther from my mind, most glorious King, than to write something that might be offered to your Majesty. *My purpose was solely to transmit certain rudiments by which those who are touched with any zeal for religion might be shaped to true godliness.* And I undertook this labor especially for our French countrymen, very many of whom I saw to be hungering and thirsting for Christ; very few who had been imbued with even a slight knowledge of him. The book itself witnesses that this was my intention, adapted as it is to a simple and, you may say, elementary form of teaching.[33]

Calvin did not intend for the *Institutes* to be a theological treatise or a presentation of systematic theology, but a guide for the development of true piety. In the opening discussion of the twofold knowledge of God and of the self in Book I, he leads the reader to recognize the priority of the knowledge of God to cultivate the virtue of piety. "For this sense of the powers of God is for us a fit teacher of piety," Calvin writes (1.2.1)—defining "*pietas*" as "that reverence joined with love of God which the knowledge of his benefits induces" (1.2.1). For Calvin, genuine piety is the fruit of knowing the immensity of God's grace and blessings on us and the expression of a lifelong response of love and reverence to God. As Hesselink observed; "pietas was [Calvin's] entire theological direction and goal, rather than merely one

---

30. Zachman, *John Calvin*, 19–20.

31. See *Inst.* 4.17.1–50; and Gerrish, "Calvin's Eucharistic Piety."

32. See Calvin, *Institutes of the Christian Religion (1536)*; Battles, *Interpreting John Calvin*, 91–116; and Hesselink, *Calvin's First Catechism*, 42.

33. Battles, *Interpreting John Calvin*, 92–93 (emphasis added).

theme in his theology."[34] Consequently, Calvin elaborates that "until people recognize that they owe everything to God, that they are nourished by His fatherly care, that He is the Author of their every good, so that they should seek nothing beyond Him–they will never yield Him willing service" (1.2.1).

For this reason, Calvin's work on the *Institutes* may be rendered as an extended elaboration of genuine *pietas*. In fact, John McNeill describes it as Calvin's "summa pietatis."[35] Indeed, Calvin would spend the next twenty-four years explicating the concept in the *Institutes*. This is not to say that Calvin did not systematically explain other theological constructs. He did. All his efforts, however, were directed at explaining how theology nurtures progress in the Christian life. As such, my work will extrapolate from the definitive 1559 Latin edition key theological constructs that serve as foundations for the spiritual life, and, arising from that, his method in spiritual guidance.

Having completed the first edition of the *Institutes*, Calvin left Basel for Strasbourg, traveling by a detour through Geneva, for the roads between the two cities were closed by religious wars.[36] He had intended to stopover in Geneva for only a night. But when Guillaume Farel, who was working zealously to reform the church there, heard that Calvin was passing through, he summoned Calvin to help in the work of restoring the church at Geneva. Calvin, however, was reluctant; preferring to be free and quiet so that he might pursue his studies. The feisty Farel, however, would not entertain Calvin's resistance but, instead, resorted to coercion to detain Calvin for the task. In Calvin's words, Farel "went so far as an imprecation, that it might please God to curse the rest and quiet I was seeking, if in so great a necessity I withdrew and refused aid and succour."[37] Horrified and shaken by Farel's imprecation, Calvin could not but remained in Geneva to help.

Calvin was hence initiated into public ministry by Farel, along with Farel's colleague from the Pays-de-vaud, Pierre Viret. As it appeared, these two reformers wielded quite a considerable influence on Calvin, for, as Zachman observed, "throughout the rest of his ministry, Calvin attempted, with varying degrees of success, to wed the prophetic zeal and tenacity of Farel (reminiscent of Luther) with the moderation and self-control of Viret (reminiscent of Bucer and Melanchthon)."[38]

34. Hesselink, *Calvin's First Catechism*, 45.
35. McNeill, "Introduction," in Calvin, *Institutes of the Christian Religion*, li.
36. Wendel, *Calvin: Origins*, 48.
37. Wendel, *Calvin: Origins*, 48.
38. Zachman, *John Calvin*, 22.

Unfortunately, Calvin's initial work at Geneva was short-lived. He and Farel were drawn into conflict with the city council and were expelled from Geneva in 1538. Calvin fled to Strasbourg, disappointed with what appeared to be a failure at Geneva. He was planning on a quiet retreat at Strasbourg. But Martin Bucer had other ideas and constrained Calvin to help with pastoring the many French religious refugees in the church there. As it turned out, the three years at Strasbourg became some of the happiest years for Calvin. In that time, Calvin got married, expanded his literary work, and served as a pastor to the church.[39] Zachman observed that "Calvin especially learned from Bucer how rightly to order the polity and worship of the church, especially with the fourfold office of teacher, pastor, elder, and deacon, and how to order the community via discipline, which Calvin came to describe as the sinews of the body of Christ."[40]

The happy years at Strasbourg, nevertheless, came to an unanticipated end in 1541. The city council at Geneva, who three years before had expelled Calvin, turned to him for help when they were at a loss on how to respond to Cardinal Sadoleto's call for the parish to return to the Roman Church. Calvin, being the pastor at heart, responded to the call for help with a letter's reply to Sadoleto, and a return to Geneva for what would become an extended stay in his work as reformer, teacher, pastor, and guide—till his death in 1564.

CALVIN FORGES HIS OWN THEOLOGICAL METHOD

Against this social-cultural and religious context, Calvin forged his own religious convictions and honed his method in his mission to guide the church. He became deeply committed to two movements that emerged at the beginning of the sixteenth century. First, the recovery of classical and patristic literature, best exemplified by Guillaume Budé and Desiderius Erasmus; and second, the recovery of the gospel in the midst of the Roman Church, best exemplified by Martin Luther and Philip Melanchthon.[41] His method echoed the call to return to the sources which, of primary concern to him, was the gospel as it was found in the Scriptures and as they were carefully expounded by the Fathers.[42]

Richard Muller posits that Calvin was probably influenced by Melanchthon's method of formulating *Loci Communes* (universal topics of

39. Selderhuis, *The Calvin Handbook*, 38–44.
40. Zachman, *John Calvin*, 22.
41. Zachman, *John Calvin*, 15.
42. Lane, *John Calvin*, 3–4.

theology) and *disputationes* (academic exercise or debates) in the way he organized his materials for the *Institutes*. Muller argues that it is "only when Calvin is recognized as a sixteenth-century formulator of an orderly series of theological *loci* and *disputationes* does the true character of his *Institutes* emerges."[43] In this light, Calvin apparently utilized the philosophical and rhetorical instruments of French humanism, and the logic and analysis of scholasticism for his purposes of formulating *loci communes* and *disputationes* in a clear and concise fashion for the instruction of teachers and pastors.

When we further note that Calvin was also firmly convinced by Luther's doctrine of justification by faith, we begin to gather a clearer idea on the method and the content he utilized to craft the *Institutes*. He adapted Melanchthon's organizing principles with the recovery of the gospel through Luther to formulate clear doctrine for the building up of Christian piety and religion.[44] The *Institutes* therefore can be seen as a set of *loci communes* and *disputationes* that serve as a theological and pastoral grid for the task of guidance in the formation of genuine piety. Specifically, they are Calvin's distinctive explication of participation in Christ which, as Billings observed, was "constituted by the *duplex gratia*, the graces of justification and sanctification, which are inseparable but distinguishable."[45] The first grace of justification is accomplished by God's free pardon in imputation—inextricably tied to union with Christ; while in the second grace of sanctification, "Calvin draws deeply upon earlier patristic and medieval theologies of participation as impartation" to explain life in the Holy Spirit.[46] Hence, the *Institutes*, explicates Calvin's distinctive understanding that participation in Christ is effectual through union with God in Christ through the Spirit.

Calvin's humanistic education and interaction with his contemporary reformers forged his self-understanding as teacher, pastor, and guide; and shaped both his strategy for organizing the church and the fundamental tenets for growth in the Christian life. His pastoral and teaching ministry was his way of participating in God's mission for the church and state. Weary of the "useless speculations of scholastic theologians and distorting glosses of the monks that led the Roman Church to ruin," Calvin believed that the way to restore the church was for godly teachers to use their gifts of learning to open access to the reading of Scripture.[47] Zachman explains that Calvin's approach was to teach the sum of doctrine to be sought in Scripture

43. Muller, *The Unaccommodated Calvin*, 188.
44. Zachman, *John Calvin*.
45. Billings, *Calvin, Participation, and the Gift*, 15.
46. Billings, *Calvin, Participation, and the Gift*, 15.
47. Zachman, *John Calvin*, 31.

in the *Institutes*, which in turn opened access to the commentaries. The commentaries then set forth with lucid brevity the true and genuine meaning of Scripture by revealing the mind of the authors of Scripture. The true teacher, therefore, acts as a guide who leads the unlearned by the hand to the goal to be sought in the reading of Scripture. In it, one learns the knowledge of Jesus Christ, who alone opens access to the Father.[48]

"Calvin knew, however, that placing Scripture in the hands of ordinary Christians would not of itself be sufficient. Godly interpreters must also be sent to the church to guide Christians in their reading of the Bible so that they might not get lost in their search for the true knowledge of God."[49] The influence of Bucer, from his time at Strasbourg, was evident as Calvin pondered over how to accomplish this. Calvin became convinced that two kinds of teaching offices were needed. First teachers (or doctors) were needed to teach the universal church its essential dogmas and doctrines of piety, and pastors were needed to apply them to their local congregations. Thus, Calvin began to entrust to teachers the responsibility to teach and guide future pastors, and to pastors the responsibility to teach and care for their respective congregations. Thus, Calvin envisioned a church in which all Christians would read Scripture for themselves, under the guidance of their pastors, who themselves would be guided by the teachers of the church catholic. The course of instruction thus passes from doctrine (*Institutes*) to Scripture (commentaries and lectures) for pastors, so that pastors might teach doctrine (catechism) and Scripture (sermons) to ordinary Christians.[50] The *Institutes*, therefore, became a rather foundational tool for guiding the Church.

THE INSTITUTES OF THE CHRISTIAN RELIGION: STRUCTURE AND MAJOR EMPHASES

We shall now turn to explore how Calvin organized the *Institutes* to convey his major theological criteria for the development of the spiritual life. The *Institutes* are organized into four "Books." Book I discuss "The knowledge of God the Creator," Book II "The knowledge of God the Redeemer in Christ," Book III is an extended discussion of "The Way in Which We Receive the Grace of Christ"—wherein we find a thorough examination of the Christian life, and Book IV a discussion of the Church as "The External Means or

---

48. Zachman, *John Calvin*, 31.

49. Zachman, *John Calvin*, 57.

50. Zachman, *John Calvin*, 61–71.

Aids by Which God Invites Us into The Society of Christ and Holds Us Therein."[51]

Charles Partee observed that while the *Institutes* were grouped into four Books, there has never been complete agreement among Calvin scholars concerning the organizing philosophy behind Calvin's theological presentation.[52] Nevertheless, four views have received major attention as summarized by Partee.[53] The first is that the *Institutes* are structured after the four articles of the Apostles' Creed: Father, Son, Holy Spirit, church. Its primary argument is that the four articles of the Apostles' Creed are correlated with the loci of the four Books. This argument is not only logical but also offers clarity on why Calvin dedicated four Books to the four major emphases contained in the Apostle's Creed, making it the most popular view among interpreters.

A second view was mooted by Edward Dowey who argued that Calvin utilized the twofold knowledge of God as Creator and Redeemer as his organizing principle.[54] Dowey posits that the knowledge of God as Creator is discussed in Book I, while the knowledge of God as Redeemer is discussed in Books II, III, and IV. Dowey derives his argument from Calvin's statement in the 1559 edition that through the universe and the general teaching of Scripture, God shows himself to be the Creator, and through the face of Christ as the Redeemer (1.2.1). The strength of this view, according to Partee, lies in its explication of Calvin's twofold distinction in his theology of the knowledge of God. However, it does not explain why Calvin does not follow that logic by dividing the *Institutes* into two books but instead chose to organize it into four.

A third view, propounded by Philip Butin maintains that the expository outline of the *Institutes* is trinitarian.[55] This view sees the work of the church (Book IV) as a continuation of the work of the Holy Spirit (Book III). In this light, there is a definite focus on the Persons and work of the triune God and on the *ecclesia* as the means through which we are schooled in the way of Christ. According to Partee, its strength lies in its focus on the Trinity but it does not fully account for Calvin's separate attention given to the ministry of the church in Book IV.

A fourth view is proposed by Charles Partee, and it focuses on the theme of Union with Christ. Partee argues that Calvin made a distinction

---

51. Calvin, *Institutes of the Christian Religion*.

52. Partee, *The Theology of John Calvin*, 35.

53. Partee, *The Theology of John Calvin*, 35–43.

54. Dowey, *Knowledge of God*.

55. Butin, *Revelation, Redemption, and Response*.

at the beginning of Book III that suggests that his previous exposition "was concerned with what Christ does *for* us and [that] the subsequent discussion will treat what Christ does *within* us"—hence powerfully affirming the emphasis on our union with Christ.[56] In his schema, the organizing thought of the *Institutes* is divided into two parts. Part One centers on "God For Us." It includes Book I–God as Creator and Book II–God as Redeemer. Part Two discusses "God With Us." It includes Book III–The Faithful Person(s), and Book IV–The Faithful Community. Partee's proposal captures the foundational emphasis in Calvin's theology, which is union with Christ by grace through faith, and possesses the logic that explains Calvin's organization of the four Books, rendering it rather persuasive.

Each of these schemas has their validity and strength. However, we recall that Calvin did not set out to write a systematic theology but a set of teachings in a systematic way. We must not, therefore, be too dogmatic about one particular view. Moreover, we keep in mind Muller's point on the influence of Melanchthon's method, which Calvin apparently used for many sections in his formulations. I will therefore draw on the strengths from each of these four major perspectives to construct an approach to spiritual guidance which, I propose, is consistent with Calvin's own theological convictions. Specifically, I find Charles Partee's view most closely aligned to Calvin's intent as stated in his preface to King Francis. I will elaborate on it further on in this chapter, and compare it with Ignatius' method in the next chapter.

CALVIN'S THEOLOGY OF THE CHRISTIAN LIFE

The Faculties of the Soul

At this point in our endeavor to identify key constructs in Calvin's theology of the Christian life, it is helpful to briefly highlight the main emphasis in each Book of the *Institutes*. We pay particular attention to Calvin's explication of the faculties of the soul for the formation of true knowledge and authentic piety. As a corrective to the philosophers' conception of the soul, which did not take into account Adam's fall, Calvin calls for "a simple definition" that reduces the cognitive faculties (understanding, reason, fantasy) and appetitive faculties (will, the capacity for anger, the capacity to desire inordinately) of the soul to the two main faculties of understanding and will (1.15.6–7).[57] Understanding refers to the ability to distinguish and is

---

56. Partee, *The Theology of John Calvin*, 40.

57. As Horton observes, "Calvin departs somewhat from the traditional restriction

equated with the discursive functions of the mind or intellect. Will refers to the ability to choose the good that the understanding deciphers and is linked to the function of the heart (1.15.8). It may be said that the faculty of understanding significantly engages in a discursive way, while the will, being linked to the heart and responding to the fruits from understanding, engages more in an affective manner. It will become evident, especially in Book III, that Calvin utilizes these two faculties, understanding and will, together with a meditative and contemplative disposition for the cultivation of true piety.

. . . in Relation to The Knowledge of God

We begin with Book I, which has as its focus "The Knowledge of God the Creator," followed by the famous aphorism that "nearly all wisdom we possess, that is to say, true and sound wisdom, consists of two parts: the knowledge of God and of ourselves" (1.1.1). John McNeill observed that this statement stands at the beginning of every edition of the *Institutes*, and sets the limits of Calvin's theology and conditions every subsequent statement.[58] Calvin explains that "no one can look upon himself without immediately turning his thoughts to the contemplation of God, in whom he "lives and moves" [Acts 17:28]" (1.1.1).While one may begin by looking at oneself, it must not end there; for, as Calvin attests, it will either lead to self-condemnation or self-aggrandizement—neither of which is a true knowledge of oneself in God. The pursuit of a knowledge of self must lead to the pursuit of a knowledge of God for, clearly, Calvin emphasizes the priority of the knowledge of God in this twofold knowledge as he adds that "it is certain that man never achieves a clear knowledge of himself unless he has first looked upon God's face, and then descends from contemplating him to scrutinize himself" (1.1.2).

However, "knowledge" (Latin *cognitio*) for Calvin, as McNeill explains, was never "mere" objective knowledge but is more akin to "existential apprehension."[59] So here, at the very beginning of the *Institutes*, we get a sense that Calvin understands true wisdom to be a two-fold knowledge that

---

of the image of God to the soul—much less to a soul thought of as an eternal spark of divinity . . . [For] Calvin argues that not only the soul, with its reasoning capacity, but the "human body" and its senses also are "ingenious." Seated in the soul, the image nevertheless "extends to the whole excellence" of humanity: clear reasoning, acute senses, and even bodily beauty." – Horton, *Calvin on the Christian life*, 63. See also, Calvin, *Institutes* 1.5.2 and 1.15.3.

58. Calvin, *Institutes of the Christian Religion*, 36 n3.

59. Calvin, *Institutes of the Christian Religion*, 35 n1.

engages not just the mind, but also apprehends the heart. God uses both the faculties of understanding (mind) and will (heart) to lead to a true knowledge of God. Indeed, Calvin will continue to emphasize that true knowledge is that which is apprehended in the heart as much as it is grasped by the mind. The mind and the heart are aspects of human apprehension that must mutually engage each other. This focus will receive increased emphasis as we examine Calvin's explanation on how the Holy Spirit applies the Scriptures to our minds and hearts to engender faith and the development of piety (3.2.6–7). Definitively, however, the knowledge of God is communicated through the Son, the second Person of the Trinity—which is Calvin's focus in Book II.

. . . in Relation to the Gospel of Jesus Christ

Book II is an elaborate explication of the gospel of Jesus Christ. It begins with a discussion of the curse upon humankind that came with the fall of Adam and contains a discussion of our human tendency to be deceived by self-admiration and so exposes the gross inadequacy of self-knowledge alone as a means to salvation. Calvin explains that God has both authored and completed the work of salvation through Jesus Christ and has revealed the way to work it into our hearts. Calvin writes: "Therefore the Lord in this way both begins and completes the good work in us. It is the Lord's doing that the will conceives the love of what is right, is zealously inclined toward it, is aroused and moved to pursue it" (2.3.9). It was Calvin's understanding that the possibility of knowing God and growing in this knowledge—which is the Gospel account of eternal life and growth therein—has been inaugurated and completed by God through Christ (John 17:3). Further, Calvin echoes Paul's teaching that while we work out our salvation with fear and trembling, it is God who works in us to will and to act according to his good purpose (Phil 2:12–13). These emphases cohere with Partee's argument that Books I and II may be summed up as God working for us.

. . . in Relation to the Holy Spirit

As we progress to Book III, we discover again Calvin's emphasis on the enjoining of mind and heart in the Christian life, first emphasized in Book I. It also becomes clear how the triune God works with us for our transformation. In his explication of how we come to a "true knowledge of Christ" through faith and the Word, Calvin underscores the necessity that "our mind must be . . . illumined and our heart strengthened" by the Holy Spirit so "that the Word of God may obtain full faith among us" (3.2.7). It is hard to miss both the emphasis on the work of the triune God, and the integration of mind and heart on how faith is engendered in us: "a firm and certain knowledge of God's benevolence toward us, founded upon the truth of the freely given promise in Christ, both revealed to our minds and sealed upon our hearts through the Holy Spirit" (3.2.7). Faith is the fruit of the Holy Spirit integrating the promises of God into our hearts and minds. Calvin explains that the Holy Spirit is "the secret energy . . . by which we come to enjoy Christ and all his benefits" (3.1.1). He is the "bond by which Christ effectually unites us to himself" (3.1.1). The testimony of the Holy Spirit is likened to a "seal upon our hearts" (3.1.1). The Spirit is the "root and seed of heavenly life in us" (3.1.2). In fact, Calvin's recognition of the critical role of the Holy Spirit in faith would lead to the emphasis that the knowledge of God is more a matter of the heart than of the mind. He writes: "that very assent itself . . . is more of the heart than of the brain, and more of the disposition than of the understanding" (3.2.8). Calvin would go on to add that "faith is much higher than human understanding. And it will not be enough for the mind to be illumined by the Spirit of God unless the heart is also strengthened and supported by his power" (3.2.33). Calvin complains that "in this matter the Schoolmen go completely astray, who in considering faith identify it with a bare and simple assent arising out of knowledge, and leave out confidence and assurance of heart" (3.2.33). To the contrary, Calvin emphasizes that "faith is a singular gift of God, both in that the mind of man is purged so as to be able to taste the truth of God and in that his heart is established therein" (3.2.33).[60]

For Calvin, it is mandatory for cognition (understanding with the mind) to work with the affections (grasp with the heart) if progress is to be realized in the Christian life. In fact, he would go so far as to emphasize that faith is effectual and brings full assurance only when it takes root in the depths of our hearts as the following section establishes so passionately:

> It now remains to pour into the heart itself what the mind has absorbed. For the Word of God is not received by faith if it flits about in the top of the brain, but when it takes root in the depth of the heart that it may be an invincible defense to withstand and drive off all the stratagems of temptation. But if it is true that the mind's real understanding is illumination by the Spirit of God, then in such confirmation of the heart his power is much

60. See also Boulton, *Life in God*, 222–228 for his emphasis that "spiritual practices" are in the first place "works of the Holy Spirit and Jesus Christ" working with us and in us for our restoration, regeneration and sanctification. They have everything to do with "divine agency and power" for our sanctification.

more clearly manifested, to the extent that the heart's distrust is greater than the mind's blindness. It is harder for the heart to be furnished with assurance than for the mind to be endowed with thought. The Spirit accordingly serves as a seal, to seal up in our hearts those very promises the certainty of which it has previously impressed upon our minds; and takes the place of a guarantee to confirm and establish them. (3.2.36)

It may be said, from this brief survey of Calvin's understanding of the role of the mind and heart with respect of faith, that Calvin's piety acknowledges the tension between theology and experience.[61] On the one hand, Calvin notes the priority of Scripture and doctrine for the engendering of faith in the mind. On the other hand, he recognizes that the assuring experience arises from the Spirit sealing the promises of Christ in the heart. Theology and experience must therefore work hand-in-hand. For Calvin, faith is engendered through the integration of Word and Spirit in the mind and heart. There might even be a priority of the apprehension of the heart by faith through the Spirit over mere intellectual comprehension.[62]

. . . in Relation to the Holy Catholic Church

Finally, in Book IV, Calvin sets the context within which we are to be nurtured in the faith. It is the holy catholic church, which he fondly refers to as our "mother" (4.1.1). Calvin writes: "I shall start, then with the church, into whose bosom God is pleased to gather his sons, not only that they may be nourished by her help and ministry as long as they are infants and children, but also that they may be guided by her motherly care until they mature and at last reach the goal of faith" (4.1.1). In fact, Calvin places such an emphasis on the role of the church for the nurturing of the believer in Christ that he utilizes a quote from Mark 10:9 as grounds for the metaphor of the church as mother: "'For what God has joined together, it is not lawful to put

61. To be sure, the division between theology and experience or doctrine and life is a post-Enlightenment phenomenon. As Horton observes, "[In modernity], we've learned to draw a line between doctrine and life, with "piety" (like "spirituality") falling on the "life" side of the ledger. The ancient church saw it differently: *eusebia* encompassed doctrine and life. It could be translated "piety" or "orthodoxy" without any confusion. Calvin assumed this overarching horizon. Doctrine, worship, and life are all of one piece. The doctrine is always practically oriented, and practice is always to be grounded in true doctrine." Horton, *Calvin on the Christian Life*, 17.

62. It is here that we notice an appeal to the practice of contemplation as opposed to meditation if we were to differentiate between the two exercises with meditation as a more discursive activity involving the mind and contemplation as a more affective activity involving the heart being acted upon.

asunder' [Mark 10:9 p.], so that, for those to whom he is Father the church may also be Mother" (4.1.1.). Calvin likened the care of the church for the believer to the way a mother would nurse her child.

The church is therefore the context wherein God's children are to be nurtured in the faith, principally through Word and Sacrament in the context of corporate worship.[63] The Word is preached as an audible means to strengthen one's faith, while the Lord's Supper, at which the Lord is mysteriously present through the Spirit, is shared as a visible word to nourish the soul. The preached Word and the visible word thus become auditory and visual means for spiritual nurture and guidance. Through much scriptural support, Calvin would go on to say that "by these words God's fatherly favor and the especial witness of spiritual life are limited to his flock, so that it is always disastrous to leave the church" (4.1.4). Calvin's comment clearly indicates that the church is the primary context through which God's children are to be guided.

CALVIN'S RULE FOR NURTURING THE CHRISTIAN LIFE

From a broad overview of the *Institutes*, we now consider some core theological criteria from Book III, chapters six to ten, which Calvin devoted to his formulation of the Christian life and his method in nurturing true piety. This segment of the *Institutes* has been published separately as a booklet—titled *Golden Booklet of the True Christian Life*—in several languages for a broader Christian audience as early as 1550. Its simpler style, spirit, and graphic language earned it a place that vies with the great Christian classics such as Augustine's *Confessions*, Thomas à Kempis's *Imitation of Christ*, and Bunyan's *Pilgrim's Progress*.[64]

At the fore in this segment, we are met with Calvin's understanding, gathered from Scripture, on the goal for the Christian life: "the object of regeneration . . . is to manifest in the life of believers a harmony and agreement between God's righteousness and their obedience, and thus confirm the adoption that they have received as sons [Gal. 4:5; cf. II Peter 1:10]" (3.6.1). The direction that Calvin sought for the Christian life is to guide the

63. As we examined in chapter three, the nurture of faith through Word and Sacrament in the context of the liturgy in corporate worship effectively enacts the mission of God to his church which, in turns, defines the mission of the church as a people sent by God into the world.

64. See Van Andel, "Preface," in Calvin, *Golden Booklet of the True Christian Life*, 9–12.

believer toward "a harmony and agreement" with God that is expressive of "God's righteousness and their obedience." Thus, he states that his goal is "to show the godly man how he may be directed to a rightly ordered life, and briefly to set down some universal rule with which to determine his duties" (3.6.1).

Calvin elaborates that this "Scriptural instruction" has "two main aspects:" first, "that the love of righteousness . . . may be instilled and established in our hearts; [and] second, that a rule be set forth for us that does not let us wander about in our zeal for righteousness" (3.6.2). First, for Calvin, the way the "love of righteousness" is established in our hearts is through God's redemptive work through the person of Jesus Christ. "Scripture shows that God the Father, as he has reconciled us to himself in his Christ [cf. II Cor. 5:18], has in him stamped for us the likeness [cf. Heb. 1:3] to which he would have us conform" (3.6.3). Discipleship, therefore, has as its goal the full expression of the life of Christ: "that our life [expresses] Christ, the bond of our adoption" (3.6.3). Discipleship is not merely effected by our verbal confession or mental assent. More than that, the knowledge of Christ must penetrate our hearts and dominate our living consciousness, in both mind and heart. Calvin explains: "For it is a doctrine not of the tongue but of life. It is not apprehended by the understanding and memory alone, as other disciplines are, but it is received only when it possesses the whole soul, and finds a seat and resting place in the inmost affection of the heart" (3.6.4). Calvin emphasizes that "it must enter our heart and pass into our daily living, and so transform us into itself that it may not be unfruitful for us" (3.6.4).

For Calvin, then, true discipleship occurs when the knowledge of Christ "penetrate[s] the inmost affections of the heart, takes its seat in the soul, and affect the whole man . . ." (3.6.4). Consequently, Calvin exhorts the believer to a life of integrity before God, in which the whole person is committed to the pursuit of godliness in Christ through the efficacious work of the Holy Spirit. Thus, the goal is "set before our eyes" as that "which we are earnestly to aim." In this direction, we press forward in full integrity, pursuing with "a sincere simplicity of mind, free from guile and feigning, the opposite of a double heart . . . where the inner feeling of the mind is unfeignedly dedicated to God for the cultivation of holiness and righteousness" (3.6.5).

Calvin recognizes the immense challenge such a life would be, but he urges the believer to press on ever so courageously, inching forward daily even if it is ever so slight.

Let each one of us, then, proceed according to the measure of his puny capacity and set out upon the journey we have begun. No one shall set out so inauspiciously as not daily to make some headway, though it be slight. Therefore, let us not cease so to act that we may make some unceasing progress in the way of the Lord. And let us not despair at the slightness of our success; for even though attainment may not correspond to desire, when today outstrips yesterday the effort is not lost. Only let us look toward our mark with sincere simplicity and aspire to our goal; not fondly flattering ourselves, nor excusing our own evil deeds, but with continuous effort striving toward this end: that we may surpass ourselves in goodness until we attain to goodness itself. (3.6.5)

Having exhorted us to such a life, Calvin now expounds on the "rule" he mentioned at the front of the section. We could summarize this rule as a direction for the Christian life that embraces the following major aspects: First, commit to the denial of ourselves (chapter 7). Do so by bearing the cross (chapter 8). Persevere by meditating on the future life (chapter 9). As a way of life, use God's good gifts for every good (chapter 10). With this brief rule, Calvin guides the believer to follow the pattern of Christ. It recalls Jesus' own attitude as described by Paul in Philippians 2:5–8.

Calvin anchors the call to the denial of self on Romans 12:1: "the duty of believers is "to present their bodies to God as a living sacrifice, holy and acceptable to him" (3.7.1). This, for Calvin—and likewise for us—is "the great thing," in that "we are consecrated and dedicated to God in order that we may thereafter think, speak, meditate, and do, nothing except to his glory" (3.7.1). The goal of self-denial is not for one's own salvation—for Christ has already won that for us—but that we might be fully abandoned to live only for God's glory. Calvin repeats three times that "we are not our own" but that "we are God's" (3.7.1). Consequently, the denial of self is "the first step" that we might depart from ourselves in order that we might apply the whole force of our ability to the service of the Lord (3.7.1). This is done through turning the mind "wholly to the bidding of God's Spirit" through the Word, so that we "may no longer live but hear Christ living and reigning" in us (3.7.1).

Here, as before, we note Calvin's emphasis on committing both mind and heart fully to the Lord. The Christian is to turn "his whole intention of mind scrupulously" to Christ and let the denial of self take "possession of [our] hearts," leaving no place for pride or self-love or any other evil that may derail us from the way of Christ (3.7.2). For Calvin, this posture purges from "our inward parts" the "deadly pestilence of love of strife and love of self," and nurtures instead "a heart imbued with lowliness and with reverence for others" (3.7.4). Consequently, the denial of self has both a Godward focus and an outward focus that free us to love and serve our neighbor. "Let this, therefore be our rule for generosity and beneficence: We are the stewards of everything God has conferred on us by which we are able to help our neighbor, and are required to render account of our stewardship. Moreover, the only right stewardship is that which is tested by the rule of love" (3.7.5). By this, Calvin has in mind the double emphasis of the law: love of God and love of neighbor.

The second movement, if it might be so called, is Calvin's rule to bear the cross (3.8.1). Here again, Christ serves as our example. The "godly mind is to climb still higher, to the height to which Christ calls his disciples: that each must bear his own cross [Matt. 16:24]" (3.8.1). Calvin explains that the cross leads us to perfect trust in God's power. "It teaches us, thus humbled, to rest upon God alone, with the result that we do not faint or yield" (3.8.3). The cross anchors our hope in God alone. It teaches us patience and instructs us in the way of obedience (3.8.4). Moreover, in God's fatherly care and discipline, the cross serves also a "medicine" for the cure of "the wanton impulse of our flesh" (3.8.5).

Rising above these benefits in cross-bearing, however, is the principal reason that we might rest fully in God's will. Calvin understands the contradictions we experience when we are beneath the cross. We wrestle with the tension between the polarities of our natural sense and of the Christ-centered sense. Our "hearts still harbor a contradiction between their natural sense, which flees and dreads what it feels adverse to itself, and their disposition to godliness, which even through these difficulties presses toward obedience to the divine will" (3.8.10). Within that tension, Calvin once more directs our attention to Scripture and find there the critical insights for the cross. "But Scripture bids us contemplate in the will of God something far different: namely, first righteousness and equity, then concern for our own salvation" (3.8.11). Consequently, we are able, despite the outer travails to the contrary, to rest with spiritual joy in God's good will: "These thoughts, I say, bring it to pass that, however much in bearing the cross our minds are constrained by the natural feeling of bitterness, they are as much diffused with spiritual joy" (3.8.11).

I gather the sense that what Calvin means by "contemplate in the will of God something far different" that we might "rest with spiritual joy in God's good will" rises beyond mere human understanding (or cognition) to a disposition of receptivity (a matter more of the heart) in which the Holy Spirit, through the Word of God, brings to the soul the assurance of God's mysterious work even in the face of difficulties arising from the cross. God, through his Word and the Holy Spirit, reaps within the disciple spiritual joy in response to the contemplative receptivity of the disciple. We might say that, for Calvin, the practice of contemplation is the disciple's inclining of heart and mind, in a disposition of receptivity, as trust in God's good will.

The Christian thus perseveres by meditating, not on the circumstances of the immediate, but on the certainty of the future hope (3.9.1). This is the third movement. Calvin is not unfamiliar with the intensity of struggles amidst the storms of reformation. He describes this life as "troubled, turbulent, unhappy in countless ways, and in no respect clearly happy; that all those things which are judged to be its goods are uncertain, fleeting, vain, and vitiated by many intermingled evils" (3.9.1). Thus, Calvin urges the Christian to "raise our eyes to heaven" (3.9.1). For Calvin, there is in fact no middle ground: "either the world must become worthless to us or hold us bound by intemperate love of it" (3.9.2). This is not to say that Calvin was not grateful for this earthly life and its goods. He was—and he has much to say on the proper use of God's good gifts. The contempt for this world is simply in dramatic contrast to love of God and eternal life. Hence Calvin exhorts: "Let the aim of believers in judging mortal life, then, be that while they understand it to be of itself nothing but misery, they may with greater eagerness and dispatch betake themselves wholly to meditate upon that eternal life to come" (3.9.4). The future hope thus serves to sustain the disciple in the present life. For "if believers' eyes are turned to the power of the resurrection, in their hearts the cross of Christ will at last triumph over the devil, flesh, sin, and wicked men" (3.9.6). Here, Calvin points the direction on the way forward in the Christian life.

In chapter ten, Calvin paints a portrait of the way we should now live: as a pilgrim—a thing Calvin was all too familiar with for much of his life. Pilgrims travel light. Pertaining to earthly goods, Calvin encourages a posture of moderation: "to use them with a clear conscience, whether for necessity or for delight" (3.10.1). It is a balanced piety that is neither "far too severe" nor far too lax (3.10.1). The former tendency would "abstain from all things that they could do without" while the latter tendency seeks "an excuse for the intemperance of the flesh in its use of external things" (3.10.1). Neither is helpful. Instead, Calvin offers a principle: "that the use of Gods' gifts is not wrongly directed when it is referred to that end to which the Author himself created and destined them for us, since he created them for our good, not for our ruin" (3.10.2). The focus here is on God the giver of all good gifts, and so all things must be utilized with that frame of reference in mind. The middle path that Calvin urges avoids the extremes of "narrow-mindedness" and "immoderation" (3.10.3). Following the apostle Paul, Calvin offers two rules: first, "those who use this world should be so affected as if they did not use it; those who marry, as if they did not marry; those who buy, as if they did not buy . . ." (3.10.4); second, "they should know how to bear poverty peaceably and patiently, as well as to bear abundance moderately" (3.10.4). These two rules essentially teach the Christian the way of temperance. To be sure, Calvin adds a third rule from Scripture, that is, that our earthly possessions are entrusted to us, and we must one day render an account of them (3.10.5). In all these exhortations, the main point for Calvin remains; to live as God has called us to live: "The Lord bids each one of us in all life's actions to look to his calling" (3.10.6). The consolation would then be: "that no task will be so sordid and base, provided you obey your calling in it, that it will not shine and be reckoned very precious in God's sight" (3.10.6).

CALVIN'S PERSPECTIVE ON CHRISTIAN PIETY

From these preceding explications of the Christian life, we gather a glimpse of Calvin's perspective on Christian piety—which he defines as "that reverence joined with love of God which the knowledge of his benefits induces" (1.2.1). Contrary to the punitive images of God that dominated his day, Calvin describes God as Father who lovingly and freely bestows his mercies and benefits upon his children. In contrast to the fearsome images, Calvin portrays the Scriptural image of God who is God "for us"—the image of God as awesome Creator, benevolent Father, compassionate Redeemer in Christ Jesus, and the Holy Spirit as seal upon our hearts. Such an image of God engenders a response of reverence and love, which is expressed in right worship. Thus, Calvin understands Christian piety to rest on a right knowledge of God. Calvin's piety embraces wholesome living images of God that leads to wholesome authentic acts of worship in reverence and love.[65]

Foundationally, Calvin's piety is a piety of Word and Spirit—the definitive means through which God communicates with us. As much as Calvin points the Christian to the Word, he equally emphasizes that the Word is confirmed by the Holy Spirit.[66] The Holy Spirit is the inner witness in our minds and hearts. For Calvin, Word and Spirit belong inseparably together: as "a kind of mutual bond" to seal the promises of God upon the heart of the believer. Calvin's definition of faith makes this clear (3.2.7). The Holy Spirit brings assurance to the believer as the Spirit enjoins the promises of God in Christ upon the disciple's mind and heart.[67] This trinitarian emphasis leads

65. *Inst.*, Book 1. See also, Zachman, *John Calvin*, 231–60.

66. *Inst.* 1.6–7, 9. See also Richard, *The Spirituality of John Calvin*, 136–73.

67. Here again, we are persuaded that contemplation of God is intimately connected to what the Holy Spirit does in us. Coe and Strobel describe contemplation as

us to a right knowledge of God. It possesses both objective and personal dimensions as it is witnessed in the inspired Word and impressed upon the receptive heart by the Spirit. Calvin's piety enjoins Bible, theology, and Christian experience. They are bound together in a way that strengthens each other. This faith knowledge will serve the Christian well in times of discernment—a subject to which we will turn in the next chapter (1.6.1–4, 1.9.3).

Further, Calvin's piety is nurtured through the practice of prayer—which we will also explore in the next chapter. He explains that prayer is "the chief exercise of faith . . . by which we daily receive God's benefits" (3.20.1). For Calvin, the practice of prayer, personal and corporate, is a necessity for sound Christian living. Calvin guides its practice through several "rules" he explicates in the *Institutes* (3.20.4–16). He also composed many prayers which serve to inspire and guide. Here, again, the Holy Spirit aids and guides the Christian to pray. I will discuss Calvin's teaching on prayer for insights on Christian guidance in the next chapter.

Finally, Calvin situates the practice of spiritual guidance within the Church. As we have noted earlier, he argued from Scripture for the offices of doctors and ministers to teach and guide the church. They, in turn, are assisted by elders and deacons (4.3.4–9). For Calvin, spiritual guidance always retains the horizon of the ecclesia as its context. It derives its basis from the confessions of the church and its instituted practices. In this regard, Word and Sacrament rightly instituted within the Church serves to nurture and to guide the Christian in the way of Christ. In fact, Calvin refers to the Lord's Supper as the enacted "visible word," the power of which rests upon the "audible word" spoken through the sermon (4.14.6). Word as "foundation" and the sacraments as "pillars" serve as an edifice that helps us to contemplate the riches of God's grace (4.16.6). B. A. Gerrish has noted that Calvin's piety was very much a "Eucharistic Piety."[68] In summary, these four major emphases—wholesome living images of God (definitively seen in Christ), the mutual bond of Word and Spirit, the daily practice of prayer, and the church as the context for spiritual guidance—reflect an understanding of Calvin's piety.

We may thus summarize Calvin's piety in the following manner. First, it is a trinitarin piety for all three Persons of the triune God participate

---

"a call to attend to the presence of God that has been made available in Christ by the Spirit." The focus is not on a certain technique, variously rendered as "contemplation" in a variety of religions and New Age practices. Rather, the focus is on "receiving the presence and love of God in Christ by the Spirit." See Coe and Strobel, "Introduction," in *Embracing Contemplation*, 6–7.

68. Gerrish, "Calvin's Eucharistic Piety"; and Gerrish, *Grace and Gratitude*.

together to establish and complete piety in the disciple. This quality is evident both in the way the *Institutes* is organized, and in the many emphases found within it; most evidently in Calvin's definition of faith. As aspects of trinitarian piety, it possesses a theological focus—depicting a wholesome picture of God the Father, merciful, loving, and benevolent. It possesses a christological focus—pointing the disciple to Jesus and the way of the cross. It retains a pneumatological focus—for it is a piety that integrates the mind and heart through the interior work of the Spirit, progressing beyond intellectual assent into heart-felt apprehension through the faith-producing work of the Spirit. Second, it is a scriptural piety, for Calvin's principles and criteria for the spiritual life are all drawn from Scripture. Scripture is the "spectacles" through which we come to know God (2.6.1), and Scripture will supply the nutrients for which to grow our life in God. The Spirit always testifies to the Word. Third, it is a balanced piety: it encourages temperance in Christian freedom, a middle path between extreme tendencies. Finally, it is a "Eucharistic piety" with a telos in eternity: each time a disciple celebrates the Lord's Supper, he looks beyond the here and now to the eternal, beyond the material to the non-material, beyond the contingent to God's good will. It is a piety that seeks to love God and neighbor in word and deed.

7

John Calvin's Method of Spiritual Guidance

WITH A GRASP OF the historical factors that shaped Calvin's theology of the Christian life and an understanding of his explication of Christian piety and its development, we continue to plumb the depths in the *Institutes* to uncover more theological criteria for founding and nurturing the spiritual life. From these collective insights, we will gather an understanding on how Calvin guided the church. It will becoming clear that Calvin's method of spiritual guidance, as seen in the *Institutes*, is framed within a two-phased process of mystical union and deepening communion with Christ.

Calvin writes, "For we await salvation from him not because he appears to us afar off, but because he makes us, ingrafted into his body, participants not only in all his benefits but also in himself . . . But since Christ has been so imparted to [us] with all his benefits that all his things are made [ours], that [we] are made a member of him, indeed one with him, his righteousness overwhelms [our] sins; his salvation wipes out [our] condemnation; with his worthiness he intercedes that [our] unworthiness may not come before God's sight. Surely this is so: We ought not to separate Christ from ourselves or ourselves from him. Rather we ought to hold fast bravely with both hands to that fellowship by which he has bound himself to us . . . And to confirm this [the Apostle Paul] uses the same reason I have brought forward: that Christ is not outside us but dwells within us. Not only does he cleave to us by an indivisible bond of fellowship, but with a wonderful communion, day by day, he grows more and more into one body with us, until he becomes completely one with us" (3.2.24).[1]

Calvin's spiritual guidance is inextricably tied to the twofold grace of justification and sanctification in his soteriology, which are his summary theological constructs that reflects his understanding of God's redemptive work in Christ and progress of our life in God. Resting upon the firm assurance of one's mystical union with Christ, Calvin charts a life-long pursuit of deepening communion with Christ through the habits of repentance and prayerful contemplation, which expresses a persevering faith in the worship of God and service to humankind. This, I propose, is Calvin's two-pronged method in spiritual guidance.

Calvin often applies many of his principles from the *Institutes* in his letters, which served to address the challenges that confront the Christian life. For example, in his letter to Viret, dated Aug 23, 1542, regarding serious differences in opinion on the Lord's Supper among the churches in the Synod of Berne, Calvin offers the following advice to pay careful attention to the reality of both union and communion with Christ in the reception of the Lord's Supper. He reminds Viret of the testimony "that there is not only figured in the Supper, but actually exhibited, that communion which we have with Christ, and that not words merely are bestowed upon us by the Lord, but that the truth and the reality agrees with the words. Moreover, [Calvin emphasizes,] that this communion is no imaginary thing, but that we are united, each individually, in one body and one substance, with Christ."[2] Calvin's letters are concrete examples of how he serves as a spiritual guide in daily life. I will include further illustrations from the letters on how Calvin applies his theology to his method of spiritual guidance as the chapter develops. For now, however, I wish to explain Calvin's twofold emphasis for the Christian life, as it is evinced in the *Institutes*.

---

1. In Johnson, *One with Christ*, 15, he emphasizes that, for Calvin, our union with Christ means that we are united to the "personal indwelling of Christ" and not just benefitting from the work of Christ. Concerned with evangelicalism's tendency to separate the work of Christ from the person of Christ in our understanding of salvation, Johnson writes that "[in] far too many evangelical expressions of the gospel, the saving work of Christ has been so distanced from his person that the notion of a saving *personal* union with the incarnate, crucified, resurrected, *living* Jesus strikes us as rather outlandish. We are content, more often than not, to refer to the "atoning work of Christ" or the "work of Christ on the cross" as the basis for our salvation. Yet, as important as such expressions are for a robust evangelical soteriology (the study of salvation), we are in dire need of the reminder that Christ's saving work is of no benefit to us unless we are joined to the living Savior whose work it is." As Johnson underscores, Calvin insisted "that we must never separate the work of Christ from his person if we wish to understand the nature of salvation."

2. Calvin, *Letters of John Calvin*, 4:333.

MYSTICAL UNION WITH CHRIST:
CALVIN'S FOUNDATION FOR THE CHRISTIAN LIFE

For Calvin, our mystical union with Christ provides a firm foundation of assurance for the pursuit of godliness. Union with Christ was his response and corrective to the Roman Church's teaching on justification by grace-assisted meritorious works.[3] For Calvin, union with Christ rests solely upon Christ's finished work of atonement and redemption, is extended to us by God's grace, and received by faith enabled by the Holy Spirit. Calvin explains:

> Let us sum these up. Christ was given to us by God's generos-ity, to be grasped and possessed by us in faith. By partaking of him, we principally receive a double grace: namely, that being reconciled to God through Christ's blamelessness, we may have in heaven instead of a Judge a gracious Father; and secondly, that sanctified by Christ's spirit we may cultivate blamelessness and purity of life. (3.11.1)

It is crucial that we understand Calvin's elaboration of this foundation for the Christian life. For Calvin, union with Christ effects the reception of the double grace of justification and sanctification, which are intimately connected yet distinct from each other. They are connected because they are both effective at the point of faith reception and are simultaneously given to the believer. One flow into the other that reflects the intimate union with Christ; and so justification continues into sanctification as a reflection of union with the whole Christ.[4] But they are also distinct; for justification, as the remission of our sins and imputation of Christ's righteousness to us is complete at the point of faith, while sanctification, as the lifelong work of cultivating blamelessness and purity of life through the Holy Spirit, is not.

Justification is complete because Christ's righteousness is imputed to us and so in the forensic act God reckons us as righteous based on Christ's righteousness. It is a judicial declaration of righteousness: we are

---

3. See Gaffin, "Justification and Union with Christ," 248–69, for a discussion of this issue. See also, Johnson, *One with Christ*, and Billings, *Union with Christ*.

4. See Gaffin's citation of Garcia, "This summary, with which Calvin opens his treat-ment of justification expresses what may be described as 'his triangulation of union with Christ, justification, and sanctification.'" Gaffin, "Justification and Union with Christ," 253. Also note Gaffin's comment that "these three elements are fairly taken as points of reference that largely determine the framework of Calvin's thinking, all told on the application of redemption, the personal appropriation of the finished salvation accomplished by Christ, with which he is formally occupied in book 3 of the *Institutes*." Gaffin, "Justification and Union with Christ," 253.

once-and-for-all declared righteous before God (3.11.1–4). Our righteousness, however, is purely based on Christ's imputed righteousness and not,
as in Osiander's mistake, of inheriting God's righteousness in our ontological selves as a crass-mixture (3.11.5–6). We do not inherit an "essential
righteousness" but an imputed righteousness through spiritual union with
Christ. So, the first grace resulting from our union with Christ is that we are
fully justified before God.

Union with Christ, however, carries a second grace that continues into
a life-long discipleship of increasing sanctification. This second grace was
simultaneously given at the point of faith but is distinct from justification.
Sanctification is now expressed, also by Holy Spirit-enabled faith, in the
ongoing practice of discipleship. It is important to note that both justification and sanctification stem from the same faith enabled by the Holy Spirit,
though their roles are distinct.

Paying careful attention to the connection and distinction between
justification and sanctification is important in view of the Roman issue of
meritorious works cooperating with grace (3.11.13–20). When we fail to
see that justification and sanctification is a two-fold grace received by faith
through the Holy Spirit as the result of union with Christ, we may be mistaken that justification can be earned by meritorious works, even when we
see them as efforts to cooperate with grace (2.2.6). In that case we may also
be tempted to work towards sanctification by our own efforts and see it as
our initiative to grow into union with God.

But, as Calvin asserts, our wills were completely disabled through
the problem of original sin and were unable even to cooperate with grace.
We were totally depraved in sin and not just incapacitated as the Roman
Church argued. The gravity of sin made it impossible to move the unregenerate will to cooperate with grace. We can only do so after being regenerated
by the saving grace of Christ, received by faith, through the agency of the
Holy Spirit (2.2.6). So, Calvin reminds us that just as we are justified by
grace through faith, we are likewise sanctified by grace through faith. We
are not on the one hand justified by faith and then subsequently sanctified
by works. Rather, for Calvin, we are both justified and sanctified by faith
through spiritual union with Christ. Consequently, justification and sanctification are intimately tied and inseparably connected to the faith reality of
union with Christ.

While both justification and sanctification are given simultaneously at
the point of faith, sanctification continues through a lifetime because of the
remnants of our sinful nature. Osiander misunderstood that we now possess the actual righteousness of God. But there is no confusion or mixture.
We are judicially reckoned as righteous before God but our growth into

increasing Christ-likeness takes a life-time because the vestiges of the flesh continue to linger in us. Hence, we must continue to exercise faith through the Holy Spirit and practice works of faith that cultivates a deepening communion with Christ toward increasing sanctification.

Without this understanding of sanctification, we might be tempted either to think that we are entirely sanctified or that we must continue to work for our sanctification through our own efforts. Our contemporary culture is significantly driven by self-agency and self-achievement, so much so that a similar mindset spills over into the spiritual life, leading some to the inclination to either work for their salvation or work at their sanctification by their own efforts. Consequently, it is vitally important to understand the basis for, continuity, and distinction, between justification and sanctification.[5]

Calvin describes justification as the main hinge of salvation. In that sense, there is a certain priority given to it. But that does not mean that we accept justification by faith, and then decide later whether we will embark on working at sanctification by faith. Justification is prior only in that it is God's "first" reckoning of us through the imputed righteousness of Christ. But justification is so tightly coupled with sanctification that it simultaneously continues into it, so much so that our works of faith in sanctification are evidence that we have indeed received by faith God's justification.

Consequently, for Calvin, works in sanctification are important as they evince the life of union with Christ. Calvin adds that though our works are never faultless, yet they are nevertheless received as good works because they are done by faith through the Holy Spirit. They are confident expressions of children who are secure before their heavenly Father. As Calvin clarifies, we are "trained through good works to meditate upon the presentation or fruition, so to speak, of those things which [God] has promised, and to hasten through them to seek the blessed hope held out to us in heaven" (3.18.3). Calvin applies this truth in a letter to the church at Geneva. Knowing that

---

5. Calvin elaborates on how this doctrine is experienced in daily living in a letter to a certain Monsieur De Saint Laurens. In it, Calvin denies the accusation of his opponents that he does not teach that good works follow justification. While Calvin, in fact, does emphasize good works, he was careful not to derive any confidence from them for justification, but rest our justification solely upon the mercy of God. See the follow extract from the letter in Calvin et al., *Selected Works of John Calvin*, 5:256: "They take occasion on this account to accuse us of making no account of good works, whereby they do us wrong; for we are far more careful to recommend holy living, than are any of our adversaries. But in order that men may not deceive themselves by an overweening confidence, we teach that we are able to do nothing whatever in our own strength, unless God guides us by his Holy Spirit, and that even when we had done all, this would afford a far too feeble ground whereon to found our justification; that we must therefore have continual recourse to the mercy of God, and to the merit and passion of Jesus Christ; and that it is there that we must rest our hope, making no account of all the rest."

the parishioners were facing severe adversities, Calvin sustains their faith by reminding them of the blessed hope they have in heaven. He urged them to "take comfort from this blessed hope" so that they might be strengthened to endure patiently and to "willingly commit all to the guidance of [God's] providence."[6]

Ultimately, the importance of understanding the connection and distinction between justification and sanctification as a double grace from union with Christ by God's grace through Holy Spirit-empowered faith, is that it must be the only and unmistakable foundation upon which we relate to God and do the work of spiritual guidance today. In Calvin's eyes, any hint of the Roman view of salvation, that of purgation leading to illumination to union, would make a mockery both of God's righteous judgment and the atoning work of Christ on the cross. As Canlis puts it: "Calvin shrugs off [the stylistic device of purgation, illumination, and union] like an old garment and exclusively focuses on the believer's ascent *en Christo* [Latin: in Christ]."[7] We cannot find our own way back to God when our wills are unregenerate, even if we try to cooperate with grace. The journey can only begin through mystical union with Christ—for it is Christ who ascended to God, and we do so only in him. Then the implications roll out in a life of increasing sanctification by faith, involving good works. Even so, sanctification will never be complete in this life but only in the eternal hope. Still, we stand assured and confident before God because of the imputed righteousness of Christ through which God has reckoned us as justified; and if justified, we will also be sanctified.

DEEPENING COMMUNION WITH CHRIST: THE HEARTBEAT OF CALVIN'S PIETY

Having laid a strong foundation for the Christian life through our mystical union with Christ, Calvin goes on to elaborate how the Holy Spirit leads

6. Calvin, *Letters of John Calvin*, 4:84. See also Calvin's letter to Philip Melanchthon in Calvin, *Letters of John Calvin*, 4:362, where he expressed the same comfort he derives from the blessed hope amid labors.

7. See Canlis, *Calvin's Ladder*, 43–49 for a discussion on communion with God through the paradigm of "ascent." There, she differentiates between Aquinas' and Calvin's views of participation in God, the former being based on a "substantial ontology," and the latter on "election." Canlis writes that a "comparison of Aquinas and Calvin reveals that, while Calvin picks up on [the scholastic scheme of "sapiential" theology, especially as seen in Aquinas' golden circle,] he also fundamentally alters it . . . [We] discover that it no longer is the story of humanity's ascent to God by grace (Aquinas), or of the soul's ascent (Augustine), but of Christ's ascent."

us to deepen our lives in God through communion with Christ. Beeke has shown that "[the] heartbeat of Calvin's practical theology and piety is communion (*communio*) with Christ."[8] Communion is the expression of participation (*participatio*) in the benefits of Christ. It is entered into via the agency of the Holy Spirit and serves as a foundational spiritual theology for growth in the Christian life.

Calvin laments that "not all indiscriminately embrace that communion with Christ which is offered through the gospel" (3.1.1). He argues that "reason itself teaches us to climb higher and to examine into the secret energy of the Spirit, by which we come to enjoy Christ and all his benefits" (3.1.1). And so, he urges us to let the Holy Spirit guide us into deeper communion with Christ. Expressing this understanding, Calvin often begins his letters with a greeting for the blessing of God's love and the grace of Christ, that comes through the communication, or power, or communion of the Holy Spirit, to be with his parishioners.[9] For Calvin, the life of faith in Christ awaits continuing growth in communion through the agency of the Holy Spirit.

In this vein, there is significant evidence in the *Institutes,* and his correspondences, that Calvin emphasizes deepening communion with God through prayer, and the practices of repentance and contemplation for growth in the Christian life. Prayer as conversation with God is to pervade our lives as disciples. We are also to engage in a life-long race of repentance that leads to increasing surrender to God. And we must nurture a posture of contemplation that leads to a deepening awareness of God's action in us. All these are aspects of growth in deepening communion with God. When these habits are nurtured through Word and Sacrament, with heart and mind, they issue in worship and service.

Prayer: The Chief Exercise of Faith

The permeating exercise for deepening communion with God, in a posture of repentance and contemplation, is prayer. Calvin describes prayer as "the chief exercise of faith" (3.20.1). It is "a communion of men with God by which, having entered the heavenly sanctuary, they appeal to him in person concerning his promises in order to experience, where necessity so demands, that what they believed was not in vain, although he had promised it

8. Beeke, "Appropriating Salvation," 273. See also *Inst.* 3.6.2, 3.8.1, 3.14.2, 3.15.1.

9. See, for example, Calvin et al., *Selected Works of John Calvin,* letters 25, 37, 344, 346, 351, 363, 414, 415 that use "by the communication of the Holy Spirit," or 85, "by the power of the Holy Spirit," or 202, "by the communion of the Holy Spirit."

in word alone" (3.20.2). For Calvin, prayer is a "colloquium"— "an intimate conversation of the pious with God" (3.20.4).

Calvin, however, was careful to guard the idea of conversation against any hint of casualness. Instead, he urges reverence and moderation "lest we give loose rein to miscellaneous requests, and lest we crave more than God allows" (3.20.16). He instructs that "we should lift up our minds to a pure and chaste veneration of him, lest God's majesty become worthless for us" (3.20.16). Nevertheless, he did not hesitate to describe prayer as "familiar" conversation with God; central to the idea of "colloquium." Steven Chase explains that this idea "connotes acquaintanceship, intimacy, friendship, and ultimately the safe, shared, and loving conversation one might find within a family . . . [Chase adds that] prayer as conversation with God is the primary speech of the true self to the true God. In prayer, we come to live and dwell in a familiar, intimate, and loving way with God."[10]

Indeed, prayer as conversation with God is not casual speech but the reverential and reflective atmosphere in which we deepen our communication with God. Just as conversation involves speaking and listening, the practice of prayer implies that we learn to speak as well as listen to God— with and without words. As Calvin argues, its power is further enhanced when joined with meditation: "Accordingly, among our prayers, meditation both on God's nature and on his Word is by no means superfluous. And so by David's example, let us not disdain to insert something that may refresh our languishing spirits with new vigor" (3.20.13). Prayer, as a primary spiritual practice, can strengthen our spirits by helping us to hear God, which is often more transforming that speaking. Prayer leads us into that deep communion which the Psalmist testifies to in the Scriptures.

Calvin's teaching on prayer is intimately connected to his teaching on faith, the Word, and the Holy Spirit. Calvin explains that just as the only way to God is by faith, the only way to pray is to be instructed by faith (3.20.1). Hence Hesselink attests that "true prayer is impossible apart from faith, stems from faith, and is a fruit of faith."[11] Faith, equally, is intimately connected to the work of the Holy Spirit, through whom we also receive the grace of Christ. Calvin describes faith as "the principal work of the Holy Spirit" (3.1.4). Further, the Holy Spirit engenders faith through the Word, which he illumines to our minds and seals upon our hearts (3.2.7). Prayer, as an exercise, is therefore intimately connected to the work of the Holy Spirit, who nurtures our faith through the illumination of the Word in our minds and hearts. Through this means, we both grow in our ability to hear God

10. Chase, *The Tree of Life: Models of Christian Prayer*, 59.
11. Hesselink, "Introduction: John Calvin on Prayer," 3.

and in our confidence to speak with God. It is therefore critical to attend to Calvin's guidance on prayer, especially as seen in how the Spirit engenders faith to receive God's grace in Christ.

As I have elaborated, Calvin premised the reception of God's grace purely upon our spiritual union to Christ by faith through the Holy Spirit (3.1.1). The Holy Spirit is "the bond that unites us to Christ," and we profit from the things spoken concerning Christ "by the secret working of the Spirit" (3.1.1). We have noted that faith is the "principal work of the Holy Spirit" (3.1.4). In his commentary on II Thess. 2:13, which he cited in the *Institutes*, Calvin emphasized that "the Spirit is the inner teacher by whose effort the promise of salvation penetrates into our minds, a promise that would otherwise only strike the air or beat upon our ears" (3.1.4). For Calvin, there is no other enabler of faith than the Holy Spirit. He is the one who builds the confidence which rests upon God's Word that is given in Christ. It is hard to miss Calvin's trinitarian emphasis in his definition of faith as he sums up these insights. Faith is "a firm and certain knowledge of God's benevolence toward us, founded upon the truth of the freely given promise in Christ, both revealed to our minds and sealed upon our hearts through the Holy Spirit" (3.2.7).

The role of the Holy Spirit in engendering faith so that we might receive God's grace through prayer is, therefore, crucial to the work of spiritual guidance. Calvin describes the Holy Spirit as "the spirit of adoption" who guides us to call God "Abba, Father." He is our "guarantee and seal" who "assures us that our salvation is safe in God's unfailing care" (3.1.3). By his secret watering, we became fruitful; by his anointing; we are nourished. His refining "fire" burns away "our vicious and inordinate desires;" and "enflames our hearts with the love of God and with zealous devotion" (3.1.3). By "the inspiration of his power he so breathes divine life into us that we are no longer actuated by ourselves, but are ruled by his action and prompting" (3.1.3). Therefore, Calvin summarily concludes that "until our minds become intent upon the Spirit, Christ, so to speak, lies idle because we coldly contemplate him as outside ourselves–indeed, far from us" (3.1.3). The regenerating work of the Holy Spirit is therefore the uncompromising means through which we learn to pray. As the principal worker of faith, the Holy Spirit guides us in the chief exercise of faith. The Spirit engenders faith in us and helps us to continually appropriate the grace of Christ in communion with God.

Consequently, Calvin frequently appeals to the action of the Holy Spirit in spiritual guidance in his letters. He often concludes his letters with prayers for the Holy Spirit to guide,[12] rule,[13] direct,[14] govern,[15] strengthen,[16] or sustain[17] his readers. Calvin recognizes that the Holy Spirit is the sanctifying power in the pursuit of Christian maturity. These correspondences tell us that Calvin consistently applies his theology of the Holy Spirit to his practice of spiritual guidance throughout his ministry.

Calvin's Reasons for Prayer

Calvin dedicates one of the longest chapters in the *Institutes* (Book 3 Chapter 20) to a discussion on prayer. He begins by offering six reasons why prayer is such an important exercise of faith (3.20.3). First, prayer inflames our hearts with a zealous and burning desire ever to seek, love, and serve God while we become accustomed in every need to flee to him as to a sacred anchor. Second, prayer guards us against any desire or wish that we may be ashamed of before God even as we learn to pour our whole hearts, even all our wishes, before him. Third, prayer prepares us to receive his benefits with true gratitude of heart and thanksgiving; our prayer reminds us that these benefits come from his hand [cf. Ps 145:15–16]. Fourthly, having obtained what we were seeking, and being convinced that he has answered our prayers, prayer leads us to meditate upon his kindness more ardently. Fifthly, prayer helps us to embrace with greater delight those things which we acknowledge to have been obtained through it. Finally, through constant practice and experience, we confirm God's providence through prayer. While we understand that God's promises never fail and that he opens the way for us to call on him in our time of need, God is quick to extend his help to us, not by "wet-nursing" us with words but by coming to our defense with present help (3.20.3).

From these reasons, Calvin helps us to see that prayer, as an exercise of faith, is of fundamental importance to our sanctification. The only way to make progress in the Christian life is to constantly appropriate God's words and apply them in prayer. In one of his letters to the brethren of Poitiers,

---

12. See Calvin et al., *Selected Works of John Calvin*, letters 159, 161, 177, 183, 187, 191, 212, 215.

13. See Calvin et al., *Selected Works of John Calvin*, letter 197.

14. See Calvin et al., *Selected Works of John Calvin*, letters 83, 84, 98, 102, 105, 134, 151, 159, 173, 338.

15. See Calvin et al., *Selected Works of John Calvin*, letters 105, 387, 391, 393, 549, 563.

16. See Calvin et al., *Selected Works of John Calvin*, letters 28, 178.

17. See Calvin et al., *Selected Works of John Calvin*, letters 389, 522, 532.

who were stretched in faith and faint-hearted, Calvin illustrates how to apply this teaching by offering the following guidance: ". . . both by prayer and continual exercise of the word of God . . . arm and fortify yourselves, in the hope that the good Shepherd who has taken you under his charge, will not forsake you in time of need."[18]

Calvin's Rules for Right Prayer

Calvin also offers specific guidelines to help us embark on the practice of prayer. First, he sets some rules for right prayer. Then, he uses the structure of the Lord's Prayer as a guide for our practice. Calvin includes teaching on public and private prayer, vocal prayers and prayers that are sung, as well as other concerns related to prayer. They require a more detailed analysis which is beyond the scope of this chapter. Here, however, I wish to highlight how Calvin guides the practice of prayer through a brief discussion of some basic rules.

Calvin offers four rules for right prayer (3.20.4–16). The first rule enjoins reverence in prayer. Calvin writes: "Now for framing prayer duly and properly, let this be the first rule: that we be disposed in mind and heart as befits those who enter conversation with God" (3.20.4). We notice Calvin's use of "mind and heart," which, as part of being the faculties of the soul, calls for the engagement of the whole person. Calvin was urging the one who prays to come in the totality of being into prayer—not half-hearted, divided, or irreverent. Calvin acknowledges that we are not always able to be integrated in mind and heart, so he reminds us that the Holy Spirit will help us and become "our teacher in prayer." The Holy Spirit "arouses in us assurance, desires, and sighs, to conceive which our natural powers would scarcely suffice" (3.20.4–5).

As a second rule, Calvin urges "that in our petitions we ever sense our own insufficiency, and earnestly pondering how we need all that we seek, join with this prayer an earnest—nay, burning—desire to attain it" (3.20.6–7). Calvin guides us to take our prayers seriously before God. Here, Calvin draws from the language of the heart as he uses words like "wishes," "desires," and "sighs." Calvin was not urging us to be flippant with our desires, for indeed he warns us against "unlawful desires." Instead, Calvin urges us to go before God with our deepest, authentic desires for the glory of God. As Hesselink notes, "the presupposition for lawful prayer is a spirit of repentance and a zeal for the Kingdom of God (3.20.7)."[19]

18. See Calvin et al., *Selected Works of John Calvin*, letter 414.
19. Hesselink, "Introduction: John Calvin on Prayer," 20.

As a third rule, Calvin instructs "that anyone who stands before God to pray, in his humility giving glory completely to God, [must] abandon all thought of his own glory, cast off all notion of his own worth, in fine, put away all self-assurance—lest if we claim for ourselves anything, even the least bit, we should become vainly puffed up, and perish at his presence" (3.20.8–10). Calvin's guidance here is that the source of our confidence in prayer is not in our own worth but solely in God's abundant mercy. Hence, the plea for the forgiveness of our sins serves as a constant refrain in our practice of prayer. Calvin writes: "the beginning, and even the preparation, of proper prayer is the plea for pardon with a humble and sincere confession of guilt" . . . "that [we] have received [our] intention to pray from God's mercy alone, and thus always have begun with appeasing him." This rule accords with the emphasis on the practice of repentance, which I will explain further on in this chapter.

The fourth rule is "that, thus cast down and overcome by true humility, we should be nonetheless encouraged to pray by a sure hope that our prayer will be answered" (3.20.11–14). Calvin returns to the counsel that prayer is ultimately an exercise of faith, and when coupled with repentance, it brings hope. Calvin writes: "For, in accordance with our previous teaching that repentance and faith are companions joined together by an indissoluble bond, although one of these terrifies us while the other gladdens us, so also these two ought to be present together in prayers" (3.20.11). Calvin recognizes that sometimes we are so troubled by our fears that we lose hope "until faith opportunely comes to [our] relief" (3.20.11). Beyond anything else, we must "follow faith as guide" (3.20.11). When we pray with faith, there is always hope. As Hesselink summarizes: "Confident faith and reverent fear go together (3.20.11; cf. 3.20.14). "Only that prayer is acceptable to God which is born . . . out of such presumption of faith and is grounded in unshaken hope" (3.20.12). But this is possible only for those who know the good news that God in Jesus Christ is "gentle and kind" to all who call upon him in repentance and faith (3.20.14; cf. 3.20.12)."[20]

In addition to the reasons and rules for prayer, Calvin also ordered his teaching on prayer after the Lord's Prayer. The prayer consists of six petitions which Calvin explicated in sections thirty-four to forty-nine in his chapter on prayer (3.20.34–49). Calvin considered the Lord's Prayer as a binding rule, not to its form but rather it's content. He writes, "In so teaching, we mean only this: that no man should ask for, expect, or demand, anything at all except what is included, by way of summary, in this prayer; and though the words may be utterly different, yet the sense ought not to

20. Hesselink, *Calvin's First Catechism*, 131–32.

vary" (3.20.49). In this spirit, Calvin also included several godly prayers to be used in the course of a day. They serve as examples for prayer in the morning, before going to school, blessing at the table, thanksgiving after a meal, and before one goes to sleep.[21]

How, then, might we summarize Calvin's guidance on prayer? Several important criteria stand out. First, we need the Holy Spirit to teach us to pray. It is the Spirit who engenders faith in us and helps us, through prayer, to appropriate the grace of Christ. We must approach God with a contrite disposition. Calvin emphasized that we must come in reverence, in "repentance and faith." We have already underscored the importance of a posture of repentance which, as we are reminded, is the fruit of faith and not its precursor for progress in the spiritual life. Here, Calvin especially applies it to the practice of prayer. Secondly, even as we come in repentance and contrition, we also come with confidence before a merciful Father and forgiving God through Christ our only Mediator (3.20.19). This gives us confidence. Calvin's *Institutes* is replete with images of a benevolent God instead of images of a punitive God, which was prevalent in his day. With this confidence, Calvin urges us to pray with certainty but not presumption. Calvin warns against doubtful prayer, for that dishonors God. It its place, Calvin encourages us to come with boldness to express our deepest desires to God. As we are reminded, prayer is the chief exercise of faith by which we daily receive God's benefits. Finally, as Calvin noted, the exercise of prayer bears the fruit of gratitude, humility, and perseverance (3.20.11–14, 30.20.50–52). Prayer transcends any hint of being a transaction with God, but instead lifts us up into true authentic communion with God. Prayer becomes the experience where we "[go into] the heavenly sanctuary" and commune with God in person concerning his honor and his Kingdom, our needs and his provision, our sins and his forgiveness, our fears, and his protection—for us, our loved ones and our enemies. Prayer is indeed the chief exercise for growth in the Christian life. This is Calvin's way of reconciling, healing, sustaining, and guiding in prayer—and, we might add, soul care.

Repentance: A Posture for Deepening Communion

Growth in deepening communion with Christ also encompasses a posture of repentance, which is a virtue that is an instrument of sanctification. For repentance, Calvin explains, is the fruit of faith: "Now, both repentance and forgiveness of sins—that is, newness of life and free reconciliation— are conferred on us by Christ, and both are attained by us through faith"

---

21. Calvin et al., *Selected Works of John Calvin*, 2:95–99.

(3.3.1). Calvin elaborates that "repentance as regeneration, [is the] sole end [that restores] in us the image of God that had been disfigured and all but obliterated through Adam's transgression" (3.3.9). This restoration is possible only through participation in Christ: "we are restored by this regeneration through the benefit of Christ into the righteousness of God" (3.3.9). As we have argued earlier, our union with Christ through participation in his death and resurrection by faith imputes to us the righteousness of Christ.

Unfortunately, in his day—and perhaps in our day too—Calvin was misinterpreted as having confused the state of our present life (that is, of experiencing the forgiveness of sins and clothed with the righteousness of Christ) with heavenly glory (3.3.9). Against this unfortunate confusion, Calvin clarifies that "this restoration does not take place in one moment or one day or one year: but through continual and sometimes even slow advances God wipes out in his elect the corruptions of the flesh, cleanses them of guilt, consecrates them to himself as temples renewing their minds to true purity that they may practice repentance throughout their lives and know that this warfare will end only at death" (3.3.9). Repentance, for Calvin, is not a once-off transaction with God for the forgiveness of sins. Rather, it is a disposition that the Christian embraces until they are taken to be with the Lord. As Calvin explained, Christian maturity is never attained in a moment but over an entire lifetime. There is "a place for growth," Calvin asserts, "in order that believers may reach this goal, God assigns to them a race of repentance, which they are to run throughout their lives" (3.3.9). Calvin's doctrine of repentance thus serves to ground an understanding of faith development, and it serves as one criterion for spiritual guidance and soul care.

Turning to God from Our Inmost Heart

Calvin elaborates on repentance under three headings (3.3.6–9). The first is turning to God from our inmost heart. Calvin writes: "When we call it a "turning of life to God," we require a transformation, not only in outward works, but in the soul itself. Only when it puts off its old nature does it bring forth the fruits of works in harmony with its renewal" (3.3.6). Calvin's attentiveness to the centrality of the heart in this matter is so strong that it bears quoting him at length:

> The prophet, wishing to express this change, bids whom he calls to repentance to get themselves *a new heart* [Ezek. 18:31]. Moses, therefore, intending to show how the Israelites might repent and be duly turned to the Lord, often teaches that it be done

with *"all the heart"* and *"all the soul"* [Deut. 6:5; 10:12; 30:2, 6, 10]. This expression we see frequently repeated by the prophets [Jer. 24:7]–[*they will return to me with all their heart.*] Moses also, in calling it *"circumcision of heart,"* searches the *inmost emotions* [Deut. 10:16; 30; 6]. No passage, however, better reveals the true character of repentance than Jer., ch. 4: "If you return, O Israel," says the Lord, "return to me . . . Plow up your arable land and do not sow among thorns. *Circumcise yourselves to the Lord, and remove the foreskin of your hearts"* [vs. 1, 3–4]. See how he declares that they will achieve nothing in taking up the pursuit of righteousness unless wickedness be first of all cast out from *their inmost heart.* (3.3.6, emphasis added)

For Calvin, the foremost concern in the practice of repentance in the Christian life is to ask God for a circumcision of the heart. Christians have to deal first with the heart if they were to experience any transformation in their lives. Mere outward penance, of any kind, is an affront to the Lord. The Lord sees the heart; and Calvin is soberly reminded of that. Repentance entails turning to the Lord from our inmost hearts.

Tutored in the Fear of the Lord

Calvin's second point for repentance is that it "proceeds from an earnest fear of God" (3.3.7). Calvin explains why the fear of God is a precursor to repentance. We fear God when we think of God's divine judgment and how God will "demand a reckoning of all words and deeds." It would be impossible for us to stand before God and so we are moved to repent. We also fear God and repent when we realize that though we might possess some virtues in life, we do not direct it to the worship of God but instead choose to relish in the praise of the world. Consequently, an earnest fear of God leads us to repentance.

Given Calvin's rationale on the fear of God, that is the fear of punishment, as a component part of repentance (which is a fruit of faith), does he then contradict his own definition of faith, which is fundamentally based on the knowledge of God's benevolence rather than judgment? The resolution is found in the precursor of repentance as "the sorrow . . . according to God." As Calvin explained, "[The apostle Paul] calls it "sorrow . . . according to God" when we not only abhor punishment but hate and abominate sin itself, because we know that it displeases God" (3.3.7). Calvin's understanding of the fear of God entails not just the fear of punishment but the concern for God's approval. Hence, it is a reverential fear that honors who God is.[22] Beeke clarifies that "[without] a pure, earnest fear of God, a person will not be aware of the heinousness of sin or want to turn from it and die to it. For Calvin, the essence of the fear of God is esteeming God's smiles and frowns to be of greater value than the smiles and frowns of men."[23]

Hence Calvin's doctrine of repentance takes a serious view of sin. For Calvin, sin is so radical that it requires a redemptive act which only God can accomplish. Metaphorically speaking, sin has so ravaged the garden of our souls that minor repairs through works of righteousness just will not suffice. The garden of our souls is not just polluted by a few weeds here and there such that some focused work on weeding will do. God must break in to do a radical transformation.

But Calvin' doctrine of repentance also takes seriously the approval of God. The virtue of repentance is not just about the avoidance of sin. It is also about seeking the approval of God. As we argued earlier, repentance as a discipline expresses our concern for God's honor and so guides us on the way of Christian discipleship.

Mortification of the Flesh and Vivification of the Spirit

The third heading that Calvin gives to repentance consists of two parts: the mortification of the flesh and vivification of the spirit. These two parts operate together and correspond to being identified with Christ in death and in the resurrection. Mortification of the flesh means "to deny our own nature," (3.3.8) that is, the sinful nature of the flesh. "Mortification is essential because, although sin ceases to reign in the believer, it does not cease to dwell in him."[24] Calvin writes, "In the saints, until they are divested of mortal bodies, there is always sin; for in their flesh there resides that depravity of inordinate desiring which contends against righteousness" (3.3.10). "Consequently, the believer is never free from sin in this life; he must always battle against it."[25] We have already noted that repentance is a life-long journey. The mortification of the flesh is, therefore, an expression of that life-long discipline. However, we are reminded that mortifying the flesh does not earn us the forgiveness of sin, for as Calvin reiterates; "repentance is not the cause of forgiveness of sins:" faith is (3.4.3). Union with Christ through faith leads to the forgiveness of sins. Repentance is the fruit of faith and

---

22. See especially *Inst.* 3.2.22–23 for Calvin's teaching on "Right fear."
23. Beeke, "Appropriating Salvation," 296.
24. Beeke, "Appropriating Salvation," 296.
25. Beeke, "Appropriating Salvation," 296.

mortification is an expression of that faith. As Beeke explains, "To place repentance before faith can produce the erroneous doctrine of preparationism, akin to Roman Catholic theology, which views works of penance as contributing to the believer's justification."[26]

It is helpful to see that "two critical aspects of mortification are self-denial and cross-bearing."[27] Calvin considers self-denial as "the sum of the Christian life" and cross-bearing is part of self-denial (3.7–8). Calvin applied this teaching on mortification in the guidance he offered to some Christians who were suffering severe persecution in the Church of Aix. "We are well aware that it is a plausible and specious opinion that it is lawful for us to avenge ourselves on a mutinous populace, because this is not resisting the order of justice; nay, that the laws themselves arm both great and small against robbers. But whatever reasons and sophistical excuses may be alleged, still our whole duty consists in practicing the lesson which the sovereign Master has taught us, viz: *to possess our souls in patience.*"[28]

If mortification of the flesh is the "sorrow of soul" and the expression of "contrition," then vivification of the spirit is "the desire to live in a holy and devoted manner, a desire arising from rebirth; as if it were said that man dies to himself that he may begin to live to God" (3.2.3). The vivification of the spirit therefore complements the mortification of the flesh as a two-pronged expression of repentance in the Christian life. Calvin explains that what follows mortification is for "the mind itself and the heart . . . [to] put on the inclination to righteousness, judgment, and mercy . . . [and] that comes to pass when the Spirit of God so imbues our souls, steeped in his holiness, with both new thoughts and feelings, that they can be rightly considered new" (3.3.8). Hence, the vivification of the spirit is a process where the Spirit of God renews our minds and hearts with new thoughts and feelings after the character of his holiness. The vivification of the spirit leads to a Spirit-renewed and Spirit-led life.

I gather a sense that the practice of the vivification of the spirit is closely linked to the disposition of contemplation which Calvin referred to at various points in the *Institutes*. It is that disposition of surrender and receptivity wherein the disciple receives God's work in his heart, leading to the inner quality of greater surrender and restedness in God. As we were reminded earlier, both mortification and vivification are exercised by participation in Christ (3.3.9). Hence, they are both efforts of faith, just as participation in Christ is by faith. What follows then are the fruits of faith,

26. Beeke, "Appropriating Salvation," 299.
27. Beeke, "Appropriating Salvation," 297.
28. Calvin, *Letters of John Calvin*, 4:187 (emphasis added).

which for Calvin, is fundamentally expressed through worship of God and service to humankind.

In this light, Calvin's explication of the posture and practice of repentance offers to the Christian a way of life in the pursuit of godliness. It continues from where we began: that is, that the Christian life is birthed through justification by faith and what follows in sanctification is also by faith, expressed in the faith-filled practice of repentance. In repentance, the Christian looks upward in God-focused reverential fear, inward in Spirit-empowered heart-felt contrition, and outward in Christ-centered mortification and vivification. These are guideposts that point the direction for Christian growth. Calvin's detailed explication of the doctrine of repentance explains why such an understanding is crucial to the work of spiritual guidance.

CONTEMPLATION IN THE CHRISTIAN LIFE

In practice, the disciplines of prayer and repentance are honed through the contemplation of God, exercised by faith, primarily through Word and Sacrament, and also through God's great universe, under the guidance and empowerment of the Holy Spirit.[29] It is when the truth concerning God, is grasped with both mind and heart, through the efficacious work of the Holy Spirit, that the disciple begins to experience a change of perspective toward God, and so these realities impact the way in which one lives to the glory of God and the service of others (1.9.3). Consequently, a posture of repentance works together with a posture of contemplation, intimately woven within the exercise of prayer, to engender growth in the Christian life.

Calvin embarks on the subject of contemplation very early on in the *Institutes*. In his renowned statement on the twin knowledge needed for true and sound wisdom, that is, "the knowledge of God and of ourselves," he goes on to comment that it is not easy to discern which one precedes the other. "In the first place, [he explains], no one can look upon himself without

---

29. As I mentioned in the previous chapter, we understand the contemplation of God to be intimately connected to what the Holy Spirit does in us. See my comments in the section on "*Calvin's Rule for Nurturing the Christian Life,*" and the preceding section for my interpretation of Calvin's use of "contemplation" in the Christian life.

In Coe and Strobel, *Embracing Contemplation*, 6–7, they describe contemplation as "a call to attend to the presence of God that has been made available in Christ by the Spirit." The focus is not on a certain technique, variously rendered as "contemplation" in a variety of religions and New Age practices. Rather, the focus is on "receiving the presence and love of God in Christ by the Spirit." See especially *Inst.* 1.1.1, 1.1.3, 1.5.1–2, and 1.5.2n6.

immediately turning his thoughts to the contemplation of God, in whom he "lives and moves" [Acts 17:28]." Yet "again, it is certain that man never achieves a clear knowledge of himself [*that is, including all humankind and all creation*][30] unless he has first looked upon God's face, and then descends from contemplating him to scrutinize himself" (1.1.2). Hence, given the inextricable link of the knowledge of our Creator God and of ourselves, the only way forward to true and sound wisdom is through a contemplative posture of knowing God and our life in Him.

I have highlighted at two points, in the preceding sections on prayer and repentance, where, in my opinion, Calvin described the exercise of contemplation as we understand it from Scripture—that is, the work of God in Christ through the Spirit in the depths of one's soul. Calvin explains in the opening chapter of the *Institutes*: Unless we are content to be either "ignorant or unmindful of [our] own misery" or conversely "content with our own righteousness, wisdom, and virtue," an honest inward glance will point us in the direction of God, both in gratitude and in reverential fear. Pondering over how we are endowed; Calvin realizes that these are "hardly from ourselves." Reflecting over our existence, Calvin recognizes that "our very being is nothing but subsistence in the one God." So, Calvin adds that "[by] these benefits shed like dew from heaven upon us, we are led as by rivulets to the spring itself" (1.1.1). This is the rhetoric of piety that is the fruit of a contemplative disposition. As we taste of the benefits from the streams of life in Christ, the Holy Spirit presses forward to lead us—renewing our minds and transforming our hearts—to the spring itself, wherein we experience true refreshment and health. This is the fruit of a contemplative disposition—yielding to the work of God in Christ through the Spirit, and experiencing in one's depths the fruit of a transformed heart.

Jones explains that Calvin uses the rhetoric of piety to inspire and guide the reader towards the disposition of *pietas (piety)*—and *pietas*, we are reminded, is "that reverence joined with love of God which the knowledge of his benefits induces" (1.2.1). She explains that "it is not surprising to discover that the rhetorical pattern that governs the flow of this chapter's [Book I:2] logic corresponds to the task Calvin has undertaken: it is a pattern designed to invoke the disposition *pietas*."[31] Through reflection and rhetoric, Calvin affirms that our endowments are all from our great God.

Following from that, we gain a humble recognition of our self: "Indeed, our very poverty better discloses the infinitude of benefits reposing in God . . . and [our] miserable ruin . . . compels us to look upward" (1.1.1).

30. See *Inst.* 1.1.2n5.
31. Jones, *Calvin and the Rhetoric of Piety*, 122.

Positively and negatively, the inward glance leads to an upward gaze. And the fruit follows. "Thus, not only will we, in fasting and hungering, seek thence what we lack; but, in being aroused by fear, we shall learn humility." As it appears the contemplative look inward and upward bears the fruit of the knowledge of God and of self; expressed in gratitude and in humility. Consequently, Calvin adds: "Thus, from the feeling of our own ignorance, vanity, poverty, infirmity, and—what is more—depravity and corruption, we recognize that the true light of wisdom, sound virtue, full abundance of every good, and purity of righteousness rest in the Lord alone. To this extent we are prompted by our own ills to contemplate the good things of God" (1.1.1). This, I propose, is "contemplation at work."

Consequently, Calvin urges us "to raise our thoughts to God, and to ponder his nature" that we might learn the fear of the Lord and live wisely (1.1.2). As piety is prerequisite to any true knowledge of God, the exercise of a contemplative disposition is a character trait of true piety, in which reverence is joined with a love of God that is derived from the knowledge of God's benefits.[32] Calvin concludes that "the pious mind does not dream up for itself any god it pleases, but contemplates the one and only true God." (1.2.2). Together with repentance, Calvin guides the Christian toward Christian growth with the practice of contemplation.

The Foci of Our Contemplation

We are reminded that contemplation serves the purpose of tutoring us in the knowledge of God and self. Calvin did not intend for contemplation to be an activity in and of itself. His sole purpose was to point us to God, and from there, we receive a derived knowledge of self. Calvin directs us to four major objects f contemplation in the *Institutes*: The Contemplation of God in his works, the contemplation of God in the Christ, the contemplation of God through Word and Sacraments, and the contemplation of the future life—all of which are enabled by the Holy Spirit.

Contemplating God in God's Great Universe

Calvin writes that "the knowledge of God shines forth in the fashioning of the universe and the continuing government of it" (1.5.1). Hence, God's "skillful ordering of the universe is for us a sort of mirror in which we can contemplate God, who is otherwise invisible" (1.5.1). Calvin notes that God

32. *Inst.*, 1.2.1.n1

"revealed himself and daily discloses himself in the whole workmanship of the universe" (1.5.1). Upon "his individual works he has engraved unmistakable marks of his glory . . ." God shows himself "in the visible splendor of his apparel . . . those insignia whereby he shows his glory to us, whenever and wherever we cast our gaze" (1.5.1). "Heaven is often called his palace," and the heavenly creatures are "an attestation of divinity." These are the "innumerable evidences" that declare his wonderful wisdom, and through which we contemplate God. For Calvin, a major avenue of wisdom comes from contemplating God in the wonders of his universe. We are to "investigate" and "observe" the universe's wonders so that our "mind[s] might rise to a somewhat higher level to look upon his glory" (1.5.2). The contemplation of God in his works can nurture in us the reverential knowledge needed for living wisely.

Randall Zachman imagines that when Calvin describes the created world as a dazzling theatre of God's glory, he infers that we are created to be spectators in the audience to behold the drama enacted before us on stage. "The performance itself must be the works of God that reveal the glory of God to us . . . As spectators of the divine performance in the world, we are to contemplate the works of God in order to discern the powers of God that shine forth in these works."[33] Zachman notes that for Calvin, "the powers that especially reveal the nature of God are eternity, wisdom, power, goodness, justice, mercy, and truth. When we behold these powers in the works of God, we are led to feel the force of these powers within ourselves; and since these powers are all good things, our feeling of these powers will lead to our enjoyment of them . . . More important, by our contemplation, feeling, and enjoyment of the powers of God that we behold in the theater of the world, we are invited, allured, and attracted to seek the God who is the source and author of all these powers, in whom alone is found human happiness and blessedness."[34]

Hence, Calvin encourages us to contemplate God in his works: "For the Lord manifests himself by his powers, the force of which we feel within ourselves and the benefits of which we enjoy. We must therefore be much more profoundly affected by this knowledge than if we were to imagine a God of whom no perception came through to us. Consequently, we know the most perfect way of seeking God, and the most suitable order, is not for us to attempt with bold curiosity to penetrate to the investigation of his essence, which we ought more to adore than meticulously to search out, but

33. Zachman, *John Calvin*, 234. See also Lane, *Ravished by beauty*, in which he discusses Calvin's depiction of God's creation as a theater of God's glory; what he says is the "surprising legacy of Reformed spirituality."

34. Zachman, *John Calvin*, 235.

for us to contemplate him in his works whereby he renders himself near and familiar to us, and in some manner communicates himself" (1.5.9).

The Problem of Sin Thwarts Our Ability to Contemplate

Unfortunately, depraved humanity thwarts the very potential of contemplating God through his wonderful works. In our depravity, we confuse the creature with the Creator, and end up in superstition and idolatry (1.5.11). Even the contemplation of our own bodies, so fearfully and wonderfully made by God, should lead us to revere God, but we do not do so because of our fallen nature. As Calvin says, we end up in vain conceit rather than the worship of God, prompting him to exhort again: "Let us therefore remember, whenever each of us contemplates his own nature, that there is one God who so governs all natures that he would have us look unto him, direct our faith to him, and worship and call upon him. For nothing is more preposterous than to enjoy the very remarkable gifts that attest the divine nature within us, yet to overlook the Author who gives them to us at our asking" (1.5.3–6, 2.1.1–3).

Since humanity has not been drawn to God by natural revelation, which really ought to have been sufficient to point us to God, God sent "another and better help . . . to direct us aright to the very Creator of the universe" (1.6.1). This is the special revelation in Christ Jesus. Calvin dedicates Book II of the *Institutes* to a thorough discussion of God's special revelation in Christ our Redeemer. It is Christ alone who has made full satisfaction for our sins before God, and hence it is through Christ alone that we are reconciled to God.

We pause here to note that, for Calvin, spiritual guidance is ultimately an act of divine revelation in Christ Jesus. Contrary to the pantheistic tendencies in today's multi-faith spiritual direction, Calvin guides the Christian back to the way God has chosen to reveal himself, that is, in the person of Jesus Christ. While natural revelation inspires, it is the special revelation in Christ that ultimately points us to the Creator. Unfortunately, many contemporary forms of guidance are content to contemplate the created world without specific reference to the Creator God who has chosen to reveal himself uniquely in Christ Jesus. Calvin's corrective for his sixteenth-century context continues to be relevant for our twenty-first-century context.[35]

Calvin attends to the problem of sin and its impact right at the beginning of Book II. Due to Adam's "original sin," his guilt is passed on to

---

35. See Coe, "The Controversy over Contemplation and Contemplative Prayer," 19–36, for a discussion of this issue.

all humankind. We inherited his corrupted nature and are entangled in his miseries. From Adam on, the deadly poison of sin is propagated to all humankind. No one is spared the ravages of sin, and no one can reverse it on their own.

Calvin's understanding of the radical nature of sin and its impact was set, in the sixteenth-century context, against the teachings of Pelagius (354–420). To Calvin's knowledge, Pelagius had argued "that Adam sinned only to his own loss without harming his posterity."[36] For Pelagius, sin "was transmitted through imitation, not propagation." Pelagius' teaching set off a body of treatises and letters by Augustine (354–430) in exposition and defense of the doctrine of original sin and man's innate depravity. Evidently, Pelagius' teachings were still embraced by some in Calvin's day. As it appeared, some were inclined to adopt the same reasoning as Pelagius for a response to the problem of sin. If sin was transmitted by imitating Adam's sinful inclinations, then perhaps righteousness could be wrought by imitating Christ's righteousness, albeit with the help of God's grace. This line of reason prompted Calvin to exclaim: "does Christ's righteousness benefit us only as an example set before us to imitate? Who can bear such sacrilege!" Calvin adds: "But if it is beyond controversy that Christ's righteousness, and thereby life, are ours by communication, it immediately follows that both were lost in Adam, only to be recovered in Christ; and that sin and death crept in through Adam, only to be abolished through Christ" (2.1.6).

Contemplating Christ through Word and Spirit

In the light of our preceding discussion, and my argument that Calvin advocates the practice of contemplation for the Christian life, the question before us, then, is whether Calvin advocated that people contemplate Christ. It is clear that the righteousness of Christ can never be earned by us through imitation, but purely by imputation. But if Christ is set as an example for us to follow, how then does the practice of following look in daily practice? As Calvin asserted in his treatment of the Christian life, we cannot coldly contemplate Christ as outside of ourselves (3.1.3). For Calvin, the answer lies in contemplating Christ in the context of his Word through his illuminating Holy Spirit. Calvin has already urged us to "embrace that communion with Christ . . . , to climb higher and to examine into the secret energy of the Spirit, by which we come to enjoy Christ and all his benefits" (3.1.1). We have already established that it is through union with Christ by faith that we are launched into a deepening communion with Christ, through

36. *Inst.*, 2.1.5, see also discussion in n8.

participation, by the efficacious work of the Holy Spirit. Hence, for Calvin, the direction for progress in the Christian life is to contemplate Christ in his Word through the Spirit.

In Calvin's spirituality, Word and Spirit work together in a "mutual bond" to seal God's truth upon the soul of the Christian (1.9.3). From the Christian's perspective, the practice that co-operates with the work of God's Word and Spirit is contemplation. Hence Calvin writes: "For by a kind of mutual bond the Lord has joined together the certainty of his Word and of his Spirit so that the perfect religion of the Word may abide in our minds when the Spirit, who causes us to contemplate God's face, shines; and that we in turn may embrace the Spirit with no fear of being deceived when we recognize him in his own image, namely, in the Word" (1.9.3).

Consequently, as a Christian by faith, through the Holy Spirit, contemplates God in the light of his Word, the knowledge of God as benevolent Father will begin to renew the mind and recalibrate the heart, bringing assurance and impetus for Christian living. The Holy Spirit, as the principal worker of faith and the "bond that unites us to Christ," leads us into greater communion with Christ so that we come to enjoy Christ and all his benefits (3.1.4). The practice of contemplation, which is really God's action on the believer, leads to deeper faith and greater surrender to God.

Calvin observes that some do not grow into this deeper communion in their Christian life: "for, as I have said, all that [Christ] possesses is nothing to us until we grow into one body with him. It is true that we obtain this by faith. Yet since we see that not all indiscriminately embrace that communion with Christ which is offered through the gospel, reason itself teaches us to climb higher and to examine into the secret energy of the Spirit, by which we come to enjoy Christ and all his benefits" (3.1.1). As Beeke notes: "The Holy Spirit always uses the faith he gives us to unite us with Christ and to give us freedom to appropriate Christ's benefits"[37] So then, Calvin urges us to "climb higher" by faith into greater communion with Christ through his indwelling Spirit.

We are reminded again that we do so only through the efficacious work of the Holy Spirit, and not through our own efforts. Calvin reminds us that the Holy Spirit "persistently [boils] away and [burns] up our vicious and inordinate desires, . . . [and then] enflames our hearts with the love of God and with zealous devotion" (3.1.3). As we noted earlier, our efforts in mortification and vivification are God-focused, Spirit-empowered, and Christ-centered. As the Holy Spirit is given to elevate Christ and glorify the Father, so the Spirit works tirelessly to sanctify us. "For by the inspiration of

37. Beeke, "Appropriating Salvation," 275.

his power he so breathes divine life into us that we are no longer actuated by ourselves, but are ruled by his action and prompting. Accordingly, whatever good things are in us are the fruits of his grace; and without him our gifts are darkness of mind and perversity of heart" (3.1.3). So, the Holy Spirit is our "inner teacher" and draws us to God our Father through Jesus the Son, bringing to mind what we have been taught by mouth (3.1.4).

For Calvin, the way to close the gap between mere mental religious assent and impotent religious practices, which were so evidenced by the Scholastic's notion of implicit faith and their subscribers, was to wholly embrace the knowledge that comes by faith through the Holy Spirit. As Calvin asserts: "Faith rests not on ignorance, but on knowledge. And this is, indeed, knowledge not only of God but of the divine will" (3.2.2). "For faith consists in the knowledge of God and Christ," Calvin adds (3.2.3). So then, a disciple of Jesus must grasp the knowledge of God's Word by faith through the Holy Spirit in order to know the will of God—and to walk in it.

Calvin notes that the apostle Paul "yokes faith to teaching, as an inseparable companion" (3.2.6). So, Calvin reminds us that there is a "permanent relationship between faith and the Word." Consequently, he warns: "take away the Word and no faith will then remain" (3.2.6). Thus, the Word, when it is imparted to us, "is like a mirror in which faith may contemplate God" (3.2.6). But faith is also intimately linked with obedience to God's will. Faith is not content with superficial knowledge of God but rather with "knowing what is his will toward us. For it is not so much our concern to know who he is in himself,[that is mere information about God,] as what he wills to be toward us" (3.2.6). So Calvin sums up the relationship between the Word and the knowledge of God's will: "Now, therefore, we hold faith to be a knowledge of God's will toward us, perceived from his Word" (3.2.6). The point of explicating all these is that a disciple of Jesus can close the gap between knowledge and practice by contemplating the Word by faith through the Holy Spirit.

Contemplating Spiritual Mysteries through Word and Sacrament

Intimately connected to the contemplation of the Word is the contemplation of the mysteries hidden in the sacraments of baptism and the Lord's Supper. Calvin explains that the sacraments are exercises that make us more certain of the trustworthiness of God's Word. Just as faith rests upon the Word of God as a foundation, the sacraments are likewise founded upon the Word and strengthen our faith like columns do for a building (4.14.6).

So, at baptism or the reception of the Lord's Supper, Calvin writes that the believer, "when he sees the sacraments with his own eyes, does not halt at the physical sight of them, but . . . rises up in devout contemplation to those lofty mysteries which lie hidden in the sacraments" (4.14.5). They act like "mirrors in which we may contemplate the riches of God's grace, which he lavishes upon us" (4.14.6). By pondering deeply upon their significance, as instructed by the Word and illumined through the Spirit, one's faith is strengthened, and we are guided further in the way of Christ. The sacraments, as "agencies of the Holy Spirit . . . in association with the Word" thus serve as "distinguishing marks of our profession of faith" before God and men and so aid our progress in our life in God. Calvin advocates that the Lord's Supper should be celebrated at least once a week, so that we are fed spiritually by God's promises in his Word (4.17.43–44).

The outcome will be illumined minds and strengthened hearts as Word and Sacrament obtains "full faith" among us. This is succinctly captured in Calvin's definition of faith: "a firm and certain knowledge of god's benevolence toward us, founded upon the truth of the freely given promise in Christ, both revealed to our minds and sealed upon our hearts through the Holy Spirit" (3.2.7). When "full faith" has been obtained, we walk in confidence before God; minds illumined and hearts aflame—putting knowledge to practice.

Contemplating the Present Life in Light of Our Eternal Hope

In this light, Calvin guides us to contemplate the present life, especially its troubles, in the light of our eternal hope. He writes: "Whatever kind of tribulation presses upon us, we must ever look to this end: to accustom ourselves to contempt for the present life and to be aroused thereby to meditate upon the future life" (3.9.1). Calvin is not advocating contempt for the world. Rather, he is cautioning the Christian against undue attention to the vanities of this life and that one becomes so bound by them that one misses the glory of our eternal hope. Yet, Calvin does not teach us to be ungrateful for the present life. Rather, he is guiding us toward a posture that expresses gratitude for God's good blessings in this life and yet "[strives] with all our heart to meditate upon the life to come" (3.9.2). For, "if believers' eyes are turned to the power of the resurrection, in their hearts the cross of Christ will at last triumph over the devil, flesh, sin, and wicked men" (3.9.6).

Calvin applied this principle in one of his letters. Writing to distressed believers dispersed in the Isles of France, he urged them to "separate [themselves] from idolatries, [and] from all superstitions, which are contrary to the service of God." Instead, they should "take courage and devote [themselves] wholly to God, who has purchased us so dearly by his own Son, and yield him the homage of body and soul, showing that we account his glory more precious than all besides; and that you set a higher value upon the eternal salvation which is prepared for you in heaven, than you do in this transitory life."[38] For Calvin, the eternal hope always serves as a source of spiritual sustenance which we should regularly meditate upon.

Through all these avenues of contemplation, Calvin's goal as guide is to direct our attention and turn our hearts to God so that we are inspired and encouraged to respond in faith and willing obedience. The outcome is a life lived more in freedom from the bondage of sin and more in character after the image of Christ.

A METHOD FOR SOUL CARE AND SPIRITUAL GUIDANCE

In this chapter, we see that Calvin's method of guidance for the Christian life is foundationally expressed through the practice of prayer in a posture of repentance and contemplation. For Calvin, the spiritual life is an integrated experience and expression of the inward and outward dimensions of faith. Knowledge of Scripture and experience of the Lord's presence work together to advance the soul. The posture of repentance and contemplation encompasses both the inward and outward dimensions of faith development. In exhorting the Christian to repentance, Calvin nurtures within the believer a humble disposition of reverence for God and of self-denial that is expressed in acts of cross-bearing and service. The contemplative posture serves as the means to deepen this disposition as the Christian learns to ponder the deep significance of God's good creation, Christ's birth, life, death, resurrection, and ascension, through Word and Spirit. This posture of repentance and contemplation leads the Christian to rest confidently in God's providence. The outcome is a deepening communion with God, through Christ, in the power of the Holy Spirit—expressed in worship to God and service to humankind for the glory of God.

---

38. Calvin, *Letters of John Calvin*, 2:433.

8

Continuity and Discontinuity in Ignatius's and Calvin's History, Theology, and Practice of Spiritual Guidance

HAVING EXAMINED IGNATIUS OF Loyola's and John Calvin's history, theology, and methodology in spiritual guidance, I will now do a comparative analysis for points of continuity and discontinuity between them. The findings from this chapter will help to clarify some of the critical points of convergence and divergence between the Ignatian and Reformed practices of spiritual guidance. I hope that these insights will promote greater understanding and learning between theologians and practitioners from these two traditions. Points of continuity can help to foster a shared emphasis in spiritual guidance across the traditions, while points of discontinuity will require mutual respect and dialogue. As with the previous chapters, I will approach this comparative analysis through the major spheres of history, theology, and methodology.

The preceding four chapters have demonstrated that Ignatius' and Calvin's personal histories have shaped their theologies of the spiritual life. We also noted how their theological assumptions influenced their methodology for spiritual guidance. We observed that Ignatius guided out of an implicit, that is, an assumed, Roman Catholic spiritual theology through an explicit methodology as seen in the text of the *Spiritual Exercises*. Calvin, on the other hand, guided out of an explicit "spiritual theology," as formulated in the *Institutes*, that was intentionally Reformed and from which an implicit method of spiritual guidance could be deduced. The historical investigation suggested that the *Spiritual Exercises* evolved chiefly out of Ignatius' own spiritual experience through which he found a way to guide others in their own spiritual progress. Calvin, on the other hand, wrestled with the diversity of theological polemics in the context of the Protestant Reformation, and hence, was very deliberate and explicit in his theological criteria. Calvin, however, was more reticent in offering a particular method for spiritual guidance, although it can be drawn out from his theological criteria and practice.

Nevertheless, both Ignatius and Calvin translated their theology into practice. For them, theology was not meant to merely be an intellectual exercise. Instead, theology served as a foundation upon which to establish spiritual practices for everyday Christian living. Their shared focus on the life "with God" was that of nurturing progress through the practice of theology, and that was their *modus operandi* in offering spiritual guidance. All things considered, it is clear that both Ignatius and Calvin ministered out of a set of core theological criteria which determined their method of spiritual guidance, and from which insights can be harvested to enrich the practice of spiritual guidance in an ecumenical context.

Two summary points stand out as we analyze the continuities and discontinuities between Ignatius' and Calvin's ways of spiritual guidance. First, they converged on a similar intent for their respective texts to serve as guides for spiritual growth. Second, while they diverged on important aspects of their respective theological assumptions for spiritual growth, they converged at some critical points on how spiritual growth occurs.

We have already noted in the preceding chapters that both Ignatius and Calvin intended for their respective texts, the *Spiritual Exercises,* and the *Institutes of Christian Religion,* to serve as guides for making progress in the Christian life. For Ignatius, his goal was laid forth explicitly in annotations one and twenty-one in the *Exercises,* which together were statements on the purpose of the *Exercises* [1, 21]—the interpretations of which I have discussed in chapter four. Calvin's goal for the *Institutes* was explicitly stated in his prefatory address to King Francis I of France— "to transmit certain rudiments by which those who are touched with any zeal for religion might be shaped to true godliness"—the explication of which I did in chapter six. This point of continuity reaffirms the legitimacy of this comparative study. Both Ignatius and Calvin endeavored through their respective texts to guide those who earnestly sought to grow in the Christian life.

However, I also discovered that their texts were vastly different in genre and organization and so make an apple-to-apple comparison difficult. Nevertheless, when I compared them through the perspective of interconnectivity that flowed from their histories to their theologies to their methods, I can analyze the points of continuity and discontinuity that emerged from the varied forces that shaped their perspectives on the Christian life.

HISTORICAL INFLUENCE

We note that both Ignatius Loyola (1491–1556) and John Calvin (1509–1564) shared several similarities having grown up in the same historical era. Both largely embraced the Catholic faith from a young age and were similarly dedicated by their parents for the priesthood. Both, however, did not fulfill their religious obligation to become priests but nevertheless became enormous shapers of the Catholic and Protestant reformations respectively. Both experienced dramatic conversions: Ignatius from the brink of death and Calvin from the zenith of unteachability. Both became great men of prayer, spiritual guides, and mission enablers.

Despite these similarities, a comparison of their personal religious histories also turned up a number of ironies. Ignatius, being somewhat of a flirtatious courtier and egocentric solider before his conversion, became a deeply devoted soldier of Christ and loyal supporter of all that the Catholic Church stood for. Calvin, in a strange reversal, went from being a rather devout Catholic to that of a fiery defender of the gospel of Jesus Christ and apologist of the Protestant Reformation. Yet both retained their fierce loyalty to the church as the mother of faith formation.[1] They also shared the same vision to free the pursuit of the spiritual life from the confines of monastic walls and to bring it into the city for the ordinary folk.

In my analysis on how their personal histories contributed to shape their theologies, I observed that, following his conversion, Ignatius' spiritual worldview was significantly shaped by the *Vita Jesu Christi* and the *Flos Sanctorum*, as well as the *Imitation of Christ*. In this regard, he was significantly influenced by medieval theology. He also largely rested his theological assumptions and paradigm on the theology of the Roman Church, in particular Peter Lombard and Thomas Aquinas. Emerging from his exposure to the *Vita Christi*, the method he adopted for the *Spiritual Exercises* revolved around meditations and contemplations on the life of Christ in the Gospels.

Calvin, on the other hand, was exposed to a broad range of influences from an early age. They included the classics, law, and the persuasions of the Christian humanists, in particular Erasmus of Rotterdam. Theologically,

---

1. See *Inst.* 4.1.1., and *SpEx* 352–370.

Calvin drew widely from the Church Fathers, fellow Reformers, but principally from Scripture for his polemical battles. Arguably, he used the method of Melanchthon for constructing the *Institutes* but anchored them on the whole counsel of Scripture.

The intersection of their lives leaves us with a rich tapestry of continuities and discontinuities from which to gather important and pertinent insights for the ministry of spiritual guidance and formation. It is with this impetus that I embark on this exploration and note first the divergent forces that shaped their respective texts.

Different Primary Impetus:
Personal Experience vs. Polemic Persuasion

First, the primary impetuses in the formation of their texts were different. It was observed that the primary impetus surrounding the formation of the *Exercises* was Ignatius' own spiritual experience[2] while those of the *Institutes* was Calvin's desire to develop a reliable guide for nurturing godliness in response to the great needs, which were especially pronounced among his fellow French refugees, during the Reformation.[3] It was especially evident from his *Autobiography* that Ignatius drew significantly from his experiences of interior spiritual movements and counter movements for his formulation of the rules of discernment and its practice. Calvin, on the other hand, drew significantly from Scripture and the Church Fathers to formulate a reliable guide to the reading of Scripture.[4] It may be said that Ignatius was primarily an exegete of spiritual experience and guided from experience through imaginative prayer using Scripture while Calvin was primarily an exegete of Scripture and guided from Scripture into the experience of deepening communion with God in prayer.

---

2. See Meissner, *Ignatius of Loyola*; O'Malley, *The First Jesuits*; Rahner, *The Spirituality of St. Ignatius*; Howard, *Affirming the Touch of God.*

3. See Calvin, "Prefatory Address to King Francis I of France," 9. The 1536 "Prefatory Address to King Francis I of France": "My purpose was solely to transmit certain rudiments by which those who are touched with any zeal for religion might be shaped to true godliness."

See also Calvin, "John Calvin to the Reader," 3. The 1559 Latin version of the *Institutes*: "it has been my purpose in this labor to prepare and instruct candidates in sacred theology for the reading of the divine Word, in order that they may be able both to have easy access to it and to advance in it without stumbling."

4. Zachman, *John Calvin*, 31.

Different Theological Persuasion:
Medieval Catholic Theology vs. Scripture and the Church Fathers

Second, the underlying theology of their texts was different. Ignatius largely assumed a Roman, and significantly Medieval, Catholic spiritual theology while Calvin sought to establish a Reformed perspective on salvation and spiritual growth that drew from the sources of Scripture and the Church Fathers. As we noted earlier, Ignatius was significantly influenced by the *Vita Jesu Christi*, *Flos Sanctorum* and *Imitatio Christi* as well as the theologies of Aquinas and Lombard. These influences led to his method of organizing the *Exercises* into Four Weeks and of utilizing the Gospels as subject matter for the various methods of prayer. He adopted the traditional Roman Catholic three ways of progress in the spiritual life and aligned the Four Weeks to the purgative, illuminative and unitive ways [10].

Calvin, on the other hand, drew significantly from the Church Fathers and the Scriptures for his purpose of formulating the *Institutes* as a guide for the cultivation of *pietas*. The 1536 edition of the *Institutes* utilized the structure of the Apostles' Creed and hence was organized into four books with corresponding foci on God the Father, Jesus the Son, the Holy Spirit, and the Church. Calvin retained this structure throughout the twenty-three years in which he expanded on the *Institutes*. Instead of the Catholic three ways, Calvin argued that the Christian life commenced through mystical union with Christ founded on the dual grace of justification and sanctification, which were coupled in a mutual bond and yet distinct. Growth in the Christian life followed through deepening communion with God through prayer and the Word, by faith through the Spirit, with both mind and heart.

Different Reactions to Ecclesial Sensitivities:
Subdued vs. Responsive

Third, their responses to the ecclesial sensitivities were different. While both Ignatius and Calvin worked from the context of the Catholic and Protestant Reformations respectively, their texts possessed quite different expressions in response to the issues of the day. For Ignatius, while there was clear evidence of his sensitivity to his ecclesial environment, such as his oblique reference to the Holy Spirit and the Rules for Thinking with the Church, he wrote the *Exercises* "not as reactions or responses to those contemporaries" but simply as a manual for "helping souls."[5] Calvin, on the other hand, responded to the theological issues that confronted his day, both from the Catholic Church

5. Howard, *Affirming the Touch of God*, 55.

and other reformers, thus introducing a polemical tone into the *Institutes*. What began as a handbook of six chapters concerning the rudiments for cultivating *pietas* evolved into a two-volume work of eighty chapters, yet without losing its primary intent as a guide for nurturing godliness.

Different Primary Audience: Individual vs. Ecclesial

Fourth, their design for the text's usage was different. Ignatius intended for the *Exercises* to serve primarily as a guide to the individual under the guidance of a spiritual director, while the *Institutes*, though designed for the individual in its first edition, was expanded to serve as a guide for the church through its teachers and pastors.[6] Arguably, Ignatius' original intent for the *Exercises* was for it to serve as a guide for the making of a religious choice.[7] This intent gave it a very specific purpose, which was to help those who were either considering to join the Society or for the making of a religious vow. Its usage was later broadened to serve as a guide for growth toward spiritual perfection and union with God. In either case, it possessed a very specific individual focus. It was a tool for personal spiritual direction. The *Exercises* were assigned according to the needs of an individual and at a pace that was appropriate to their spiritual growth through the perceptive guidance of a spiritual director.

The *Institutes*, on the other hand—especially as seen in the final 1559 version—were crafted to guide teachers and pastors for their work at guiding Christians in an ecclesial context. That did not preclude the suitability for individual use, especially as we recall that the original 1536 version was designed as a catechetical pocketbook, and as evinced through his application of the principles in his letters to a variety of individuals. Whether used individually or corporately, the *Institutes* possessed a set of guiding principles that were derived from the Scriptures and Christian doctrine for the purpose of individual and corporate spiritual guidance.

Similar Personal Piety: Trinitarian and Kingdom-focused

Despite these differences in historical influences, I observed that both Ignatius and Calvin guided out of a piety that was focused on the Trinity and the Kingdom of God. They dedicated their lives to be wholly lived for the glory of God. They followed the example of Christ in self-denial and

6. See Zachman, *John Calvin*.
7. Guibert, *The Jesuits*, 127.

cross-bearing, and embraced the virtues of humility and love so that they served as Christ did. They were men of prayer and deep reflection, and were guided by the impulse of the Holy Spirit. Although they lived in the world, they did not live according to the world but wholly embraced God's mission for their world. Their foci on spiritual formation and guidance were their efforts to usher the dawning of God's Kingdom on earth. Although they had vastly different personal histories, they shared a similar commitment to God and his Kingdom purposes. These expressions of piety were foundationally grounded upon their theology, the comparative analysis to which I will now turn.

THEOLOGICAL CRITERIA FOR GUIDANCE

Continuity: The Doctrine of the Triune God as Foundation for the Christian Life and Guidance

A core continuity between Ignatius and Calvin was that they both founded their theology of the Christian life upon the doctrine of the Trinity. In our examination of Ignatius, we observed that the doctrine of the Holy Trinity constituted his foundational understanding of the Christian God. For him, God as Trinity comprises God the Creator, Jesus the Redeemer, and the Holy Spirit the Guide (see especially [101–109]). Calvin, similarly, interpreted God to be the Holy Trinity: Father, Son, and Holy Spirit (see especially *Inst.*1.13.1–29). For both Ignatius and Calvin, the Christian understanding of the triune God, who they also respectfully addressed as the "Divine Majesty" in their historical context, is the non-negotiable foundation for an understanding of our creation, redemption, and growth in the Christian life. For them, it was because God had revealed himself in creation and redemption that they could then speak of regeneration in the Christian life. This theological understanding of God unequivocally marked their spiritual theology and practice of spiritual guidance as distinctively Christian.

The roles of the Three Persons in God's plan of salvation were clearly described in their theological schemas. The first Person of the Trinity was referenced foremost as the Father or Creator ([23]; Book I). The Second Person is the Son, who is God incarnate, Jesus Christ our Redeemer ([102]; Book II). Reference to the Third Person, however, was oblique in Ignatius, though interpreters have consistently demonstrated that Ignatius referred to the Holy Spirit.[8] For Calvin, however, the Holy Spirit was explicitly mentioned as the primary Agent who engenders faith in the elect, unites them

---

8. See Palmer, *On Giving the Spiritual Exercises*.

to Christ, and guides them to receive the benefits that Christ has accrued for the faithful (Book III).

Calvin's elaborate pnuematology significantly sets him apart from Ignatius. Calvin's repeated mention and elaboration of the Spirit's work served as a crucial emphasis for guidance and growth in the Christian life (3.1.1). The emphasis on the Holy Spirit will receive further elaborations in the ensuing sections. Presently, the point is made that the foundational understanding of the triune God defined both Ignatius's and Calvin's self-understanding as creatures, who were ravished by sin but now redeemed, and from which their mission for life were defined and now focused. The implication of this foundational understanding on God's self-revelation, redemption in Christ, and sanctification through the Sprit, cannot be overstated. It fundamentally grounds the possibility for and sets the basic direction for Christian spiritual guidance.

Knowing God as the Trinity profoundly shaped their images of God. Rather than the punitive images that were prevalent in their time, they experienced God to be the loving and merciful Father, humble and gracious Son, and zealous yet gentle Holy Spirit [56–61]. These healthy images of God not only served to correct the faulty images that were repugnant then but served as assurances for guidance in the Christian journey now.

Both Ignatius and Calvin emphasized that a trinitarian foundation implied that life must be lived only for the worship, service and glory of God. Hence Ignatius declared in the First Principle and Foundation [23] that humankind was created to "praise, reverence, and serve God our Lord" and that every decision in life must be made "solely [for] the service, honor, and glory of the Divine Majesty" [16]. The *Spiritual Exercises* thus sought to nurture the disposition of freedom, exemplified by the virtue of indifference, so that a disciple of Jesus would not be dominated by inordinate desires but rather live only for the greater glory of God. This understanding defined the ultimate horizon for the Christian life, what Ignatius described as "the end for which [we] are created."

Likewise, Calvin understood a trinitarian foundation to mean that a Christian lives only for the greater glory of God (1.2.1–2). He wrote: "We are consecrated and dedicated to God in order that we may thereafter think, speak, meditate, and do, nothing except to his glory" (3.7.1). This perspective served as the ultimate horizon on being a disciple of Jesus. It meant being empowered through the Holy Spirit to live only for the glory of God. For Calvin, the Christian life must always be lived from the perspective of bringing glory to God, through the secret energy of the Holy Spirit, because of the grace that came through Jesus the Christ.

For Ignatius and Calvin, the doctrine of the triune God fundamentally undergirded their material theological criteria for spiritual guidance. It explains our life in God and presents the practice of spiritual guidance with an integrative focus. In salvation and in spiritual growth, a Christian embraces the work of all the Persons of the Trinity—just as salvation and spiritual growth are accomplished through the action of the triune God. A Christian is redeemed by the atoning work of Jesus, grows through the sanctifying work of the Holy Spirit, and lives for the greater glory of God. The benevolence of the Father comes to us through the grace of our Lord Jesus, whose word is illumined in our minds and sealed upon our hearts through the Holy Spirit. An understanding of the interpenetrating work of the triune God defines the integrative nature of the practice of spiritual guidance—which are the efforts at translating our theology into a lived reality.

Discontinuity: The Problem of Mariology

Thus far, the foundational doctrinal understanding of the triune God is a major point of continuity between Ignatius of Loyola and John Calvin. A discontinuity emerged when Ignatius appealed to Mary as a mediatrix to God the Father [63]. For Calvin, the only mediator between God the Father and humankind is Jesus Christ the Son (3.20.19). Ignatius' appeal to Mary marked a departure from Calvin and became a major point of discontinuity.

As we noted earlier, Ignatius rested his theology of spiritual guidance upon the theology of the Roman Church, which included the traditional teaching on Mary. Ignatius thus translated this understanding into his method, and so invoked "Our Lady" as the mediatrix in prayer, the use of which was especially evident in the triple colloquy [63]. While Calvin held a respectful view of Mary as the earthly mother of our Lord, he refused to accept the extra-biblical teaching that invoked Mary as mediatrix. For Calvin, the only way to the Father was through the Son. Since the Son has atoned for all our sins and merited God's grace and salvation for us, we have confidence before God and there was no need for any other mediators apart from Christ (2.6.1, 2.17.1–6).

For Calvin, there was no other basis for justification before God except through the righteousness of Christ. Even grace-assisted works could not contribute in any way to justification. Calvin's perspective made Ignatius' appeal to meritorious works problematic [20, 44, 87]. For Calvin, there was nothing that could lend to a more secure justification or standing before God other than the imputed righteousness of Christ; not Mary nor the saints and certainly not our works.

Discontinuity: Catholic and Reformed Orders of Salvation

The discontinuity stemming from the problem of Mariology is further accentuated when we consider the phrase in Ignatius' First Principle and Foundation "by this means to save his soul." I have already discussed the various interpretations of what the phrase might have meant for Ignatius. As I have clarified, if by it Ignatius intended for the *Spiritual Exercises* to serve as means for the accrual of meritorious works toward justification before God, then it was clearly a point of discontinuity with Calvin. Calvin rested the assurance for justification solely in the meritorious work of Jesus alone (2.17.1–6). The Pelagian and semi-pelagian heresies revealed that there was no place for meritorious works on our part to secure our justification before God.

Hence, a core theological discontinuity between Ignatius and Calvin laid in their different understandings of the order of salvation. Ignatius adopted the traditional Catholic "three ways" of spiritual progress involving continuous conversion, through the will cooperating with grace, and so aligned the *Spiritual Exercises* to guide one from purgation, through illumination, to union. Calvin, however, grounded the order of salvation causally on mystical (or spiritual) union with Christ, through faith bestowed by the Spirit, in a two-fold grace of justification and sanctification followed by a lifestyle of deepening communion.[9]

Having derived his theology from the Roman Church, Ignatius would have subscribed to the decree concerning justification from the Council of Trent in 1547, which affirmed the medieval system of meriting justification through grace-assisted works. The decree appealed to the "predisposing grace of God through Jesus Christ" and states "that they who by sin had been cut off from God, may be disposed through His quickening and helping grace to convert themselves to their own justification by freely assenting to and cooperating with that grace."[10] In this Tridentine understanding, the will was moved to cooperate with the predisposing grace to secure justification: "so that, while God touches the heart of man through the illumination of the Holy Ghost, man himself neither does absolutely nothing while receiving that inspiration, since he can also reject it."

Calvin, however, objected to the notion of preparatory grace or that the will was capable to cooperate with grace before it was regenerated. For Calvin, sin has so ravaged the human will that it was in complete bondage

9. As Muller explains; "faith, bestowed by the Spirit, is the instrument of union and of the first grace, justification; regeneration-sanctification is the second grace; and repentance is effected by the union." Muller, *Calvin and the Reformed Tradition*, 210.

10. See Schroeder, *Canons and Decrees of the Council of Trent*, 29–34, 39–41.

and was unable to respond until it was regenerated by God's special grace through union with Christ (2.2.6, 2.2.27). Calvin, therefore, rejected the notion that the unregenerate could move the will to cooperate with predisposing grace and be justified. For Calvin, justification rested solely on God's mercy and the work of the Holy Spirit who unites us to Christ. Those who were spiritually united to Christ receive the imputation of his righteousness and were reckoned as righteous before God, not on account of their works, but solely on the righteousness that belonged to Christ alone (Book II). Calvin, therefore, argued that it was only upon regeneration by justifying grace through faith that the will was capable then to respond to God's further sanctifying grace.

Discontinuity: In Relation to Sin and Its Impact

The foundational differences in the causality of salvation were, in turn, linked to the different understandings of sin and its impact.[11] For Ignatius, sin was an impediment that hindered cooperation with God's will and must be incrementally, but decisively, removed with the help of predisposing grace, so that there would be increasing freedom to cooperate with God. The *Spiritual Exercises* thus sought to foster freedom from inordinate attachments to secure a spiritual freedom to respond to God and his will.

Calvin, on the other hand, argued that sin has completely held the will in bondage to such an extent that one was unable to long for the good without the Holy Spirit (2.2.27). Spiritual freedom is only possible through mystical union with Christ by grace through faith. It is only upon being engrafted into Christ that we receive God's Spirit who sets us free to respond to His sanctifying grace.

Ignatius, moreover, differentiated between mortal and venial sins and applied the practice of penance for their absolution [82–89]. Calvin, however, argued that we were so ravaged by original sin that there is no part of us that was unaffected by it. All the parts of the soul, our minds, hearts, and senses, were possessed by sin (2.1.8–11). After being justified by grace through faith, we fight against sin and practice acts of repentance as the vestiges of sin continue to wage a war against the development of our faith. Nevertheless, for Calvin, acts of repentance are the fruit of faith rather than the precursor to faith.

An issue that arises from the different understandings of sin and its resolution is the problem of assurance. For Ignatius, acts of penance have

11. See Muller, *Calvin and the Reformed Tradition*, 161–210, for a discussion of this subject from the Reformed perspective.

meritorious value and contributed to the purgation of post-baptismal sin. The problem, however, is that one cannot be certain how much penance is sufficient for the full remission of sin. This uncertainty results in a lack of assurance before God—and may even accentuate punitive images of God in the exercitant despite the *Exercises'* testimony of a merciful God. This perspective might explain why Ignatius' appealed to the Virgin Mary to intercede before the Father. Perhaps this is a reason why Protestant versions of the *Spiritual Exercises* first emphasize the unconditional love of God as preparatory exercises.[12]

For Calvin, however, Christ has made full satisfaction for sins and has removed both penalty and guilt. The believer who is united to Christ by grace through faith receives the full remission of sin and finds in God not a punitive Judge but a gracious Father (2.6.1; 3.11.1). In Calvin's theological perspective, there is assurance of the forgiveness of sins from Christ's work of substitutionary atonement on the cross. There is now no need and no place for meritorious acts of penance.[13]

Nevertheless, recent interpreters of the *Exercises* have not emphasized the work of penance but have instead emphasized the image of a merciful and loving God.[14] Rather than a punitive Judge, the *Exercises* communicate to the exercitant the image of a gracious and forgiving God. This is consistent with the image that Calvin communicates through the *Institutes*, particularly on his definitions of faith and the exercise of prayer, both of which emphasizes God's benevolence founded upon the freely given promise in Christ.

Discontinuity: Grace and Human Effort for Spiritual Progress

Apart from the preceding points of discontinuity between Ignatius and Calvin, there is also a pronounced difference in their understanding of the relationship between grace and human effort for spiritual growth. While both Ignatius and Calvin emphasize that God's grace is needed for the spiritual life, Ignatius, in adopting the traditional Roman Catholic position, combines God's grace and meritorious works as conditions for continual conversion and growth in the spiritual life toward eventual union with God. Calvin, on the other hand, emphasized that while progress in the spiritual life is not *without* works, it is nevertheless not *through* works that one grows

12. See Warner, *Journey with Jesus*.

13. See Bradley, "Historical Reflections on Substitutionary Atonement," 12–16, for a discussion on this issue.

14. See, for example, English, *Spiritual Freedom*.

into union with God (3.16.1). For Calvin, union with God begins with the free and unmerited grace of God that imputes the righteousness of Christ to the believer and hence justifies the person before God. A second grace is also given, enabling works, so that the Christian can participate by faith through the Holy Spirit and grow into deeper communion with God (3.14.9).

For Ignatius, progress is attained through the gradual removal of inordinate attachments in the purgative way and the imitation of Christ in the illuminative way. Growth in the spiritual life is best described as ordering the human will to cooperate with God's grace toward union with God. For Calvin, however, growth in the spiritual life is only possible through participation in God via union with Christ by faith through the Spirit.

It should be noted that while the text of *the Spiritual Exercises* apparently advocates a form of purgative effort that emphasizes the attainment of freedom through human effort cooperating with grace, a number of recent interpretations of the *Spiritual Exercises* have all emphasized the priority of grace operating through these efforts.[15] As seen in chapters four and five, while there was a sustained emphasis on the priority of grace, for Ignatius, human effort is required to cooperate with God's infused grace so that the human will is moved to cooperate with God's will. Hence, while the text of the *Spiritual Exercises* appears to be semi-pelagian, its interpreters have all sought to emphasize the indispensability and priority of grace.

However, for Calvin, the issue here is not the question of human effort cooperating with grace but rather the problem of invoking the human will before it has been regenerated. For Calvin, an unregenerate will is not capable of cooperating with God. It is only after the Holy Spirit has bestowed the gift of faith through God's grace that one can be moved to exercise one's effort in response—and again only by faith through the Holy Spirit. Hence, there is a difference between Ignatius's and Calvin's understandings of the relationship between grace, faith, and human effort. While both Ignatius and Calvin emphasize human effort and grace, Ignatius proceeds by ordering the human will through human effort in response to God's infused grace, while Calvin renders as priority God's mercy and grace apprehended by faith as causal for the response of human effort.

These theological bases for Ignatius and Calvin fundamentally set the direction and method for growth in the spiritual life. For Ignatius, the fundamental commitment secured in the Foundation sets the direction of progress through the purgative, illuminative, and unitive ways to its culminating exercise in the Contemplation to Attain Love expressed in works

---

15. See, for example, Cusson, *Biblical Theology and the Spiritual Exercises*; Palmer, *On Giving the Spiritual Exercises*; and English, *Spiritual Freedom*.

of service for the glory of God. For Calvin, a secure footing is first assured through union with Christ through the two-fold grace of justification and sanctification before a life of deepening communion with God is nurtured through prayer and expressed in service to humanity for God's glory.

METHODOLOGY

Ignatius's translation of his theological assumptions into his method thus significantly emphasizes the cooperation of the will with predisposing grace, as the expression of love, in a Christocentric focus. In the First Week, through the purgative way, he sought with the help of grace, to rid the will of inordinate desires so that one may hear and respond to the call of Christ the King. In the Second Week, through the illuminative way, the exercitant, through self-abnegation, seeks to imitate Christ and resolves to choose only the way of Christ. The choice of one's disposition in life is then offered to God, which in the Third Week, is confirmed through the determination to identify with Christ even in suffering and death on the cross. The Fourth Week thus celebrates one's full surrender to love, and hence spiritual freedom, in the unitive way.

Calvin is likewise Christocentric as he emphasizes the primacy of Spirit-enabled faith to appropriate the twofold grace of justification and sanctification through mystical union with Christ. His method rests on God's initiating mercy and grace to first regenerate the will, previously held in bondage by sin, through the Holy Spirit that unites one to Christ. The regenerated will is then guided, by the same Holy Spirit-enable faith, to appropriate the grace of Christ in a life of deepening communion with God in prayer, through the disciplines of repentance and contemplation, and expressed in a life of service to God and humankind in love.

Despite the similar focus on Christ, Ignatius's and Calvin's methods of guidance see both points of continuity and discontinuity due to their different theological assumptions on various aspects of the Christian life. Ignatius's Catholic theology clearly threads through his entire methodology, while Calvin was clearly reticent with offering a method in the same way that Ignatius did. This explains why the contemporary tendency to adopt methods for spiritual formation without an understanding of their theological premise and historical context can mislead practitioners to assume that methods that appear similar share the same theological assumptions. While the methods may look similar across the traditions, or faiths, the theological assumptions underlying the practices may, in fact, be very different. Here, it is observed that a major discontinuity between Ignatius and Calvin lies in their different theologies of justification which, consequently, lead to divergences in their methodologies for spiritual progress.

If, however, the differences on the means of justification between Ignatius and Calvin are resolved and both their texts serve as methods for sanctification, then it will be rather interesting to observe where their continuities lie. Still, care must be taken to differentiate Calvin's emphasis on the role of faith through the Holy Spirit—and always by grace, from Ignatius's emphasis on the will cooperating with grace. It is important to note that, for Calvin, the faith that justifies is the same faith that sanctifies. Sanctification, therefore, is also through faith, now exhibited through faith-filled works in grateful response to God's mercy (3.17.8-10). Ignatian spirituality tends not to overtly emphasize yielding to the Holy Spirit although its criteria for discernment implicitly refers to the Holy Spirit and are firmly anchored upon the theological virtues of faith, hope, and love. For Calvin, there is neither justification nor sanctification apart from the secret work of the Holy Spirit in our lives. Nevertheless, points of continuity may offer important insights for guidance in the spiritual life. I will point out these possibilities in the comparison that follows.

Continuity: Foundational Attitudes in Prayer

It is important to note that both Ignatius and Calvin emphasized praying with the right attitudes and virtues. Both the *Spiritual Exercises* and the *Institutes* were dedicated to nurture virtues that lead to true godliness. Ignatius directs us to enter into prayer "with magnanimity and generosity" toward God and to offer to him our "entire will and liberty" that God may guide us "according to His most holy will" [5]. This posture threads through all the prayer exercises and culminates in Ignatius's famous prayer: "Take, Lord, and receive all my liberty, my memory, my understanding and my entire will, all that I have and possess. Thou hast given all to me. To Thee, O Lord, I return it. All is Thine, dispose of it wholly according to Thy will. Give me Thy love and Thy grace, for this is sufficient for me" [234].

Calvin instructs us to enter into prayer, seeking to love and serve God with our whole hearts in gratitude and thanksgiving, so that we may meditate on his kindness and call upon him for our every need (3.20.3). We enter into prayer with reverence, humility, and confidence as we earnestly seek what we want before God so that, in attaining our request, we may give all glory to God (3.20.4-14). Fundamentally, both Ignatius and Calvin emphasized the attitude that, in prayer, we offer to God our entire self without reserve.

Continuities and Discontinuities on Purgation and Repentance

On closer examination, however, we discover degrees of continuity and discontinuity as we compare Ignatius's and Calvin's perspectives on purgation and repentance. They converge in their emphasis on repentance as an act of heartfelt contrition and grateful response to God for his love and mercy. Both of them emphasized that self-examination, self-denial and cross-bearing are virtues necessary for progress in the Christian life. However, they differ in their opinions on the practice of purgation. Calvin's view is not in agreement with Ignatius's that the practice of purgation is needed for making satisfaction for post-baptismal sins (see [87], 3.3.2).

The Ignatian method embarks on the purgative way through the exercises of the Examen and the confession in the First Week. Their function is to assist with the efforts at repentance and purgation, meant to satisfy the penalty for post-baptismal sins. Fundamentally, Ignatius sought to guide the exercitant toward a basic disposition, assisted by grace, to nurture a lifestyle of self-examination in thought, word, and deed for the identification and removal of inordinate attachments, to grow in self-knowledge, and to cultivate the virtues of humility and seeking the greater good. Methodologically, Ignatius sought first to address the problem of sin and to remove the impediments that hinder spiritual progress. Though negatively focused on sin, the examinations are nevertheless done in the light of a merciful and loving God [61]. Though significantly focused on gathering self-knowledge, the knowledge of God is interwoven into the exercises of the First Week.

While Calvin presents the practice of repentance as a race throughout life in sanctification, repentance was not meant to satisfy the penalty of post-baptismal sins (3.3.9). For Calvin, Christ has removed both the guilt and the penalty through his substitutionary atonement. Hence, Calvin treats the subject of sin after discussing the knowledge of God and of Christ and the gospel. As such, Calvin discusses repentance as a fruit of faith rather than a precursor to faith. It is only when one has received the unmerited grace of God by faith through the Holy Spirit that one begins to respond to the fatherly love of God in a posture of repentance. For Calvin, it is the picture of a benevolent God, so clear in his definition of faith, that results in the practice of repentance to mortify the flesh and yield to the Spirit. Repentance that flows from Holy Spirit-enabled faith is, therefore, an expression of deep remorse for having grieved God through our sin and a response of gratitude to God's mercy rather than an effort at satisfaction for sin (3.4.26–30, 3.3.9).

To be sure, Ignatius emphasizes God's great mercy and sacrificial love in the First Week [53]. In that colloquy, the exercitant contemplates Christ upon the cross and dying for our sins. The reflection questions were geared toward gratitude expressed in action: "What have I done for Christ?" "What am I doing for Christ?" "What ought I to do for Christ?" In this pivotal exercise of the First Week, the exercitant is guided to experience God's love in a deep and moving way. The exercise does bear the fruit of gratitude and draws out a loving response in action that is characteristic of Ignatius's active spirituality. Yet, due to its emphasis on doing something for Christ, it runs the risk of nurturing the need to work as a response to Christ rather than simply a deep gratitude for Christ's saving grace and love that can never be earned nor repaid but nevertheless bears the fruit of the worship of God and service to humankind.

Embarking with a focus on an examination of conscience and meditations on sin can be emotionally strenuous to an exercitant—and lead to spiritual and emotional anxiety. That is why Warner's protestant adaptation of the *Exercises* begins with preparatory exercises that assure the exercitant of God's unconditional love.[16] The preparatory exercises, however, are not part of the *Spiritual Exercises*. While Calvin notes that the knowledge of God and of self are linked by many bonds, he reasons that the right beginning to a knowledge of self is to begin from a knowledge of God. He argues: "it is certain, that man never achieves a clear knowledge of himself unless he has first looked upon God's face, and then descends from contemplating him to scrutinize himself . . . for if you contemplate yourself, that is sure damnation" (3.2.24). Consequently, Calvin chose to structure the *Institutes* to begin with the knowledge of God the Creator before proceeding to the knowledge of God the Redeemer in Christ, and within that a discussion of the problem of sin and God's provision of satisfaction in Christ.

Continuities and Discontinuities in Prayer and Discernment

As we consider the practices of prayer and discernment, we again discover degrees of continuity and discontinuity between Ignatius and Calvin due to their different theological emphasis at various points. Ignatius's method sought to cultivate a deep awareness of the movements of the spirits through imaginative prayer. It is a practice that threads through the entire Four Weeks. Through the various meditations and contemplations, especially as they are applied to the grace sought and the "*iq quad volo*"—the "what I want and desire"—attention is drawn to the experiences of the affections of consolations and desolations in the soul. This method of cultivating interior awareness of the movements of the spirits trains the exercitant to be aware

16. Warner, *Journey with Jesus*, 57–77.

of and to recognize the quality and trajectory of these movements—and to admit or to reject them. This method that involves a deep knowledge of the affections in one's experience is distinctively Ignatian.

As we saw, the criteria for judging the interior movements were given in the Rules of Discernment for the First Week [313–327] while more rules were given for the subtler movements in the Second Week [328–336]. Fundamentally, consolations are signaled by the increase of faith, hope, and love—the theological virtues, while desolations are the opposite. More subtle discernment in differentiating between true and false consolations involve tracing the beginning, middle, and end of an affective movement to see if it tends toward God or not. It is in this light that the practice of discerning the quality and trajectory of our affectivity becomes so foundational for ascertaining God's leading and will. As such, the knowledge of God's guidance was significantly wrought through the awareness and assessment of these affective movements, and they served as the means that trains us to be familiar with the mind of Christ.

Calvin did not present discernment in the systematic way that Ignatius did. Still, he emphasized a deep affective knowledge of God's assurance. Calvin's approach focused on prayer as the chief exercise of faith and linked it to the way prayer reaps the fruit of assurance through faith. Through it, Calvin nurtured a holy familiarity with God that is so important to discernment. His definition of faith emphasizes the work of the Holy Spirit in our minds and hearts that leads to a firm and certain knowledge (3.2.7). Prayer, as an exercise of faith, thus reaps the benefit of a deep assurance of God's benevolence, which leads to a familiar sense of God's presence. That is why Calvin says that "the knowledge of faith consists in assurance rather than in comprehension" (3.2.14).

Calvin's way of discernment, therefore, emphasizes an assurance that rests on the Holy Spirit's work of faith in our minds and hearts. The Holy Spirit, as our "inner teacher," illumines the Word in our minds and seals its promise in our hearts as a way of guidance. For Calvin, discernment arises from that profound resonance with God as the Holy Spirit seals the word of God in our inner beings to engender a certain assurance of God's leading. Hence Calvin writes: "for by a mutual bond the Lord has joined together the certainty of his Word and of his Spirit so that the perfect religion of the Word may abide in our minds when the Spirit, who causes us to contemplate God's face, shines; and that we in turn may embrace the Spirit with no fear of being deceived when we recognize him in his own image, namely, in the Word" (1.9.3). Calvin testifies that "there is a far different feeling of full assurance that in the Scriptures is always attributed to faith" (3.2.15). It puts beyond doubt God's goodness to us as we feel its sweetness and experience it in ourselves. For this reason, Calvin adds, we derive confidence from faith, and from confidence, in turn, boldness (3.2.15). Consequently, for Calvin, discernment stems from a deep assurance of faith that reaps the fruit of holy familiarity with God in accord with the testimony of Scripture through the illumination of the Spirit.

While Ignatius did not explicitly refer to the Holy Spirit in his Rules for Discernment, he did imply that the power behind the "good spirit" was in fact the work of the Holy Spirit. So then, it may be said that Ignatius sought to nurture in the exercitant a deep awareness of how the Holy Spirit moves interiorly through the affections in accord with the theological virtues of faith, hope, and love. The want of faith, hope, and love was, therefore, an indication that it was not consistent with God's leading.

Calvin, on the other hand, explicitly teaches that the Holy Spirit is the principal agent through which intimacy with God is nurtured, and from which wisdom and discernment is wrought. Without the Holy Spirit, our minds are dark and our hearts perverse and we can be deceived even by our own hearts. It is only when the Holy Spirit "persistently [boils] away and [burns] up our vicious and inordinate desires, [that he] enflames our hearts with the love of God and with zealous devotion" (3.2.3). In this sense, Calvin describes a consolation that reflects a "far different feeling of full assurance" that is attributed to faith. Through "feeling its sweetness and experiencing it in ourselves," we reap a deep familiarity with God and discern in our inner beings God's leading (3.2.15).

Continuity: Relish of the Truth with Mind and Heart in Deepening Communion

It is significant that both Ignatius and Calvin sought to integrate the cognitive (the understanding) and the affective (the will) powers of the soul as means toward deepening communion with God. In Ignatian prayer, the three powers of the soul—the memory, understanding, and will—are moved, first to recall the truths of Scripture, then to explore their content with the understanding, to relish them deeply and move the will to respond to God's bidding. In Ignatian prayer, the knowledge of God and his will are gained through a deep knowledge of one's interior affections. That is why Evan Howard describes Ignatian discernment as "an affectively-rich act of knowing."[17] Calvin, likewise, points to the importance of integrating the faculties of the soul to deepen one's knowledge of God. He writes: "[the knowledge of Christ] is not apprehended by the understanding and memory

17. See Howard, *Affirming the Touch of God*, 1–12.

alone, as other disciplines are, but it is received only when it possesses the whole soul, and finds a seat and resting place in the inmost affection of the heart" (3.6.4). Calvin places the emphasis on the understanding and the will as the truly fundamental faculties of the soul (1.15.4–7). For him, the understanding is the cognitive power (the mind) that moves the will (the affections or the heart), under whose control is choice. Calvin explains that "our mind must be otherwise illumined, and our heart strengthened, that the Word of God may obtain full faith among us" (3.2.7) The continuity between Ignatius and Calvin on the integration of mind and heart in prayer informs the understanding that spiritual direction is an art that integrates knowledge and practice, involving the cognitive and affective aspects of our lives.

Further, we note that while the three powers of the soul function together as a unit in Ignatian prayer, special emphasis is placed upon the heart. Ignatius reminds us that it is not the aim of the mind to amass much information but to gather spiritual understanding to move the heart to respond to God in generosity. Hence, he explains that "it is not much knowledge that fills and satisfies the soul, but the intimate understanding and relish of the truth" [2]. For this reason, Ignatius's closest associate Jerome Nadal (1507–1580) writes that it "is in the heart that we find the beginning of every grace and of every spiritual understanding."[18] The pivotal point in spiritual transformation lies in the heart. Calvin, likewise, places his emphasis on the centrality of the heart in the exercise of faith. He writes that assent "is more of the heart than of the brain, and more of the disposition than of the understanding" (3.2.8). In fact, Calvin applied this disposition of the heart to the controversy of the Lord's mysterious presence in the Supper. In this regard, he wrote: "I rather experience than understand it. Therefore, I here embrace without controversy the truth of God in which I may safely rest" (4.17.32). As Calvin emphasized, progress in the Christian life is made only when the knowledge of God "possesses the whole soul, and finds a seat and resting place in the inmost affection of the heart" (3.6.4). It is, therefore, very significant that both Ignatius and Calvin pointed to the centrality of the heart in the living the Christian life. This point of continuity acts as a very strong bond between the Ignatian and the Reformed traditions on the work of spiritual guidance—and of Christian spiritual formation.

The integration of the mind and heart explains the reason why the practice of meditation and contemplation contribute so significantly to spiritual growth and guidance. Through these exercises of deep communion with God, one relishes and internalizes the truth of God's word and

18. Cusson, *Biblical Theology and the Spiritual Exercises*, 106.

develops a holy familiarity to the voice of Christ, through the Holy Spirit. With practice, one learns to discern the guidance of the Spirit of Truth and obeys the will of God. In this regard, both Ignatius and Calvin affirm that it is only in keeping the Word of God in our hearts that we learn to obey and serve him for his glory.

This disposition of familiarity and obedience is honed through the faith-based practice of daily conversation with God—which both Ignatius and Calvin sought to nurture in all they guide ([54], 3.20.4). Ignatius consistently concludes a prayer exercise with a colloquy that draws out a better response to God in reverential communion [53, 61, and 63]. Calvin urges prayerful communion with God as the chief exercise of faith (3.20.1). For them, spiritual guidance is ultimately about disposing another to the grace of God in a deepening communion by faith through the Holy Spirit in the heart.

For both Ignatius and Calvin, a deepening communion with God through the integration of mind and heart is, however, not an end in itself. This deepening communion must be expressed in daily living and issue in a life of service to God and humankind. Ignatius emphasized that love must be expressed in deeds [230]. This emphasis treads through the *Exercises* from the Foundation [23] to the Contemplation to Attain Love [230–237], and receives special attention in several meditations (see, for example, the three classes of men [149–157] and three kinds of humility [165–168]). Calvin, likewise, emphasizes that our love for God must be expressed in concrete ways in our daily living: "But [the knowledge of Christ] must enter our heart and pass into our daily living, and so transform us into itself that it may not be unfruitful for us" (3.6.4). He emphasized that the efficacy of our life in God "ought to penetrate the inmost affections of the heart, take its seat in the soul, and affect the whole [person] a hundred times more deeply than [mere talk]" (3.6.4). Both Ignatius and Calvin understood that spiritual formation must issue in a transformed life that participates in the mission of God.

CONCLUDING REMARKS

Through its comparative analysis, this chapter has highlighted points of continuity and discontinuity between Ignatius and Calvin in the spheres of historical influence, theological criteria, and methods of practice in spiritual guidance. We saw that, despite being contemporaries with each other historically, they were influenced by quite a different range of cultural, political, ecclesial, and personal experiences. These different historical influences significantly shaped their theological horizons and led to major points of discontinuity in their theological criteria for the ministry of spiritual guidance. Nevertheless, they shared a common theology of the Trinity, which foundationally grounded their Christian faith and set their approach on guidance as distinctively Christian.

While they diverge on several points in their method of spiritual guidance, they also converge on important points. These points of divergences and convergences were directly influenced by their theological criteria and so underscores this work's thesis that methods in spiritual guidance emerges from one's theological assumptions, which in turn were shaped by one's historical influences. The points of continuity and discontinuity between these two great traditions in the Christian church, nevertheless, possess potential for mutual enrichment through a constructive interpretation. It is to this potential that we turn in the final and concluding chapter in this work.

9

A Constructive Interpretation

IN THE OPENING CHAPTER, I proposed that genuine enrichment across the traditions requires, firstly, that one gains an in-depth knowledge of one's own spiritual tradition, especially in the connections between its history, theology, and spiritual practice. Secondly, I proposed that authentic ecumenical enrichment requires an honest appraisal of the continuities and discontinuities between traditions. My work, thus far, has attempted to accomplish these two goals through a comparative study of Ignatius of Loyola and John Calvin as spiritual guides.

Having examined the continuities and discontinuities in the histories, theologies, and methods of spiritual guidance between Ignatius Loyola and John Calvin, I will now conclude with a constructive interpretation on how these two traditions could enrich each other. Here, I wish to make a few suggestions that, I hope, will lead to a constructive dialogue between the two traditions.

TRINITARIAN FOUNDATION

As a point of departure, we note that both Ignatius and Calvin shared a piety that was founded on the Trinity and God's mission. This shared trinitarian foundation fundamentally defines them as distinctively Christian in their theological orientation and faith commitment. It is from this Christian theological foundation that they sought to live out their life's mission as spiritual guides.[1] This shared Christian foundation makes it possible for us

1. Note how mission historian Scott Sunquist similarly derives an understanding of

to creatively explore how the two traditions, the Ignatian and the Reformed, can potentially enrich each other. This exploration might then serve as a case study for explorations across other Christian traditions in an ecumenical context.

ORDERS OF SALVATION

While Ignatius and Calvin have a shared trinitarian foundation for their piety, their methods of spiritual guidance were nevertheless influenced by their personal histories and their bias in various aspects of their theologies; the points and implications of which this study have sought to explicate. Arguably the deepest discontinuity between the Ignatian and Reformed traditions lie in their different orders of salvation. The problem principally revolves around the question of atonement and satisfaction for sins. This is a colossal issue, and it is beyond the scope of this study to treat it in the full. Nevertheless, my work has attempted to illuminate some of the intricacies of this issue.[2]

THE ROLE OF THE HOLY SPIRIT

As a way forward in ecumenical enrichment, however, my study proposes that it will be worthwhile for the two traditions to return once more to Scripture and historical theology in a joint study of its teachings on the role of the Holy Spirit in relation to the functions of grace, faith, and human effort. These are important vectors that could clarify how the two traditions can close the gap between their different understandings on salvation and spiritual progress. As it appears, a major tension between the two traditions revolves around pneumatology, their understanding of the agency of the Holy Spirit with respect to the will's response to God's grace as an exercise of faith.

I have pointed out the problem of illuminism in historical context which may help to explain why Ignatius was less explicit about the role of the Spirit in his theology and methodology. Calvin, on the other hand, was very deliberate in emphasizing the role of the Holy Spirit in his theology and method. The construction of a shared pneumatology may help to clarify the

---

Christian mission from a trinitarian theological foundation. See Sunquist, *Understanding Christian Mission*.

2. See Bradley, "Historical Reflections on the Substitutionary Atonement," for a good discussion on the subject.

Holy Spirit's role in activating the will to respond to grace or in engendering faith, and this may help with bridging this gap between the traditions.

The issue of the Holy Spirit's agency is linked to the issue of human initiative. I have observed that both Ignatius and Calvin affirmed the role of human effort for progress in the Christian life. However, they had different perspectives on how human effort is to be exercised. Ignatius emphasizes that the will cooperates with grace while Calvin places his emphasis on a Holy Spirit-enabled faith that appropriates the grace of Christ. Nevertheless, Ignatius's implicit theology of the Holy Spirit meant that his assumptions on the exercise of human effort to cooperate with grace did involve the agency of the Holy Spirit. This infers that it is with the Spirit's help that the will is moved to cooperate with grace.

Jesuit theologians Harvey Egan and Michael Ivens have both argued that Ignatius in fact appealed to the Holy Spirit in the *Exercises*. Egan writes: "Now that the dangers and exaggerations of illuminism are scarcely present the exercitant must be explicitly told that the Exercises will evoke, strengthen, and make more explicit the ever-present experience of the Holy Spirit."[3] Ivens affirms Egan's call and adds "that it must be strongly emphasized today that the rules for discernment are essentially concerned with recognizing the action in human consciousness of the Holy Spirit."[4]

In the light of Egan's and Iven's contributions, it may be said that Ignatius's understanding of the Spirit's role in spiritual growth is very closely aligned with Calvin's. For Ignatius, the Holy Spirit actively engages the will that seeks God. For Calvin, the Holy Spirit is the prime mover behind the expressions of human effort to appropriate the grace that Christ has procured for us. These human efforts are the exercises of faith, but they are always done through grace and with the help of the Holy Spirit. Greater clarity on the role of the Holy Spirit with respect to the functions of grace, faith, and human effort will help to deepen mutual understanding between the Ignatian and Reformed traditions.[5]

3. Egan, *The Spiritual Exercises*, 122.

4. Ivens, *Understanding the Spiritual Exercises*, 211.

5. See Tan and Gregg, *Disciplines of the Holy Spirit*, for an emphasis on the integral role of the Holy Spirit for a dynamic and growing Christian life. Tan writes that the "Spirit-filled life is the Christ-directed life by which Jesus lives his life in and through us in the power of the Holy Spirit."

SPIRITUAL DISCERNMENT

A consideration of the agency of the Holy Spirit in sanctification leads to the question of discernment. Discernment, as we observed, plays a central role in the ministry of spiritual guidance. The possibility for discernment is in turn grounded in a trinitarian understanding of God and the reality of his Spirit indwelling us. Both Ignatius and Calvin recognized the important function of discernment in the Christian life, and they both emphasized the roles of the Word and the Spirit in its practice.

Ignatius honed the posture of discernment through the practice of imaginative prayer using Scripture. Through this method, he brought to awareness the different affections that were experienced by the exercitant. The rules of discernment then helped to clarify the quality and trajectory of these interior movements and so guided one on how to discern the authentic movements of the Spirit.[6] Calvin, on the other hand, utilized a broader approach to discernment that also involved the mutual bond of the Word and Spirit in prayer. For Calvin, the Holy Spirit brings about a deep assurance of God's leading through the promises of Scripture. Immersion in Word and Spirit reaps a deep familiarity with God that serves as a basis for discerning the guidance of God.

While the "Rules for Discernment" offers specificity in the Ignatian approach, Ivens notes that discernment as a practice requires a wider context for honing our ability to listen to God. He writes that discernment needs a set of spiritual qualities that include "an attitude of presence to God's word in all its mediations, and hence a sense of the Church and an openness to God's word in Scripture, prophecy, situations, events; and more particularly, . . . the growing interiorized knowledge of Christ that leads to the feel of his 'mind'."[7] This wider listening context serves as an important backdrop to the specifics of the Ignatian rules of discernment. By way of creative integration across the traditions, we might consider Calvin's broader approach to discernment as a complement to the Ignatian rules of discernment. Calvin's thorough study of the Scriptures, evident both in the *Institutes* and the commentaries, with a sharp eye for the essential role of the church in Christian formation, serves as a robust guide to nurture the "mind of Christ."[8]

---

6. See Ivens, *Understanding the Spiritual Exercises*, 211–13.

7. Ivens, *Understanding the Spiritual Exercises*, 205.

8. See Bolton, *Life in God*, 29–45, for Matthew Bolton's description of how Calvin and his fellow reformers in Geneva transformed the church into a "sacred schoolhouse" for Christian formation; a change that not only impacted the church but the entire city of Geneva.

On the other hand, Calvin's way of discernment can also benefit from the Ignatian rules of discernment. While Calvin consistently appeals to the experience of the Spirit's assurance, he did not distill those experiences into a set of "rules" as Ignatius did. The Ignatian "rules" can offer greater precision to Calvin's way of discernment, especially as seen in its criteria for assessing the quality and trajectory of the affections. The Reformed approach to discernment can also benefit from Ignatian imaginative prayer, as it is appropriately practiced, to serve as a good means to bring to awareness the diversity of spirits that act upon the soul. The guidance from the rules for discernment brings greater specificity to a general sense of the Spirit's leading.

In this regard, our comparative study has pointed out the more individually inclined nature of the *Spiritual Exercises* while Calvin's approach to spiritual guidance consciously retained an ecclesial perspective. This subtle, but very important, difference underscores the importance of retaining an ecclesial or corporate context for the exercise of personal discernment—a concern which I addressed in chapter three. Having said that, we note that contemporary authors from both the Ignatian and Reformed traditions have emphasized the important role of the church in the practice of Christian discernment, and so do curb the perennial danger of individualism that is so prevalent in contemporary spirituality.

The insights that emerge from a comparison of the Ignatian and Reformed ways offers a more robust practice of discernment in the Christian life. Both Ignatius and Calvin converged on their emphasis for the integration of mind and heart for spiritual transformation, with a special focus on the inner assurances of the heart. The complementarity of their ways of discernment therefore contributes to the nurture of the Christian life as a lived reality, and so offers a constructive integration that benefits both the traditions.

SPIRITUAL THEOLOGY AND SPECIFIC STEPS

The constructive integration on discernment leads to the possibility of integrating other major strengths of the two traditions in a manner that contributes to the work of spiritual guidance for the Ignatian and the Reformed traditions respectively. We have already noted the favorable comments and appropriations across these two traditions seen in Catholic lay theologian Lucien Richard's retrieval of Calvin's spirituality, and James Wakefield's and Larry Warner's appropriation of the *Spiritual Exercises* for an evangelical audience.[9] Drawing on the major strengths from the two traditions will be strategically constructive for ecumenical cooperation if care taken to retain an eye on their respective historical and theological distinctives.

Broadly speaking, the Ignatian *Spiritual Exercises*, the strength of which lies in its methodical approach to guidance, can potentially benefit from a strong spiritual theology as found in Calvin's *Institutes of the Christian Religion*. Conversely, Calvin's method of guidance can benefit from the specificity of the Ignatian method as seen in its text and process. This broad proposal addresses the common observations that the *Exercises* lack a robust explicit spiritual theology while the *Institutes*, as reflective of the larger Protestant emphasis, lack a more deliberate super structure for spiritual growth.[10]

This broad proposal does not overlook the difficulties encountered between the two traditions as seen in the points of discontinuity identified in this work, in particular their theological assumptions. The differences will have to be acknowledged and surmounted. Nevertheless, the distinctive strengths from these two traditions can be creatively adapted by theologians and practitioners of spiritual guidance from the two traditions as they are deemed appropriate for their tradition.

For example, the Ignatian tradition can benefit from Calvin's teaching on union with Christ through the twofold grace of justification and sanctification which offers to the exercitant a deep sense of assurance in God as a point of departure for the life-long journey of Christian formation. The Ignatian tradition can also benefit from an explicit theology of the Holy Spirit, which, for example, affirms the agency of the Spirit in guiding us to Christ—then of Christ bringing us to the Father.[11] Those from the Reformed tradition can, in turn, benefit from the Ignatian *Exercises*, such as the Examinations of Conscience and of Consciousness,[12] the practice of imaginative prayer, and the Rules for Discernment.

Specifically, the retrieval of Calvin's teaching on Word and Spirit can enrich the Ignatian understanding of preparatory grace in imaginative

9. See also, Aronis, *Developing Intimacy with God*, on his adaptation of the *Spiritual Exercises* for modern disciples of Jesus. Also of note was the conference on Ignatius and Calvin at Saint Patrick's College at Maynooth, Ireland. See, McConvery, *Living in Union with Christ in Today's World*.

10. See, for example, Chan, *Spiritual Theology*, 15–39, on his observations about the lack of a super structure for spiritual growth in Protestant spiritual theology.

11. See Canlis, *Calvin's Ladder*, for an excellent work that discusses our participation in the life in God. She discusses our "ascent" by the Spirit into the Son, and in the Son to the Father.

12. See Aschenbrenner, "A Check on Our Availability: The Examen," for a good reinterpretation of the Examen for daily practice.

prayer. Ignatius's use of imaginative prayer does have elements of potential danger when it is misapplied, especially when one reads into (eisegesis) rather than out of (exegesis) a biblical text or when it is used as a form of imitation rather than of participation in Christ.[13] Anchoring a gospel text upon a proper exegesis before engaging in imaginative prayer and contemplation can circumvent this potential danger. As the Ignatian *Exercises* tend toward an explicit methodology with an implicit theology, they can benefit from a robust Reformed theology of Word and Spirit. Calvin's teaching on the mutual bond between the Word and Spirit can enrich the practice of imaginative prayer and contemplation.

For the Protestant audience, it is important to note the difference between Catholic and Reformed orders of salvation and explicitly rest the *Spiritual Exercises* upon a Protestant theology of justification and sanctification through spiritual union with Christ. Here, Calvin's teaching from the *Institutes* can serve as an alternate spiritual theology for the *Exercises*. This construction will address the points of discontinuity in theology between the Ignatian and Reformed traditions while opening possibilities for exploration on their points of continuity. Resting the *Exercises* upon a Reformed theological basis will not detract the *Exercises* from their formational intent if care is taken to identify the exercises that can or cannot be adapted for use. For example, the practices that appeal to Mary in prayer or of penance rest upon radically different theological assumptions and so cannot be integrated into a Reformed theology of spiritual formation. Calvin provided a different theological basis for the practice of prayer and repentance. The Ignatian exercises of self-examination, meditation, and contemplation, however, can be integrated if care is taken to adjust the theological assumption from that of working toward union with Christ with human effort cooperating with grace (the Ignatian way) to that of working from union with Christ by grace through Holy Spirit-enabled faith (the Reformed way). As such, the extent to which exercises can be constructively integrated depends on the extent to which the theological assumptions can be navigated. The criterion for decision lies in whether a practice is in keeping with one's theological conviction. This important consideration underscores this work's concern that greater care must be taken, especially in an ecumenical context, where the mixing and matching of spiritual practices may be made

---

13. We note that whether in Ignatian imaginative prayer using Scripture or the practice of prayerful reading of Scripture (*Lectio Divina*), there is an assumption that the practice is premised on a proper understanding of the biblical context and text wrought through the discipline of study and analysis. See, for example, Wilhoit and Howard, *Discovering Lectio Divina: Bringing Scripture into Ordinary Life*, for their discussion of this practice.

without due consideration for their theological assumptions. Practices (or forms) that look similar may, in fact, have very different undergirding theological assumptions.

It is nevertheless acknowledged that the Reformed tradition's inertia on articulating a method for spiritual progress has impoverished its audience. I have attempted to demonstrate that a method can be elicited from Calvin's doctrine of the spiritual life in the *Institutes*. A critical retrieval and application of the *Exercises* upon a Reformed theology may in fact offer a method of spiritual progress for those in the Reformed tradition. The Ignatian examination of consciousness, practice of imaginative prayer, and discernment of spirits can be utilized with Calvin's source of assurance, wrought through spiritual union with Christ, to kindle a robust confidence for decision-making.

PERSPECTIVE AND MISSION

Further to these ideas on constructive integration, I wish to highlight two further points that my work addresses in relation to the practice of spiritual direction, especially in an ecumenical context. The first is the need to make and retain the tri-perspective of history, theology, and method in spiritual guidance by both the directee and the director. Often the danger in an ecumenical context lies in the temptation to separate the formation of spiritual experience from theological reflection. The separation of theology from practice invariably leads to a fragmented approach to spiritual guidance and formation. However, a directee's personal history inevitably shapes her theology of God and her approach to the spiritual life. A director will benefit from being very conscious of how the directee's personal history impacts her theology, for example, with regards to her images of God and of herself. A skillful director who is conscious of these connections will then be more careful in suggesting exercises to help with the directee's efforts at making spiritual progress. They also offer clues that explain the times when the directee seem to be hindered by resistances or stagnation. Keeping the tri-perspective in view will offer a more comprehensive perspective for the practice of spiritual guidance.

Similarly, the director should also be conscious of how her personal history and theology impacts her practice of spiritual guidance. It is often a good practice for the director to inform the directee of her theological orientation before embarking on a direction relationship. As spiritual direction is significantly about theological reflection on spiritual experience, being clear about where the director and directee stand theologically is an important precursor to good spiritual direction. In addition, sometimes while giving guidance the vestiges of our flesh or old hurts surface to influence our ability to attend. Being aware of how these dynamics impact us as directors helps with keeping an eye out for how they may get in the way of offering spiritual guidance. Often, it is helpful for spiritual directors to share these issues with their supervisors. These issues are naturally accentuated in an ecumenical context where there is greater variance or variety of theologies, apart from personal histories. Taking the care to be open to the tri-perspective is a way forward to a better practice of ecumenical spiritual direction.

This leads to the point on missiological engagement across the traditions. My work has pointed to the similar trinitarian and scriptural foundations across the Ignatian and Reformed traditions. While, admittedly, there are historically held theological differences across the traditions, a recent text from the gospels reminds us of Jesus words that "anyone who is not against us is for us" (Mark 9:40, NLT). These words serve as an apt reminder that ecumenical engagements in the world Christian movement calls for a spirit of honesty and wisdom, and of humility and openness. While there are clearly points of convergence and divergence across the traditions, the spirit of ecumenism calls us to see that the enemy is not one's brothers and sisters in the Christian faith. It helps to note that both Ignatius of Loyola and John Calvin "drew from the same well-springs of renewed evangelical fervor."[14] While Ignatius may have preserved the more traditional dimensions of medieval theology, he nevertheless, "envisioned the integration of ancient spirituality in the wider social world with an evangelical spirit."[15] Calvin, likewise, regarded the Christian's work in the world as being a spiritual vocation through which one could give greater glory to God. In this regard, both Ignatius and Calvin shared the same vision of "a deeper spiritual life coupled with active ministry in the world" as truly reflective of their fundamental concern in spiritual guidance and missiological engagement.[16] Keeping in view this foundational impetus helps us to retain the big picture in the call, and continuing story, of God to his work in the world.

The preceding ideas may serve as points of departure for further constructive dialogue between these two traditions in the Christian Church. Their shared burden on spiritual guidance, trinitarian foundation, and Christocentric focus that nurtures the virtues of self-denial, humility, and love, envisions that the Christian life is best lived in partnership with God's mission. These are traits that serve as bridges that can mutually enrich both

14. Irvin and Sunquist, *History of the world Christian movement*, 117.

15. Irvin and Sunquist, *History of the world Christian movement*, 117.

16. Irvin and Sunquist, *History of the world Christian movement*, 117.

the traditions. While it is important to be discerning on the particularities of a tradition's history, theology, and methodology for spiritual guidance, it is nevertheless healthy to be open on how certain aspects of one tradition can enrich another. On this note, I will now conclude with some summative comments on the main thrust of this work.

SUMMARY REMARKS

The presenting problem of this work is the issue of ahistorical and atheological spiritual direction, which is an issue that is particularly accentuated in an ecumenical setting. When spiritual direction is reduced to mere practice, it fails to be faithful to the historical context and guiding theology of each tradition's heritage and it will hinder rather than help in the work of spiritual direction across the traditions.

This work thus proposes the thesis that the practice of spiritual direction must carefully attend to the connection between a tradition's history, theology, and methodology for spiritual direction before help can be meaningfully offered across the traditions. As this work has shown, a tradition's history influences its theology which in turn shapes its method of spiritual direction. It is when we attend to these connections that we notice the continuities and discontinuities across the traditions. The awareness of continuities and discontinuities across the traditions thus prompts us to be more faithful and honest in retrieving a tradition's history, theology, and practice, which then helps to further our ecumenical engagements.

My historical treatment in chapter two illustrated the connections between a tradition's history, theology, and its practice of spiritual direction. We saw that a tradition's unique historical setting shaped its set of theological convictions which then influenced its way of spiritual guidance. In a sense, then, there is really no possibility of an ahistorical and atheological method of spiritual practice; for every method and practice has its underlying theological assumptions and historical context. This observation issues a strong caution for any tendency to simply embrace a spiritual practice without due consideration for its underlying theology or historical precedent.

As we observed, however, a tradition's practice of spiritual direction emerges from its theological assumptions. As such, I devoted chapter three to a discussion of the theological considerations for the practice of spiritual direction. In that chapter I presented a brief history of spiritual theology and discussed several major theological dogmas that must serve as the foundational theological criteria for a Christian practice of spiritual direction. In the chapter I made the point that the practice of spiritual direction is fundamentally theological in orientation and so calls attention to the underlying theology of any practice of spiritual guidance.

With those important preliminaries in place, my work then proceeded onto a comparative study of Ignatius of Loyola and John Calvin with respect to their histories, theologies, and methods of spiritual guidance. In the respective chapters on Ignatius and Calvin I explicated how their social, political, religious, and personal histories shaped their theologies of the Christian life from which emerged their methods for spiritual guidance. The clarity with which their personal histories shaped their personal theologies, which in turn influenced their methodologies, strongly demonstrated that careful attention must be given to the interconnectivity between history, theology, and practice in the ministry of spiritual guidance. In those chapters especially, I explicated why Ignatius and Calvin guided in the ways they did.

My comparative analysis in chapter eight then highlighted the points of continuity and discontinuity between the Ignatian and Reformed traditions. The chapter showed that though they belonged to the same historical period in the Christian church, their different personal histories resulted in rather different theologies and methods, although there were also points of similarity. This observation underscores the importance of paying careful attention to a directee's personal history, theological biases, and the ensuing spiritual practices in the work of spiritual guidance. A tri-perspective of history, theology, and spiritual practice is critical to a more comprehensive practice of spiritual guidance.

The points of convergence and divergence that the comparative chapter unearthed helped us to understand where difficulties are encountered between the Ignatian and Reformed traditions, but also on how they could potentially complement each other in the ministry of spiritual guidance. My constructive integration thus went on to suggest ideas on how the two traditions can enrich each other through the complementation of their strengths.

Fundamentally, my work draws attention to the importance of retaining a tri-perspective of history, theology, and method in the ministry of spiritual direction. This tri-perspective is important both for understanding one's own spiritual tradition and the broad range of Christian traditions. The connection between a tradition's or an individual's personal history, theology, and practice makes this tri-perspective a mandatory vision for the ministry of spiritual direction. It also furthers the potential for enrichment across the traditions in the practice of spiritual direction in an ecumenical context—rendering the practice truly missional in the world Christian movement.

Bibliography

Addison, Howard A. *Show Me Your Way: The Complete Guide to Exploring Interfaith Spiritual Direction*. Woodstock, VT: SkyLight Paths, 2001.

Aelred, Rievaulx. *Spiritual Friendship*. Edited by Marsha L. Dutton. Translated by Lawrence C. Braceland. Collegeville, MN: Cistercian, 2010.

Allen, Diogenes. *Spiritual Theology: The Theology of Yesterday for Spiritual Help Today*. Cambridge, MA: Cowley, 1997.

Allen, Joseph J. *Inner Way: Toward a Rebirth of Eastern Christian Spiritual Direction*. Brookline, MA: Holy Cross Orthodox, 2000.

Anselm. *The Letters of Saint Anselm of Canterbury*. Translated by Walter Fröhlich. Cistercian Studies Series. Kalamazoo, MI: Cistercian, 1990.

Armstrong, Regis, ed. *Francis of Assisi: Early Documents. Volume II. The Founder*. New York: New City, 2000.

Aronis, Alexander Basile. *Developing Intimacy with God: An Eight-Week Prayer Guide Based on Ignatius' "Spiritual Exercises."* Makati City, Philippines: Union Church of Manila, 2003.

Aschenbrenner, George A. "A Check on Our Availability: The Examen." *Review for Religious* 39.3 (1980) 321–24.

———. *Stretched for Greater Glory: What to Expect from the Spiritual Exercises*. Chicago: Loyola University Press, 2004.

Athanasius of Alexandria. *The Life of Antony*. Translated by Tim Vivian, Apostolos N Athanassakis, and Rowan A. Greer. Kalamazoo, MI: Cistercian, 2003.

Au, Wilkie. "Review of *Journey with Jesus: Discovering the Spiritual Exercises of Saint Ignatius*, by Larry Warner." *Journal of Spiritual Formation and Soul Care* 4.1 (2011) 3.

Aumann, Jordan. *Spiritual Theology*. Westminster, MD: Christian Classics, 1987.

Bakke, Jeannette A. *Holy Invitations: Exploring Spiritual Direction*. Grand Rapids: Baker, 2000.

Barry, William A. *Spiritual Direction and the Encounter with God: A Theological Inquiry*. Mahwah, NJ: Paulist, 2004.

Barry, William A., and William J Connolly. *The Practice of Spiritual Direction*. New York: HarperOne, 2009.

Battles, Ford Lewis. *Interpreting John Calvin*. Edited by Robert Benedetto. Grand Rapids: Baker, 1996.

Beeke, Joel R. "Appropriating Salvation: The Spirit, Faith and Assurance, and Repentance." In *A Theological Guide to Calvin's Institutes: Essays and Analysis*, edited by David W. Hall and Peter A. Lillback, 270–300. Phillipsburg, NJ: P & R, 2008.

Benedict. *The Rule of St. Benedict in English*. Edited by Timothy Fry. Collegeville, MN: Liturgical, 2019.

Benner, David G. *The Gift of Being Yourself: The Sacred Call to Self-Discovery*. Downers Grove, IL: InterVarsity, 2004.

Bennett, Melvin Joseph. "John Calvin and Ignatius of Loyola as Spiritual Guides for Today." D.Min. diss, Christian Theological Seminary, 1994.

Billings, J. Todd. *Calvin, Participation, and the Gift: The Activity of Believers in Union with Christ*. Changing Paradigms in Historical and Systematic Theology. Oxford: Oxford University Press, 2007.

———. *Union with Christ: Reframing Theology and Ministry for the Church*. Grand Rapids: Baker Academic, 2011.

Boulton, Matthew Myer. *Life in God: John Calvin, Practical Formation, and the Future of Protestant Theology*. Grand Rapids,: Eerdmans, 2011.

Bradley, James E. "Historical Reflections on the Substitutionary Atonement." Edited by Joel B. Green. *Theology, News & Notes* 59.2 (2012) 12–16.

Bradley, James E., and Richard A. Muller. *Church History: An Introduction to Research, Reference Works, and Methods*. Grand Rapids: Eerdmans, 1995.

Browning, Don S. *A Fundamental Practical Theology: Descriptive and Strategic Proposals*. Minneapolis: Fortress, 2010.

Buckley, Suzanne M., ed. *Sacred Is the Call: Formation and Transformation in Spiritual Direction Programs*. New York: Crossroad, 2018.

Bumpus, Mary Rose, and Rebecca Bradburn Langer, eds. *Supervision of Spiritual Directors: Engaging in Holy Mystery*. Harrisburg, PA: Morehouse, 2005.

Burrows, Mark S. "*Devotio Moderna*: Reforming Piety in the Later Middle Ages." In *Spiritual Traditions for the Contemporary Church*, edited by Robin Maas and Gabriel O'Donnell. Nashville: Abingdon, 1990.

Butin, Philip Walker. *Revelation, Redemption, and Response: Calvin's Trinitarian Understanding of the Divine-Human Relationship*. New York: Oxford University Press, 1994.

Byrne, Lavinia. *Traditions of Spiritual Guidance*. Collegeville, MN: Liturgical, 1990.

Calvin, Jean. *Calvin's Commentaries*. Translated by Calvin Translation Society. Grand Rapids: Baker, 1999.

———. *Golden Booklet of the True Christian Life*. Translated by Henry J. Van Andel. Grand Rapids: Baker, 1952.

———. *Institutes of the Christian Religion*. Edited by John T McNeill. Translated by Ford Lewis Battles. Philadelphia: Westminster, 1960.

———. *Institutes of the Christian Religion: Embracing almost the whole sum of piety, & whatever is necessary to know the doctrine of salvation; a work most worthy to be read by all persons zealous for piety, and recently published ; preface to the most Christian King of France, wherein this book is offered to him as a confession of faith*. Translated by Ford Lewis Battles. Grand Rapids: H. H. Meeter Center for Calvin Studies and Eerdmans, 1986.

———. *John Calvin: Writings on Pastoral Piety*. Edited and translated by Elsie Anne McKee. New York: Paulist, 2001.

———. *Letters of John Calvin*. Edited by Jules Bonnet. New York: Franklin, 1973.

———. *Selected Works of John Calvin: Tracts and Letters*. Edited by Henry Beveridge. Translated by Jules Bonnet. Grand Rapids: Baker, 1983.

———. *The Piety of John Calvin: An Anthology Illustrative of the Spirituality of the Reformer.* Edited and translated by Ford Lewis Battles. Grand Rapids: Baker, 1978.

Calvin, Jean, and I. John Hesselink. *On Prayer: Conversation with God.* Louisville: Westminster John Knox, 2006.

Calvin Studies Society, and David L Foxgrover. *Calvin and Spirituality: Papers Presented at the 10th Colloquium of the Calvin Studies Society, May 18–20, 1995, Calvin Theological Seminary. Calvin and His Contemporaries : Colleagues, Friends and Conflicts : Papers Presented at the 11th Colloquium of the Calvin Studies Society, April 24–26, 1997, Louisville Theological Seminary.* Grand Rapids: Published for the Calvin Studies Society by CRC Product Services, 1998.

Canlis, Julie. *Calvin's Ladder: A Spiritual Theology of Ascent and Ascension.* Grand Rapids: Eerdmans, 2010.

Caraman, Philip. *Ignatius Loyola.* London: Collins, 1990.

Casiday, Augustine. *Tradition and Theology in St. John Cassian.* Oxford Early Christian Studies. Oxford: Oxford University Press, 2007.

Cassian, John. *John Cassian, the Conferences.* Translated by Boniface Ramsey. Ancient Christian Writers 57. Mahwah, NJ: Paulist, 2000.

Cassian, John, and Boniface Ramsey. *John Cassian, the Institutes.* Ancient Christian Writers 58. New York: Paulist, 2000.

Chadwick, Owen. *John Cassian.* Cambridge: Cambridge University Press, 2008.

Chan, Simon. *Liturgical Theology: The Church as Worshiping Community.* Downers Grove, IL: IVP Academic, 2006.

———. *Spiritual Theology: A Systematic Study of the Christian Life.* Downers Grove, IL: InterVarsity, 1998.

Charleston, Steven. "A Graph of Spirituality: Understanding Where We Are Going by Knowing Where We Have Been." In *Still Listening: New Horizons in Spiritual Direction*, 183–98. Harrisburg, PA: Morehouse, 2000.

Chase, Steven. *The Tree of Life: Models of Christian Prayer.* Grand Rapids: Baker Academic, 2005.

Chin, Clive S. "*Unio Mystica* and *Imitatio Christi*: The Two-Dimensional Nature of John Calvin's Spirituality." PhD diss, Dallas Theological Seminary, 2002.

Chittister, Joan. *The Rule of Benedict: Insights for the Ages.* New York: Crossroad, 1992.

———. *Wisdom Distilled from the Daily: Living the Rule of St. Benedict Today.* San Francisco: HarperSanFrancisco, 1991.

Chryssavgis, John. *Soul Mending: The Art of Spiritual Direction.* Brookline, MA: Holy Cross Orthodox, 2000.

Coe, John. "Spiritual Theology: A Theological-Experimental Methodology for Bridging the Sanctification Gap." *Journal of Spiritual Formation and Soul Care* 2.1 (2009) 4–43.

———. "The Controversy over Contemplation and Contemplative Prayer: A Historical, Theological, and Biblical Resolution." In *Embracing Contemplation: Reclaiming a Christian Spiritual Practice*, 19–36. Downers Grove, IL: InterVarsity, 2019.

Coe, John H., and Kyle C. Strobel, eds. *Embracing Contemplation: Reclaiming a Christian Spiritual Practice.* Downers Grove, IL: InterVarsity, 2019.

Conroy, Maureen. *Looking into the Well: Supervision of Spiritual Directors.* Chicago: Loyola University Press, 1995.

Cusson, Gilles. *Biblical Theology and the Spiritual Exercises: A Method toward a Personal Experience of God as Accomplishing within Us His Plan of Salvation*. St. Louis: Institute of Jesuit Sources, 1988.

Dalmases, Câadido de. *Ignatius of Loyola, Founder of the Jesuits: His Life and Work*. Translated by Jerome Aixala. Vol. 1. 2 vols. Series II-Modern Scholarly Studies about the Jesuits in English Translations 6/2. St. Louis: Institute of Jesuit Sources, 1985a.

———. *Ignatius of Loyola, Founder of the Jesuits: His Life and Work*. Translated by Jerome Aixala. Vol. 2. Series VIII-Biographies. St. Louis, Missouri: The Institute of Jesuit Sources, 1985b.

Déchanet, Jean. *William of St Thierry: The Man and His Work*. Cistercian Studies Series 10. Spencer, MA: Cistercian, 1972.

Demacopoulos, George E. *Five Models of Spiritual Direction in the Early Church*. Notre Dame, IN: University of Notre Dame Press, 2007.

———. *The Book of Pastoral Rule*. Crestwood, NY: St. Vladimir's Seminary Press, 2007.

Demarest, Bruce A. "Reading Catholic Spirituality." In *Reading the Spiritual Classics: A Guide for Evangelicals*, edited by Jamin Goggin and Kyle Strobel, 115–30. Downers Grove, IL: IVP, 2013.

———. *Soul Guide: Following Jesus as Spiritual Director*. Colorado Springs: NavPress, 2003.

Dougherty, Rose Mary. *Group Spiritual Direction: Community for Discernment*. New York: Paulist, 1995.

Dowey, Edward A. *Knowledge of God in Calvin's Theology*. Grand Rapids: Eerdmans, 1994.

Dreyer, Elizabeth, and Mark S Burrows. *Minding the Spirit: The Study of Christian Spirituality*. Baltimore: Johns Hopkins University Press, 2005.

Dubay, Thomas. *Fire Within: St. Teresa of Avila, St. John of the Cross, and the Gospel, on Prayer*. San Francisco: Ignatius, 1989.

———. *Seeking Spiritual Direction: How to Grow the Divine Life Within*. Ann Arbor: Servant, 1994.

Edwards, Tilden. *Spiritual Director, Spiritual Companion: Guide to Tending the Soul*. New York: Paulist, 2001.

———. *Spiritual Friend*. New York: Paulist, 1980.

Egan, Harvey D. *The Spiritual Exercises and the Ignatian Mystical Horizon*. Vol. 5. Study Aids on Jesuit Topics 4. St. Louis: Institute of Jesuit Sources, 1976.

English, John J. *Spiritual Freedom: From an Experience of the Ignatian Exercises to the Art of Spiritual Guidance*. Chicago: Loyola University Press, 1995.

Fleming, David L, Ignatius, and Institute of Jesuit Sources. *Draw Me into Your Friendship: A Literal Translation and a Contemporary Reading of The Spiritual Exercises*. St. Louis: Institute of Jesuit Sources, 1996.

Foster, Richard J. *Streams of Living Water: Celebrating the Great Traditions of Christian Faith*. New York: HarperCollins, 1998.

Francis, de Sales, Jeanne-Françoise de Chantal. *Francis de Sales, Jane de Chantal: Letters of Spiritual Direction*. Translated by Péronne Marie Thibert. Selected and introduced by Wendy M. Wright, and Joseph F. Power. Classics of Western Spirituality. New York: Paulist, 1988.

Fryling, Alice. *Seeking God Together: An Introduction to Group Spiritual Direction*. Downers Grove, IL: InterVarsity, 2008.

Gaffin, Richard B., Jr. "Justification and Union with Christ." In *A Theological Guide to Calvin's Institutes: Essays and Analysis.*, edited by David W Hall and Peter A Lillback, 248–69. Phillipsburg, NJ: P & R, 2008.

Gallagher, Timothy M. *A Handbook for Spiritual Directors: An Ignatian Guide for Accompanying Discernment of God's Will.* Chestnut Ridge, NY: Crossroad, 2017.

Garcia, Mark A. "Life in Christ: The Function of Union with Christ in the 'Unio-Duplex Gratia' Structure of Calvin's Soteriology with Special Reference to the Relationship of Justification and Sanctification in Sixteenth-Century Context." PhD diss., University of Edinburgh, 2004.

George, Timothy, and Alister E McGrath, eds. *For All the Saints: Evangelical Theology and Christian Spirituality.* Louisville: Westminster John Knox, 2003.

Gerrish, B. A. "Calvin's Eucharistic Piety." In *Calvin and Spirituality: Papers Presented at the 10th Colloquium of the Calvin Studies Society, May 18–20, 1995, Calvin Theological Seminary. Calvin and His Contemporaries: Colleagues, Friends and Conflicts: Papers Presented at the 11th Colloquium of the Calvin Studies Society, April 24–26, 1997, Louisville Theological Seminary*, edited by David L. Foxgrover. Calvin Studies Society Papers. Grand Rapids: CRC, 1995.

———. *Grace and Gratitude: The Eucharistic Theology of John Calvin.* 1993. Reprint, Eugene, OR: Wipf & Stock, 2002.

Goggin, Jamin, and Kyle Strobel. *Reading the Christian Spiritual Classics: A Guide for Evangelicals.* Downers Grove, IL: IVP, 2013.

Green, Thomas H. *Weeds among the Wheat: Discernment, Where Prayer & Action Meet.* Notre Dame, IN: Ave Maria, 1984.

Guenther, Margaret. *Holy Listening the Art of Spiritual Direction.* Cambridge, MA: Cowley, 1992.

Guibert, Joseph de. *The Jesuits, Their Spiritual Doctrine and Practice: A Historical Study.* Edited by George E Ganss. Translated by William J Young. Chicago: Institute of Jesuit Sources, 1964.

———. *The Theology of the Spiritual Life.* New York: Sheed & Ward, 1953.

Habsburg, Maximilian von. *Catholic and Protestant Translations of the "Imitatio Christi", 1425–1650: From Late Medieval Classic to Early Modern Bestseller.* St. Andrews Studies in Reformation History. Farnham, UK: Ashgate, 2011.

Hall, David W., and Peter A Lillback, eds. *A Theological Guide to Calvin's Institutes: Essays and Analysis.* Phillipsburg, NJ: P & R, 2008.

Hauerwas, Stanley, and Samuel Wells. *The Blackwell Companion to Christian Ethics.* Malden, MA: Blackwell, 2004.

Hausherr, Irénée. *Spiritual Direction in the Ancient Christian East.* Cistercian Studies Series 116. Kalamazoo, MI: Cistercian, 1989.

Hernandez, Wil. *Henri Nouwen and Spiritual Polarities: A Life of Tension.* New York: Paulist, 2012.

Hesselink, I. John. *Calvin's First Catechism: A Commentary: Featuring Ford Lewis Battles' Translation of the 1538 Catechism.* Columbia Series in Reformed Theology. Louisville: Westminster John Knox, 1997.

———. "Introduction: John Calvin on Prayer." In *On Prayer: Conversation with God,* 1–37. Louisville: Westminster John Knox, 2006.

Holmes, Urban T. *A History of Christian Spirituality: An Analytical Introduction.* New York: Seabury, 1980.

Holt, Bradley P. *Thirsty for God: A Brief History of Christian Spirituality.* 2nd ed. Minneapolis: Fortress, 2005.

Horton, Michael Scott. *Calvin on the Christian Life: Glorifying and Enjoying God Forever.* Wheaton, IL: Crossway, 2014.

———. *The Christian Faith: A Systematic Theology for Pilgrims on the Way.* Grand Rapids: Zondervan, 2011.

Houdek, Francis Joseph. *Guided by the Spirit: A Jesuit Perspective on Spiritual Direction.* Chicago: Loyola University Press, 1996.

Houston, J. M, and Kenneth N Pearson. *Alive to the Love of God: Essays Presented to James M. Houston by His Students on His 75th Birthday.* Vancouver, BC: Regent College, 1998.

Houston, James M. "Christian Spirituality: A Contextual Perspective." In *For All the Saints: Evangelical Theology and Christian Spirituality,* 27–38. Louisville: Westminster John Knox, 2003.

Howard, Evan B. *Affirming the Touch of God: A Psychological and Philosophical Exploration of Christian Discernment.* Lanham, MD: University Press of America, 2000.

Howard, Evan B. "Experience." In *Dictionary of Christian Spirituality,* edited by Glen G Scorgie, Simon Chan, Gordon T Smith, and James D. Smith III. Grand Rapids: Zondervan, 2011.

Ignatius. *A Pilgrim's Journey: The Autobiography of Ignatius of Loyola.* Translated by Joseph N Tylenda. Collegeville, MN: Liturgical, 1985.

———. *Ignatius of Loyola: the Spiritual Exercises and Selected Works.* Edited by George E Ganss. Classics of Western Spirituality. New York: Paulist, 1991.

———. *Letters of St. Ignatius of Loyola.* Translated by William J Young. Chicago: Loyola University Press, 1959.

———. *The Constitutions of the Society of Jesus and Their Complementary Norms: A Complete English Translation of the Official Latin Texts.* Translated by Jesuits. Series I--Jesuit Primary Sources in English Translations. Saint Louis: Institute of Jesuit Sources, 1996.

———. *The Spiritual Exercises of St. Ignatius: Based on Studies in the Language of the Autograph.* Translated by Louis J Puhl. New York: Vintage, 2000.

Ignatius, and Michael Ivens. *Understanding the Spiritual Exercises: text and commentary ; a Handbook for Retreat Directors.* Translated by Michael Ivens. Leominster, UK: Gracewing, 1998.

Irvin, Dale T., and Scott Sunquist. *History of the World Christian Movement,* Vol. 2: *Modern Christianity from 1454–1800.* 2 vols. Maryknoll, NY: Orbis, 2012.

Johnson, Marcus Peter. *One with Christ: An Evangelical Theology of Salvation.* Wheaton, IL: Crossway, 2013.

Jones, Alan W. *Exploring Spiritual Direction.* Cambridge, MA: Cowley, 1999.

Jones, Cheslyn, et al., eds. *The Study of Spirituality.* London: SPCK, 2000.

Jones, Serene. *Calvin and the Rhetoric of Piety.* 1st ed. Columbia Series in Reformed Theology. Louisville: Westminster John Knox, 1995.

José Ignacio Tellechea Idígoras. *Ignatius of Loyola: The Pilgrim Saint.* Chicago: Loyola University Press, 1994.

Julian and John-Julian. *The Complete Julian of Norwich.* Brewster, MA: Paraclete, 2009.

Kannengiesser, Charles. "The Spiritual Message of the Great Fathers." In *Christian Spirituality: Origins to the Twelfth Century,* 61–88. New York: Crossroad, 1985.

Kelsey, Morton T. *Companions on the Inner Way: The Art of Spiritual Guidance.* New York: Crossroad, 1983.

Lane, Anthony N. S. *John Calvin: Student of the Church Fathers.* Grand Rapids: Baker, 1999.

Lane, Belden C. *Ravished by Beauty: The Surprising Legacy of Reformed Spirituality.* Oxford: Oxford University Press, 2011.

Lane, Dermot A. *The Experience of God: An Invitation to Theology.* Dublin: Veritas, 1981.

Latourette, Kenneth Scott. *A History of Christianity: Volume 1: To A.D. 1500.* New York: HarperCollins, 1975.

Leclercq, Jean. "Western Christianity." In *Christian Spirituality: Origins to the Twelfth Century*, 113–32. New York: Crossroad, 1985.

Leech, Kenneth. *Soul Friend: Spiritual Direction in the Modern World.* Harrisburg, PA: Morehouse, 2001.

Liebert, Elizabeth Ann. "The Process of Change in Spiritual Direction: A Structural Developmental Perspective." PhD diss., Vanderbilt University, 1986.

———. "The Process of Change in Spiritual Direction: A Structural-Developmental Perspective." PhD diss., Vanderbilt University, 1986.

Lommasson, Sandra. "Widening the Tent: Spiritual Practice across Traditions." In *Sacred Is the Call: Formation and Transformation in Spiritual Direction*, edited by Suzanne M. Buckley, 161–70. New York: Crossroad, 2005.

Lonsdale, David. *Eyes to See, Ears to Hear: An Introduction to Ignatian Spirituality.* Maryknoll, NY: Orbis, 2000.

———. "Traditions of Spiritual Guidance: Towards a Theology of Spiritual Direction." *The Way* 4.32 (1992) 312–13.

Louth, Andrew. "The Cappadocians." In *The Study of Spirituality*, edited by Cheslyn Jones et al., 161–67. London: SPCK, 2004.

Lovelace, Richard. "The Sanctification Gap." *Theology Today* 29 (1973) 363–69.

Maas, Robin, and Gabriel O'Donnell, eds. *Spiritual Traditions for the Contemporary Church.* Nashville: Abingdon, 1990.

Mabry, John R. *Noticing the Divine: An Introduction to Interfaith Spiritual Guidance.* Harrisburg, PA: Morehouse, 2006.

———, ed. *Spiritual Guidance across Religions: A Sourcebook for Spiritual Directors and Other Professionals Providing Counsel to People of Differing Faith Traditions.* Woodstock, VT: Skylight Paths, 2014.

Macario and Nicodemo. *Early Fathers from the Philokalia: Together with Some Writings of St. Abba Dorotheus, St. Isaac of Syria, and St. Gregory Palamas.* Translated by E. Kadloubovsky and G. E. H. Palmer. London: Faber & Faber, 1981.

Malloy, Richard G. *Spiritual Direction: A Beginner's Guide.* Maryknoll, NY: Orbis, 2017.

Marshall, I. Howard. *Christian Experience in Theology and Life: Papers Read at the 1984 Conference of the Fellowship of European Evangelical Theologians.* Edinburgh: Rutherford House, 1988.

May, Gerald G. *Care of Mind, Care of Spirit: A Psychiatrist Explores Spiritual Direction.* San Francisco: Harper & Row, 1992.

McConvery, Brendan. *Living in Union with Christ in Today's World: The Witness of John Calvin and Ignatius Loyola: Conference Papers from St. Patrick's College, Maynooth.* Dublin: Veritas, 2011.

McGinn, Bernard. *The Essential Writings of Christian Mysticism*. New York: Modern Library, 2006.

McGinn, Bernard, and Patricia Ferris McGinn. *Early Christian Mystics: The Divine Vision of the Spiritual Masters*. New York: Crossroad, 2003.

McGinn, Bernard, et al. *Christian Spirituality: Origins to the Twelfth Century*. New York: Crossroad, 1985.

McNeill, John Thomas. *A History of the Cure of Souls*. London: SCM, 1952.

Meissner, William Walter. *Ignatius of Loyola: The Psychology of Saint*. New Haven: Yale University Press, 1992.

Meredith, Anthony. *The Cappadocians*. Crestwood, NY: St. Vladimir's Seminary Press, 1995.

Merton, Thomas. *Spiritual Direction & Meditation*. Collegeville, MN: Liturgical, 1987.

Michael, Chester P. *An Introduction to Spiritual Direction: A Psychological Approach for Directors and Directees*. New York: Paulist, 2004.

Moon, Gary W, and David G Benner. *Spiritual Direction and the Care of Souls: A Guide to Christian Approaches and Practices*. Downers Grove, IL: InterVarsity, 2004.

Mulholland, Robert M. *The Deeper Journey: The Spirituality of Discovering Your True Self*. Downers Grove, IL: InterVarsity, 2006.

Muller, Richard A. *Calvin and the Reformed Tradition: On the Work of Christ and the Order of Salvation*. Grand Rapids: Baker Academic, 2012.

———. *The Unaccommodated Calvin: Studies in the Foundation of a Theological Tradition*. Oxford: Oxford University Press, 2000.

Nataraja, Kim. *Journey to the Heart: Christian Contemplation through the Centuries-an Illustrated Guide*. Maryknoll, NY: Orbis, 2012.

Neafsey, James. "The Human Experience of God." In *Sacred Is the Call: Formation and Transformation in Spiritual Direction*, edited by Suzanne M. Buckley, 19–26. New York: Crossroad, 2005.

Nicodemus, Makarios, and Kallistos. *The Philokalia: The Complete Text*. Translated by G. E. H Palmer and Philip Sherrard. London: Faber & Faber, 1979.

Nouwen, Henri J. M. *Reaching Out: The Three Movements of the Spiritual Life*. Garden City, NY: Image, 1986.

Nouwen, Henri J. M, et al. *Spiritual Direction: Wisdom for the Long Walk of Faith*. San Francisco: Harper San Francisco, 2006.

Oden, Thomas C., and Don S. Browning. *Care of Souls in the Classic Tradition*. Philadelphia: Fortress, 1984.

O'Donnell, Gabriel. "Mendicant Spirituality." In *Spiritual Traditions for the Contemporary Church*, 83–99. Nashville: Abingdon, 1990.

———. "Monastic Life and the Search for God." In *Spiritual Traditions for the Contemporary Church*, 55–73. Nashville: Abingdon, 1990.

Ó Laoghaire, Diarmuid. "Celtic Spirituality." In *The Study of Spirituality*, edited by Cheslyn Jones et al., 216–25. London: SPCK, 1986.

O'Malley, John W. *The First Jesuits*. Cambridge: Harvard University Press, 1993.

Palmer, Martin E. *On Giving the Spiritual Exercises: The Early Jesuit Manuscript Directories and the Official Directory of 1599*. St. Louis, MO: The Institute of Jesuit Sources, 1996.

Partee, Charles. *The Theology of John Calvin*. Louisville: Westminster John Knox, 2008.

Pennington, M. Basil. *Praying the Holy Scriptures*. Brewster, MA: Paraclete, 2012.

Peters, Greg. "On Spiritual Theology: A Primer." *Journal of Spiritual Formation and Soul Care* 4 (2011) 5–26.

———. "Spiritual Theology: A Historical Overview." In *Reading the Christian Spiritual Classics: A Guide for Evangelicals*, edited by Jamin Goggin and Kyle Strobel, 79–94. Downers Grove, IL: InterVarsity, 2013.

———. "The Medieval Traditions." In *Reading the Christian Spiritual Classics: A Guide for Evangelicals*, edited by Jamin Goggin and Kyle Strobel. Downers Grove, IL: InterVarsity, 2013.

Peterson, Eugene H. *The Contemplative Pastor: Returning to the Art of Spiritual Direction.* Grand Rapids: Eerdmans, 1993.

Phillips, Susan S. *Candlelight: Illuminating the Art of Spiritual Direction.* Harrisburg, PA: Morehouse, 2008.

Rahner, Hugo. *The Spirituality of St. Ignatius Loyola: An Account of Its Historical Development.* Westminster, MD: Newman, 1953.

Rahner, Karl, and Helmuth Nils Loose. *Ignatius of Loyola.* London: Collins, 1979.

Reed, Angela H., et al. *Spiritual Companioning: A Guide to Protestant Theology and Practice.* Grand Rapids: Baker Academic, 2015.

Reiser, William E. *Seeking God in All Things: Theology and Spiritual Direction.* Collegeville, MN: Liturgical, 2004.

Reynolds, Stefan, and Esther De Waal. "St Benedict." In *Journey to the Heart: Christian Contemplation through the Centuries—An Illustrated Guide*, 148–58. Maryknoll, NY: Orbis, 2012.

Richard, Lucien. *The Spirituality of John Calvin.* Atlanta: John Knox, 1974.

Riche, Pierre. "Spirituality in Celtic and Germanic Society." In *Christian Spirituality: Origins to the Twelfth Century*, 163–76. New York: Crossroad, 1985.

Ruffing, Janet. *Spiritual Direction: Beyond the Beginnings.* New York: Paulist, 2000.

Runia, Klass. "Towards a Biblical Theology of Experience." In *Christian Experience in Theology and Life Papers Read at the 1984 Conference of the Fellowship of European Evangelical Theologians*, edited by I. Howard Marshall, 175–98. Edinburgh: Rutherford House, 1988.

Schneiders, Sandra M. "A Hermenuetical Approach to the Study of Christian Spirituality." In *Minding the Spirit: The Study of Christian Spirituality.*, 49–64. Baltimore, MD: Johns Hopkins University Press, 2005.

Schroeder, Henry Joseph. *Canons and Decrees of the Council of Trent.* St. Louis: Herder, 1941.

Schwanda, Tom. *Soul Recreation the Contemplative-Mystical Piety of Puritanism.* Eugene, OR: Pickwick Publications, 2012.

Scorgie, Glen G., Simon Chan et al., eds. *Dictionary of Christian Spirituality.* Grand Rapids: Zondervan, 2011.

Selderhuis, H. J. *The Calvin Handbook.* Grand Rapids: Eerdmans, 2009.

Sheldrake, Philip. *Spirituality and History: Questions of Interpretation and Method.* Maryknoll, NY: Orbis, 1998.

———. *Spirituality and Theology: Christian Living and the Doctrine of God.* London: Darton, Longman & Todd, 2004.

Shore, Paul J., and Ludolf von Sachsen. *The Vita Christi of Ludolph of Saxony and its influence on the Spiritual Exercises of Ignatius of Loyola.* Studies in the Spirituality of Jesuits. St. Louis: Seminar on Jesuit Spirituality, 1998.

Silf, Margaret. *Inner Compass: An Invitation to Ignatian Spirituality*. Chicago: Loyola, 2007.

Sittser, Gerald L. "The Desert Fathers." In *Reading the Spiritual Classics: A Guide for Evangelicals*, 195–220. Downers Grove, IL: InterVarsity, 2013.

Smith, Gordon T. *Listening to God in Times of Choice: The Art of Discerning God's Will*. Downers Grove, IL: InterVarsity, 1997.

———. *Spiritual Direction: A Guide to Giving & Receiving Direction*. Downers Grove, IL: InterVarsity, 2014.

———. *The Voice of Jesus: Discernment, Prayer, and the Witness of the Spirit*. Downers Grove, IL: InterVarsity, 2003.

Spearritt, Placid. "Benedict." In *The Study of Spirituality*, 148–57. London: SPCK, 2004.

Spitz, Lewis W. "Desiderius Erasmus." In *Reformers in Profile*, edited by B. A Gerrish. Philadelphia: Fortress, 1967.

Stewart, Columba. *Cassian the Monk*. Oxford Studies in Historical Theology. New York: Oxford University Press, 1998.

Sullivan, John. *Spiritual Direction*. Washington, DC: ICS, 1980.

Sunquist, Scott. *Understanding Christian Mission: Participation in Suffering and Glory*. Grand Rapids: Baker Academic, 2013.

Tamburello, Dennis E. *Union with Christ: John Calvin and the Mysticism of St. Bernard*. Columbia Series in Reformed Theology. Louisville: Westminster John Knox, 1994.

Tan, Jimmy Boon-Chai. "Discernment in Times of Transition: Guidance from the Spiritual Exercises of St. Ignatius of Developing Leaders." ThM thesis, Fuller Theological Seminary, 2006.

———. "Retaining the Tri-Perspective of History, Theology and Method in Spiritual Direction: A Comparative Study of Ignatius of Loyola and John Calvin." PhD diss, Fuller Theological Seminary, 2014.

Tan, Siang-Yang. *Counseling and Psychotherapy*. Grand Rapids: Baker Academic, 2011.

Tan, Siang-Yang, and Douglas H. Gregg. *Disciplines of the Holy Spirit: How to Connect to the Spirit's Power and Presence*. Grand Rapids: Zondervan, 1997.

Tanquerey, Adolphe. *The Spiritual Life; a Treatise on Ascetical and Mystical Theology by the Very Reverend Adolphe Tanquerey*. Translated by Herman Branderis. Tournai Belgium: Desclée, 2000.

Thibodeaux, Mark E. *Ignatian Discernment of Spirits for Spiritual Direction and Pastoral Care: Going Deeper*. Chicago: Loyola, 2020.

Thomas, à Kempis. *The Imitation of Christ : A Modern Reading*. Translated by Bernard Langley. Crowborough, UK: Highland, 1983.

Thompson, Bard. "Ulrich Zwingli." In *Reformers in Profile*, edited by B. A Gerrish. Philadelphia: Fortress, 1967.

Thornton, Martin. *English Spirituality: An Outline of Ascetical Theology according to the English Pastoral Tradition*. London: SPCK, 1963.

———. *Spiritual Direction: A Practical Introduction*. London: SPCK, 1984.

Tidball, Derek J. "Christian Theology in a World Crying Out for Experience." In *Christian Experience in Theology and Life Papers Read at the 1984 Conference of the Fellowship of European Evangelical Theologians*, edited by I. Howard Marshall, 1–15. Edinburgh: Rutherford House, 1988.

Toner, Jules J. *A Commentary on Saint Ignatius' Rules for the Discernment of Spirits: A Guide to the Principles and Practice*. Series III—Original Studies, Composed in English 5. St. Louis: The Institute of Jesuit Sources, 1982.

Treier, Daniel J., and David Lauber. *Trinitarian Theology for the Church: Scripture, Community, Worship*. Downers Grove, IL: IVP Academic, 2009.

Van Engen, John H. *Devotio Moderna: Basic Writings*. New York: Paulist, 1988.

———. *Sisters and Brothers of the Common Life: The Devotio Moderna and the World of the Later Medieval Ages*. Philadelphia: University of Pennsylvania Press, 2008.

Vanhoozer, Kevin J. "Triune Discourse: Theological Reflections on the Claim That God Speaks." In *Trinitarian Theology for the Church: Scripture, Community, Worship*, edited by Daniel J. Treier and Dauvid Lauber, 50–78. Downers Grove, IL: IVP Academic, 2009.

Vest, Norvene, ed. *Still Listening: New Horizons in Spiritual Direction*. Harrisburg, PA: Morehouse, 2000.

———, ed. *Tending the Holy: Spiritual Direction across Traditions*. Harrisburg, PA: Morehouse, 2003.

Von Habsburg, Maximilian. *Catholic and Protestant Translations of the Imitatio Christi, 1425–1650: From Late Medieval Classic to Early Modern Bestseller*. St. Andrews Studies in Reformation History. Farnham, UK: Ashgate, 2011.

Wakefield, James L. *Sacred Listening: Discovering the Spiritual Exercises of Ignatius Loyola*. Grand Rapids: Baker, 2006.

Ward, Benedicta. "Gregory the Great." In *The Study of Spirituality*, edited by Cheslyn Jones et al., 277–79. London: SPCK, 1986.

———. "Spiritual Direction in the Desert Fathers." In *Traditions of Spiritual Guidance*, 3–15. Collegeville, MN: Liturgical, 1990.

———. *The Sayings of the Desert Fathers The Alphabetical Collection*. Kalamazoo, MI: Cistercian, 1984.

Warner, Larry. *Journey with Jesus: Discovering the Spiritual Exercises of Saint Ignatius*. Downers Grove, IL: InterVarsity, 2010.

Webster, Douglas D. *Finding Spiritual Direction: The Challenge and Joys of Christian Growth*. Downers Grove, IL: InterVarsity, 1991.

Wendel, François. *Calvin: Origins and Development of His Religious Thought*. Translated by Philip Mairet. Grand Rapids: Baker, 1997.

Wilhoit, James C., and Evan B. Howard. *Discovering Lectio Divina: Bringing Scripture into Ordinary Life*. Downers Grove, IL: InterVarsity, 2012.

Willard, Dallas. *Renovation of the Heart: Putting on the Character of Christ*. Colorado Springs: NavPress, 2002.

Williams, Daniel H. *Retrieving the Tradition and Renewing Evangelicalism: A Primer for Suspicious Protestants*. Grand Rapids: Eerdmans, 1999.

Wilson, Terence L, ed. *Daily Office Readings: Year One, Volume 1*. New York: Church Publishing, 1983.

Zachman, Randall C. *John Calvin as Teacher, Pastor, and Theologian: The Shape of His Writings and Thought*. Grand Rapids: Baker Academic, 2006.

Index

www.ingramcontent.com/pod-product-compliance
Lightning Source LLC
Chambersburg PA
CBHW060331100426
42812CB00003B/950